Harriot Mackenzie

Evolution Illuminating the Bible

Harriot Mackenzie
Evolution Illuminating the Bible
ISBN/EAN: 9783337096687

Printed in Europe, USA, Canada, Australia, Japan

Cover: Foto ©Lupo / pixelio.de

More available books at **www.hansebooks.com**

EVOLUTION

ILLUMINATING THE BIBLE

BY

HARRIOT MACKENZIE.

LONDON:
SIMPKIN, MARSHALL, KENT, & CO., LIMITED.
EDINBURGH AND GLASGOW: JOHN MENZIES & CO.
1891.

[*All Rights Reserved.*]

TO
T. H. HUXLEY, LL.D., F.R.S.,
AS A
TOKEN OF ADMIRATION
AND A
TRIBUTE TO HIS GENIUS.

PREFACE.

It is evident that the material views advanced by our leading men of science are causing a class of Christians much anxiety. One object I had in writing this volume was to draw the attention of this class to the fact that our Lord clearly advanced such views, when he defined man in his natural state as a unit of Body and Mind—graphicly classed by Him as "that which is born of the Flesh is Flesh,"—put in contrast with the new sentiment conversion imparts, defined as one "born of the Spirit, Spirit."—John iii. 6. He was instructing Nicodemus on this vital principle of Christianity, who recognised Jesus as a teacher come from God, and came to be taught by Him. Nicodemus, like many in our day, who are startled by materialism, was greatly amazed when informed of the necessity of being "born again" before he could see the kingdom of heaven. But such is the case.

Thus, then, I meet the objection, or rather the fears of the class I refer to, by showing we have the highest of all authority for accepting the material views advanced by such authors as Spencer, Bain, and Huxley, &c. It is on the authority so rendered, which these words of our Lord's indicate, that I hold it to be a duty as well as a privilege to accept the material conception of body and mind so advanced.

In adopting this course, the first point to be considered was spontaneous generation. Could a rational explanation be anticipated to account for it as conditions that may have led to develop organic life. Reasoning thus, I saw in Light, as a disturber of elements, the most probable force to do so, as one of the most powerful chemical agents; therefore, the most probable originator of the vaguest possible form of sensation—which is Life.

Sensation I anticipated to have been developed as the equivalent of the shock produced in parting the atoms of a very stable compound molecule, under some exceptionally favourable condition which lead toward this end. Sensation, so developed, I inferred, would be reproduced when these atoms reunited as the equivalent of another shock; further, that such atoms would retain in their constitution the vaguest possible form of sensation, and therefore have a tendency to unite among themselves, just as we know organic atoms to have. Sensation, so developed, would, according to natural laws, grow in complexity, as shocks under changed conditions, multiplied until, after countless ages of this vital force on our planet, body and mind in the human forms was produced capable of developing human intelligence as the equivalent of the forces at work within and without the human organism, proclaiming how that organism is affected by its environment.

I applied to Body and Mind the materialistic conception these conditions indicate, to illuminate the words our Lord referred to, so as to enable the converted Christian to comprehend with clearness the nature of the new life-giving power, union with Christ in conversion imparts, called by Him a being " born of the Spirit, Spirit." This is a mental experience more or less familiar to all who have been born again, that is, united to Christ in conversion.

Taking such a view of Life " Natural" and Life "Spiritual," I had no hesitation in anticipating conditions that may have developed spontaneous generation. Viewing vital forces as equivalent to conditions inherent in matter itself, so ordered of God as to develop a phase of the most rudimentary form of sensation, which is Life ; a force co-existent with all vital organisms. For to feel, or to be capable of feeling, is what constitutes a living organism. Plant life is no exception. Plants absorb substances that sustain them, and bend toward the life-sustaining rays of the sun. Plant life thus indicates its appreciation of conditions that sustain it; therefore in its own way feels or is sensitive. Proceeding on these lines, I do not hesitate to accept the fact that nervous structure develops sensation. Conditions that lead up to prove that conscious states are developed of human nervous structure, and so far as their origin is concerned are inseparable therefrom.

However, I show once created consciousness the co-relative of Ego and its equivalent, on the death of the organism will, as Ego, sustain itself as a disembodied spirit, by absorbing energy from its medium to form conscious states, which are the equivalent of sensation—the form of activity wherein immortality rests. Because it is a form of vitality inseparable from disembodied human personality, soul or Ego. In possession of an Ego so created and endowed, I show we have that living unit our Lord came to redeem. The process that secures the redemption thereof is what I aim at making plain and intelligent, as the change Our Lord indicates, in the "Verily, verily, I say unto you, except a man be born again, he cannot see the kingdom of heaven."—John iii. 3. When instructing Nicodemus, who had come to render Jesus homage, he was greatly startled by these important words, which our Lord so unfolded as to enable Nicodemus to perceive that the change referred to was only possible for a man to experience while on earth. Yet this change was so momentous and of such vast importance, as far to surpass anything that could happen to a human being hereafter, even during that immortal individual's onward existence through Eternity.

CONTENTS.

CHAPTER I.

The Developing Properties inherent in matter lead to Spontaneous Generation—Life so produced sustains itself by transforming dead matter into Living Forms, . . . PAGES 1—16

CHAPTER II.

Life as sensation viewed in its Progressive Form, 17—25

CHAPTER III.

A short account of the Mechanical Process at work in Developing Conscious States by the human nervous structure, . 26—60

CHAPTER IV.

The Life-Sustaining property of the Blood, , 61—78

CHAPTER V.

Memory and its Laws, . . 79—110

CHAPTER VI.

Vital Energy in its Automatic Form, 111—139

CHAPTER VII.

Process Creating and Developing Immortal Soul, 140—168

CHAPTER VIII.

Will guided by Motives, ... 169—183

CHAPTER IX.

The Social Organism—What is it? Human in its Origin—Immortal in its Destiny, ... 184—211

CHAPTER X.

The Bible Illuminating Evolution is Illuminated Thereby, 212—276

CHAPTER XI.

Human Depravity finds its Antidote in Christianity, 277—308

CHAPTER XII.

Christianity—Its End and Origin, 309—331

CHAPTER XIII.

Vital Christianity—What is it? Loving and Working, 332—350

CHAPTER XIV.

Intellectual Christianity—What is it? Do Good Works and Live. Into which a few remarks on Brain Structure enters, 351—367

CHAPTER XV.

Mysteries of Christianity explained in Scientific Language, 368—393

EVOLUTION ILLUMINATING THE BIBLE.

CHAPTER I.

THE DEVELOPING PROPERTIES INHERENT IN MATTER LEAD TO SPONTANEOUS GENERATION—LIFE SO PRODUCED SUSTAINS ITSELF BY TRANSFORMING DEAD MATTER INTO LIVING FORMS.

WE must assume throughout our whole argument that the Laws of Nature reveal God's mode of working as the Intelligence who created universal space. Matter viewed thus in its developing properties, is created by God, in order to produce the intelligent beings of our race, whose imaginative faculty enables them to anticipate future events in the world's history which God in His foreknowledge has decreed to bring to pass. By this view in the imaginative faculty of our race revealed truth finds its correlative. This theory of the God of matter and of humanity is not ante-scientific—on the contrary, it rests on a true scientific basis. For when the anticipated conception in the imagination of an individual is in harmony with God's design, he signifies approval of it through the medium of a special revelation understood as such by the individual so inspired.

Inherent in matter, which is a product of God, are the laws of unity in nature which recent scientific investigation has brought to light. This unity will eventually enable the student of nature to explain the world, including its social

A

organism, as a systematic whole, which the phenomena of nature have combined to produce.

Thus may human intelligence deal with matter and its laws. But to explain whence matter came is beyond the power of Natural Science. Here, so far as it is concerned, eternal silence must reign. Revelation alone can bridge the gulf. It tells us that God is the originator of all.

This gap in Science is however being gradually filled up, which makes it apparent that there is no break in Nature in the way hitherto inferred from God's interference. For Matter has been proved capable of transformations so varied and so remarkable, that no limit can be assigned to its power of adaptation, change, and efficiency.

Every Molecule is placed in its position by attractions and repulsions due to the nature of the Molecules themselves. It thus comes to pass, that matter displaying in special circumstances the structural power exhibited in crystallisation, as well as in different and more complex circumstances, manifests the organic power witnessed in vegetable and animal life. All demonstrates the potentiality inherent in matter (itself a production of God), giving expression to the Laws with which His foreknowledge concerns itself.

Certain it is, that prior to the creation of universal space, all was in form conceived by God.

Our own section of the system of universal space in its developing capacity is graphically defined by Professor Huxley in his "Physical Basis of Life." He says, "Plants are the accumulators of the powers which animals distribute and dispense. But it will be observed that the existence of the matter of life depends on the pre-existence of certain compounds—namely, carbonic acid, nitre, and ammonia. Withdraw any one of these three from the world and all vital phenomena come to an end. They are related to the protoplasm of the plant as the protoplasm of the plant is to that of the animal. Carbon, hydrogen, oxygen, and nitrogen are all lifeless bodies. Of these, carbon and oxygen unite in certain proportions and under certain conditions to give rise to carbonic acid; hydrogen and oxygen produce water; nitrogen and hydrogen give rise to ammonia. These new compounds, like the elementary bodies of which they are composed, are lifeless. But when they are brought together under certain conditions they give rise to the still more complex body protoplasm, and this protoplasm exhibits the phenomena of life. I see no break in this series of steps in molecular complication, and I am unable to understand why the language which is applicable to any one term of the series may not be used to any of the others. We think it fit to call different kinds of matter carbon, oxygen, hydrogen, and activities of these substances as the properties of matter of which they are composed. When hydrogen and oxygen are mixed in certain proportions, and the electric spark is passed through them, they disappear, and a quantity of water equal in weight to the sum of their weights appears in their place. There is not the slightest parity between the passive and active powers of the water and those of the oxygen and hydrogen which have given rise to it. In some way or another the properties of the water result from the properties of the compound elements of the water. We do not assume that something called aquosity entered into and took possession of the oxide of hydrogen as soon as it was formed, and then guided the aqueous particles to their place in the facets of the crystal or amongst the leaflets of the hoar-frost. Does anybody quite comprehend the *modus operandi* of an electric spark which traverses a mixture of oxygen and hydrogen? What justification is there then for the assumption of the existence in the living matter of a something which has no representative or correlative in the not-living matter which gives rise to it? What better philosophical status has "vitality" than "aquosity"? and why should "vitality" hope for a better fate than the other of Huxley's "itys which have disappeared"? My answer to this question is—We Christians have no right to assume that vitality has a different fate from the other forces referred to, till in the advancing series of organic life we arrive at the human form with its marvellously constituted brain and nervous structure. These combining to produce the most highly endowed vital force known to us, give birth to human intelligence in creating "Sentient Personality," which is developed as conscious states technically called the energy of self-conservation, soul, or ego. This form of vitality cannot cease its activity on the death of the organism, but as an immortal unit maintains its individuality in functioning the conscious states which the human organism and environment give birth to in creating the ego, the immortal part that Christianity takes to do with.

It is evident "that what is called vital force is simply mechanical and chemical force transformed through the special conditions under which it acts. The human body is as incapable of generating force as a steam engine or a galvanic battery. It only distributes the forces which it receives from the world without, and varies its manifestations to the senses. Its walking and climbing, pulling and pushing, respiration and digestion, assimilation and exertion, can be shown to be either a mechanical or chemical operation." Yet in "Sentient Personality" the human organism developes the immortal form of force we call Ego.

A part of God's fore-ordained plan was that nature should develop vital force. This being so, the case is just what we are entitled to expect, that "the life of the body and its functions are manifestations of the same generic principle as the life of the soul and its functions." For it is evident that the bodily organism and its environment develop the soul or Sentient Personality which is the immortal part of man's being. This is God's way of working through nature. Now the whole range of nature is subject to the same laws. There is only a difference of degree between the highest mental and the lowest vital faculties. There is no absolute break or distinction, but on the contrary a continuous progression along the entire psychological line." . . "The doctrines of the correlation of forces and of development are as applicable to the explanation of mind as of life. Mind is force—the highest development of force—the force which is accumulated in the brain and nerves; and the mental is as exactly correlated with vital and with physical force as these are with each other. It may be proved by a variety of scientific considerations that all forces come under the same generalisation. Motion, heat, and light may be transformed into sensation, emotion, and thought, and these can be reconverted into motion, heat, and light."

This is man's definition of God's mode of working in Nature—the Universe of Space, representing, we shall say, God's First-born. This plan of His is a specimen of how He regulates the successive manifestations of His will in Nature to suit the requirements of the developments towards immortality made by our race in its onward movement through eternity. We become acquainted through Physical Science with the Universe of Space; while Evolution, which deals with the Laws at work therein, teaches us our relation to it. These Laws we, as Christians, acknowledge as the correlative of God's decrees which Nature supplies. These decrees proclaim our Father's mode of working as One Who, in the course of race-development which St. Paul so vividly describes in Rom. viii. 19-22, gradually unveils to us His hidden purposes. With St. Paul's shout of victory sounding in our ears we can turn to poor suffering humanity and say, that although it is true that "the whole creation groaneth and travaileth in pain together until now," yet deliverance is sure to come at last.

There can be no doubt that "as surely as every future grows out of the past and present, so will the physiology of the future gradually extend the realm of matter and law until it is co-extensive with knowledge, with feeling, and with action" (Prof. Huxley.) Mind embodied in the Ego is co-existent with the realm of matter and law composed of energy which finds expression in conscious states as the correlative. For mind, which embodies human intelligence, includes all that is known of matter and law, and mind and matter thus qualified embraces our immortal race in its units. In accepting the materialism which the doctrine of evolution necessarily includes, what have we, as Christians, to fear? If we view it in the light the Christian records reveal, do we not find that it, like them, acknowledges that God was the originator of all, that His laws are the agents evolution employs to secure the immortality of the race? Seen from this standpoint, the doctrine of evolution satisfies the legitimate claims of unity of design in Nature. From the standpoint of evolution, the law that regulates life is that of vital force, sustained in the survival of the fittest.

Further, wherever there is a nervous element, vital force is as clearly defined in the very lowest forms as in the highest. Vital force always conforms to the law of attraction and repulsion, by attracting what sustains life and repelling what does not. Defined briefly, vitality is the force explained in human language as attracting a pleasure and repelling a pain. For such is the law that sustains and governs Life. In recognising this, we demonstrate Life itself by giving the condition whereon it rests. Vitality so understood is the very condition which gives birth to the nervous structure which it has created to serve as its support. It uses this system henceforth as its medium to repel what we shall agree to call pain, and attract what we shall call pleasure. It is, of course, well known that these terms cannot be applied in their literal sense where there is no brain organism, for in that case, although the action of Life is the same, these sensations are absent. The Brain is the seat of conscious states. It enables consciousness to feel, as pleasure and pain, vital force, in attraction and repulsion, and, however complicated such actions may be in the highest forms of life, they are at the root of every vital movement on our planet. Therefore life, as we know it, must centre in the double effort to attract and repel, for attraction and repulsion are the forces that show the action of that vitality (governed by the law of affinity), which attracts pleasure and repels pain. Affinity seems to be the law that governs all forms of force, organic and inorganic. Sensation, feeling, or life, attracts what gratifies (that is what sustains) it, and repels what weakens it. We have thus proved that affinity does regulate organic life. The Law therefore that creates Sensation or Life, must be the affinity that attracts pleasure and repels pain wherever there is a brain organism.

When Life can be explained as a form of force so simple as this, we may justly infer that it originates through the action of Light, as a disturber of elements; for light is well known as a powerful chemical agent. That light, as such, does store itself up, is proved by decomposing the compound—molecule carbonic acid—on the green leaf of the tree in which light, as force, is absorbed, to reappear in equal proportions when the wooden fibre is burned.

Life is wholly dependent on the energy dispensed by the sun. If the sun ceased to shine, all life, such as we know it on our planet, would terminate. The inference this leads to is that the Sun is the origin of Life, of Sensation, and of Immortality too. For it builds up the human organism which develops conscious states (the equivalent of the immortal Ego or Sentient Personality)—the highest and most enduring because the immortal form of the sun's energy. For every conscious state is the correlative of the energy that forms it. Both conditions are coexistent. With this proposition accepted, the question that arises is—What induces Sensation? or let us say—What causes the condition that leads up to what we know as Sensation in its most rudimentary form? For an organism to feel, or to be capable of feeling, constitutes a living form. Life centres in a consciousness of differences, however vague. From this point it is quite permissible to view spontaneous generation, as originating in conditions, causing the vaguest possible conception of change. Such change might occur thus: Suppose the process of storing up light to be going on during the sun's presence in some part of our planet, under exceptionally favourable circumstances. The sun sets (or ceases to shine at least on that place), and thus leaves this process subject to a changed condition, which generates a shock. This shock consists of the most rudimentary form of sensation, as the result of the altered circumstances. When the sun returns to shine, and the process of accumulating its rays is resumed, changed condition again takes place, and in the fresh shock produced thereby, there is embodied the very vaguest consciousness of change. These conditions would henceforth be inseparable, and would reappear together, multiplying in complexity just as the shocks, through various reasons, might increase in variety; each distinctive kind of shock generating the structural form that corresponded to it. Viewed from the human standpoint, the nature of the shock might be stated thus—When the storing up process ceases, a shock of lowered vitality or weakness is felt; when the process is resumed, a shock of strength or increased vitality is perceived. The presence and absence of the sun may in this way actually develop that feeblest possible form of sensation, above referred to as consciousness of change, or in one word, Life. For to feel is to live. And the battle of life centres in the affinity that draws towards it what strengthens, and refuses what weakens. It seems quite reasonable to suppose that changes so simple as this were all that were required to produce organic matter. For is not God all and in all? and spontaneous generation demonstrates His Law which bridges the gulf between organic and inorganic matter. Life, as pleasure and pain, is known to us as a state that gratifies, associating with a condition that depresses. Sensation, the condition that distinguishes a living organism from a dead organism, is thus created; indeed it is the law of life. The case, as above stated, may have been the very conditions that generated life. Anyhow, in these conditions we have cause and effect, found to be so related as may have been capable of developing vital force. The sun as a powerful chemical agent, dispersing radiant matter, may have produced this law of cause and effect, from which the forces we call vital, spring.

The sun, as an agent capable of acting as a chemical force, is a powerful disturber of those atoms, which we on our cool planet call elements. This being so, Spontaneous Generation may have developed by the action of the sun breaking up some very stable combination—say, carbonic acid. The elements of such a molecule in parting, we shall infer, would have the most rudimentary form of sensation induced in them, and this sensation all such elements so parted would retain. They, in consequence, would combine among themselves, as we know the organic atoms do, and in doing so, generate the sensation called "consciousness of changed condition." This feeling may be partaken in by the elements of all such compound molecules. Under the conditions we have imagined we would have created in the carbon and oxygen (the ingredients of the compound, carbonic acid) this sense (although a very feeble one) of altered condition which, we shall say, is peculiar to all liberated parts of a molecule thus broken. This sense is equivalent to, say, the general sensation that every vital organism possesses in itself, if these conditions are accepted. It has been shown that under those circumstances, a compound molecule is capable, both as a unit and when broken up into parts, charged with vitality, of building up a living organism which would increase in complexity in proportion to the complexity of the shocks, until the human brain and nervous structure, which produces and includes in its units the intellect of the race, was developed.

We do know that the oxygen and carbon are liberated

on the green leaf of the tree—the carbon going to build up the woody fibre. Further, that in the burning process of the tree, these elements again unite, and proclaim their union in developing the equivalent of light and heat absorbed when liberated.

However, that sensation might have sprung from such data as I have given, is all that I am concerned with, for these show the basis on which vitality rests, and supply a working hypothesis to enable us to comprehend how the light and heat of the sun may transform dead matter into a living organism. For we have, by this time, made it quite clear that vital force is capable of transforming dead matter into a living form. This is the condition that sustains life as we know it. Does not the blood carry into all parts of the body what was dead matter, but which is transformed into living matter when it becomes part of the tissue of our living bodies. This marvellous transformation, which is constantly taking place in our daily experience, is as wonderful as that which took place when dead matter was first transformed into a living form in, say, Spontaneous Generation. But we are so familiar with the fact that it passes unnoticed.

Let us strive to contemplate the magnitude of the change that has taken place on our planet in the effects that this form of force (the conversion of non-living Substances into living beings or forms) has produced. The origin of it may have been as simple in form as the process I have described of the effect produced by the ray of the sun. Yet it is a force capable of developing all the varied forms of organic life found on our earth.

Man as the head of the series, is capable of feeling and of reasoning, as well as of anticipating, far reaching conclusions (a gift which a well informed imaginative faculty confers), and in predicting conditions yet to be realized. Individuals so constituted, are the medium God makes use of to forecast the future, which He in His foreknowledge has decreed. For in creating matter, God included the laws that produce all. Such laws are seen in great complexity in the forces at work in the social medium that surrounds us, and of which we form part. Wonderful this is indeed when we realize that the social organism is the result of this force. We have seen that this force once developed has power to convert lifeless matter into living substances; and into these the immortal part of man, in the shape of energy, finding expression in conscious states, enters as the human soul. It is when we contemplate all this that we begin to perceive the marvellous transformation that has taken place by the development of vital force, since it came to be one of the forces of our planet. It is no exaggeration to say, this force has changed the face of the earth. It has done so. For although organic life may have been in its origin no more complex than that of perceiving the change the sun's presence or absence indicated, yet it has eventually altered the whole appearance of the globe. It has also filled it with human beings, forming the social medium into which we are plunged at birth, and of which we then begin to form part.

The force we call vital which has produced all, begins and ends with Sensation. For Sensation—a consciousness of differences—is the distinguishing quality of all living organisms, whether animal or vegetable. It is an indisputable fact that in the lowest forms of life it is impossible to distinguish between animal and plant life. Some Naturalists have in fact classed some forms as vegetable life which others have classed as the animal kingdom. It is true of animal and plant life that the true function of living matter is manifested by both kingdoms. Both show by their activities that they possess the vitality of sensation, *i.e.*, the power to feel and to discriminate. This capacity is shown in their attracting what sustains, and repelling what weakens. This power of vitality is always the same wherever we meet with it. It is a force which, once developed, has the property of perpetuating and increasing itself by absorbing none-living matter and transforming it into its kind by vitalizing it. This is done (to quote an authority)—" Not otherwise than a spark of fire grows into a flame and continues to spread when it meets with suitable elements." The function which living-matter imparts to dead-matter is power to feel. It imparts the vitality with which it is itself endowed, and converts none-living substances into sentient matter with wonderful rapidity. Thus it transforms the inanimate forces of nature into living forms, having the power to feel, to know, and to think. In the human form it approaches God through Christ in prayer, in adoration, and in love, being capable of glorifying God and of enjoying Him for ever. This is the expression of the highest form of intellectual emotion, that a living human being in our world, or any other, is capable of. Yet, marvellous as the human form with the powerful intellect is, it also has sprung from the lowest forms of life. One of these elementary forms is seen in "the gory dew, a dark red slimy film not unfrequently to be seen on damp walls and in shady places."

In plant life, when cells group themselves together, the phenomena of life becomes more distinctly marked; and where their natural affinity is gratified, we may see the plant gradually incline to where the excitation comes from.

Plants automatically turn towards the sun. The clinging plant perceives points of support, the insect-eating plant is sensitive to its touch, and every flower feels the light and strives to bend its head towards it. Botanists have shown that some flowers feel the effect of light so strongly as to fold up at night, and unfold themselves in the morning. So strongly as this, do some mark their sense of satisfaction and its opposite when their affinities are affected. The water-lily hides in the water at night, but its natural affinities being gratified by the sun, the flower is called out of its hiding place by it. When you examine the sensitive plants, you find species with their leaves beautifully divided, being again and again pinnate into a great number of small leaves, of which the pairs close upwards when touched. On repeated or rougher touching, the leaflets of the neighbouring pinion also close together, and all the pinions in turn sink down till at last the stalk itself hangs down, and the whole leaf looks withered. If the stem is shaken, all the leaves exhibit the same phenomena. After a short time, the leaf if shaken, rises, and the leaflets stand upright again. We have in this shrinking plant the very phenomena giving expression to pain, when in the highest forms of life vitality is attacked. For we all know how innerving pain is, and how prostrated we are when greatly pained, either physically or mentally. See how the child or the dog cringes under the smart of the lash. Also mark how both assume their usual expression when the pain and its cause pass away. Man then stands erect, and so does the dog and the plant, each in its own way. The effect being such, we are compelled to recognize sensibility and life as identical, because these phenomena hold good under all conditions, marking the distinction between dead and living matter. Since they hold good in all forms of organic life, we are led to the conclusion that between the effect of rough handling in the sensitive plant referred to, and that of pain in man, the distinction is simply one of degree, not of kind. And we must remember pain is a phenomenon of life. Further, the degree which marks the distinction is to be measured by the progress made in the nervous system, which reaches its climax in the human form.

Life is so developed that the human nervous system makes us the constituents of the social organism, and the social medium is the condition that creates and maintains the moral element in us. For we are social and moral units being surrounded by the men and women of our race, and having mutual interests which develop the moral element in us. All spring from sensation or vital force, which possesses the inherent power of transforming dead matter into living substances, and also of developing morality out of selfishness. For the individual finds it to his interest to combine with the community, so as better to secure his individual well-being. The power of man's intellect enables him to arrive at this conclusion.

Intellect is defined by Bain in his "Mind and Body," as the *senses of feeling*, classified as three : Discrimination, Similarity, and Memory—" these three functions, however they are mingled and inseparably mingled in our mental operations, are yet totally distinct properties, and each the ground work of a different superstructure." Intellect, thus defined, is the product of sensations of this simple nature; yet it is capable of developing the marvellous capacities which the intellectual growth of our race displays in producing a Newton, a Darwin, a Stuart Mill, &c., as well as the Christian Martyrs, beginning with St.

Stephen and St. Paul. All such martyrs, in possessing the new sense that Conversion develops, were capable of analyzing and discriminating the change in their mental state that follows it. St. Paul, however, was the great master Apostle, far surpassing all the others in defining the mental changes conversion produces. Though the change is a manifestation of the Spirit of God in the human soul, take note it is the power the human intellect confers which enables man to perceive the change wrought, as such, in his mental state. It is therefore the Intellect, and the Intellect alone, that gives expression to the mental change that accompanies conversion in making that change apparent to the individual.

CHAPTER II.

LIFE AS SENSATION VIEWED IN ITS PROGRESSIVE FORM.

I HAVE stated conditions from which spontaneous generation may have sprung, anticipating what may have caused sensations, the equivalent of Life, of Biology—yes, and of Intellect too. For to live is to feel, and to be capable of feeling constitutes a living organism. And of such in its progressive form is the human Brain, the seat of sensation, the structure of mind.

I shall now proceed by tracking out the working of the machinery which provides the base that leads to the glorious result of developing and perfecting human intelligence. This is a form of intelligence, I hold, to culminate in producing the moral and religious elements, phenomena always accompanied with a human brain structure, which is so rich, so varied, and so delicate, that the Almighty in revealing truth directs the movements of man through it. An element is intended to indicate an ideal conception or combination, and may be used in a very broad or a very narrow sense, just as the subject matter may indicate. It may, indeed, be applied to the moral or religious structures in man, structures indispensable in securing his well-being, because they take concern with morality and religion, though all springs from sensation which is life; and memory cells are the produced forms of intelligent life, sensibility being the condition that creates cells, as well as the link that makes its effect felt in uniting cell to cell, and bringing the cells into contact with the surrounding medium. For if there was no sensibility, there could be no perception, no memory, no intelligence, such as the higher beings possess, to attract what gratifies and repel what is disagreeable. Even the essential tendency of the lowest forms of life is revealed by seizing upon substances that gratify their affinity. For such is the indispensable condition of life, both in the vegetable and animal world. It reveals its affinity by seizing on substances that strengthen it and avoiding those that weaken it.

We know that vegetable life turn automatically to the sun, which gratifies their affinity, and they may be said to awaken when he appears, and sleep when he is absent. Some flowers droop their heads when the sun is absent, and fold their leaves to array themselves in the most attractive form that their nature will permit of when he is present, by raising their heads and unfolding their flowers and their leaves, as much as to say, I awaken and rejoice to welcome thy life-giving rays, showing my joy in thy presence by unfolding all the beauty I possess to captivate these insects which may enable me to deck myself yet more gaily in virtue of the pollen they will leave: for they, too, rejoice in thy life-giving power, O Sun. In the animal kingdom, sensation in its origin presents the very same phenomena which are to be found in the vegetable kingdom.

In the white corpuscles, sensibility is purely histologically understood as the phenomena which is nominally present in living beings. In the elementary form of animal life, sensibility is diffused among all the cells in a general way by an organized tissue. However, as we ascend the series, the form becomes more complicated; new factors appear, gifted with special aptitudes, capable of performing such and such functions. The form becomes more perfected by differentiated functions being distributed through the organism which belong to the lowest form of a nervous system. In this system natural selection is seen to be at work in the organism, and the equal division of labour soon makes that apparent—conditions which mark the outline of the nervous system in its progressive form by providing each part with its special work. This is the process through which the organism becomes perfected; through the operation of its nervous structure guided by the force at work. This finds expression in the intellectual conception of natural selection—the selective power of the force—we call vital, which creates and perfects the nervous system. This system has sprung from types so simple that their bodies are formed of one cell. Little by little in the progressing animal form cells multiply and become united one to another. As these cells group themselves together, the phenomena of sensation become more distinctly marked. Nervous ganglisms begin grouping themselves together, and adding to their number and complexity as the work of evolution goes on, until we arrive at the well marked point where the force is destined to form the spinal axis which accumulates and gives birth to conditions, which produce Vertebrate species, with its complicated nervous system—the system which is henceforth the great dispenser of sensibility, destined to collect, to concentrate, and to disperse the subtle forces stored up therein, which can so well give expression to the currents, so as best to secure what will gratify life's affinities and dispel what is distasteful to them. This action is perfected through the development of the superior ganglion defined as the brain united to the spinal axis. The brain united becomes the crowning edifice of the nervous structure into which sensation of every form is drained, condensed, and transformed. From this point the nervous system becomes a central force, which conducts excitations and moulds them into activities capable of being co-ordinated into motor reaction. It now comes to pass that the forces of the nervous system are brought under control dispersed in a methodical form by the forces being directed. To one group is allotted the function of sensibility ; to another the function, so to speak, of motive activity : say, required to regulate our speaking, walking, writing, &c. To another group is allotted the silent work of sustaining organic life, principally through the automatic action which regulates the heart and the lungs.

The fact is that the nervous system has been produced as the equivalent of sensations vitality has given birth to ; and as such is by life used as a means to a yet higher end, that of providing vital force with a support to act through in its ceaseless movement, ever ready to catch at a pleasure or repel a pain. This is the end life force ever has in view. The means whereby it most effectually secures this is by the intervention of the nervous structure it has created, and finds so useful to farther its ends in transforming sense impressions into human intelligence ; and at a further stage, to carry the desires human intelligence begets into execution. This double part performed by the nervous structure is only seen in its perfection in the human organism regulated by the optic thalamus and the corpus striatum—structures I shall have occasion to refer to further on.

In the activities of the human nervous structure it is clearly apparent that the forces which unite in forming human intelligence, animated by the energy of self-conservation, are the forces which attract all forms of sensations, conscious or unconscious, to their own habitation in the brain. Such is the action of the nervous current of life. It gives expression to its own quality of what we shall call dynamic electricity or heat, which the nervous system condenses and conducts. As I hold Locker's views that energy is radiant matter, the probability is that the nervous structure, during the ages vitality has formed one of the forces of our planet, has been built up of the substance we call energy through the law of inheritance as the structure sensibility created. Certain it is, in its own way, every sensation adds to the volume or potency of structure.

The human form itself is a product of vital activity, with its marvellous nervous structure implanted therein. Bereft of vitality, the human form could not have been, because it is in life itself, having the vital property of transforming dead forms of matter into a living organism, that produced the human form, as well as all zoological forms. Shortly, it is this property of vital force that creates all living forms whatsoever, and has created all such forms. The marvellous human brain, the seat of human intelligence, is no exception. For in the brain the units of sense impressions group themselves together in developing their conceptions of human intelligence. The truth is, the conditions in the abstract on which human intelligence rests are to be found in the wonderful properties possessed by the nervous structure, which embraces the human organism. That it is so, may be proved by many methods of study. The method adopted by Dr. Luys has enabled him to produce wonderful results. The method of study adopted was to apply the microscope to very thin sections of the brain cut horizontally and vertically, and then photograph them. These slices, when placed in position, showed everything in their normal form, making them visible to the eye, altering nothing, but rendering the most minute forms visible just as they appear in the human brain. By placing in position and comparing the section horizontally and vertically, Dr. Luys had everything very much as in its normal form. By this process can be traced out the working and movements of the most minute forms of the nervous structure with wonderful clearness. Through this method, Dr. Luys was able to trace up through the bowels the threads of the nervous system from their origin in the cell ganglion of the bowels, on through the organism and complicate tissue of the brain, to be absorbed in the habitation prepared for them in the cortical substance of the cerebral brain, which is the seat of sensation proper in the highest forms of the vertebrate animal. These white threads of the nervous system are the sympathetic conducting fibres through which the bowels make their complaints of pain to the sphere of psycho-intellectual life, whose office it is to interpret the sensations perceived as pain. They set the human machinery in motion so as to have the cry of pain relieved. This is effected through the agency of the corpus striatum appealing to the little brain, whose office it is to execute the commands, either through the organs of speech, or writing, &c. So complicated as this, is the action which human intelligence confers on life—energy to repel a pain when it feels its vitality attacked.

The condition which includes all that is required is as simple as this. When the stored up traces of vital energy localised in the few cell ganglion of the bowels have their vitality attacked, they are set in motion, and a wave of nervous current rushes up with their complaint to the brain, the intellectual structure in man whose function it is to give the needed warning that the vitality of Sentient Personality is attacked. Immediately this takes place, the means is used to have the cause removed, and the case made public. When we see the stately carriage of the family physician drive up to the hall door, the doctor briskly step out and in haste enter the chamber of his wealthy patient, racked on a bed of pain, surrounded by all the modern comforts and luxuries which life-energy, acting through the human form, animated by the desire to increase a pleasure, has produced. For all beautiful and useful things displayed in the noble mansion were designed to gratify some one as trophies left by pleasure-seeking vitality. While this force passes on desirous to create new objects of beauty and usefulness that would gratify still farther. For such is the action of life—a force ever in motion, catching at a pleasure and repelling a pain.

Human intelligence is stimulated by striving to gratify others, and thereby secure the individual pleasure that approval gives. However, human nature is so varied in its choice, that one may retain as a pleasure what another, differently constituted, would avoid as a pain. This accounts for the variety of tastes the human race has manifested in all ages and under all conditions in its pleasure-seeking effort to sustain human vitality, as pleasure is the medium through which life gathers strength, feeds, and grows; and has toward the end of the 19th century produced the marvellous complexity that our social environments display. All is created to gratify some section of that medium. Nevertheless, a race so intelligent as this has developed all as the equivalent of sensations that group themselves into ideas.

All forms and varieties left to posterity by those that

have gone before, may be viewed as traces left of the life-sustaining sensation of pleasure or the death-threatening sensation of pain by a race who as individuals are animated by self-preservation. Reasoning this, all must allow that the tiny spot that first marked the abode of sensation has gathered marvellous strength represented by all that the race has accomplished.

A race endowed with the imaginative and inventive capacities, is capable of inspiring the individual geniuses it begets to higher and yet higher attainments. And yet all spring from sensation and may be stated thus. Every sensorial impression has itself a local habitation in the brain and forms a base of thought because capable of reproducing itself in thought. Further sensations, which are constantly arising, do not press away but become the inhabitants of memory cells. Memory cells in the bygone ages of the race sensation has created as the base self-consciousness rests in and acts through. The molecular activity of sensations have abiding forms in the human brain, the production of the sensorial motor system, which in its normal state functions so harmonously as to produce rational thought The sensorial motor combinations of molecular activity in the brain provides the material for thought that speech gives expression to.

The human form in its brain and nervous structure, which has taken countless ages to develop, is a production, when viewed from the standpoint of evolution, guided by motives, has been capable of developing the force we call rational self-direction, and as such is fitted for the work assigned it.

There can be no reasonable doubt but that the degree which marks the inferior intelligence of a dog and the superior intelligence of man, rests in the human form and its complicated brain and nervous structure. For sensation is the base of consciousness, and consciousness develops ideal conception of the most complex order in forming the molecular activity which the impressions coming from the external world provides as the sensations that represent the individual's external surrounding. In this process we have the rational explanation given of how the inward man, St. Paul referred to, is created. Such is the process whereby the brain has acquired the power that leads up to what we call human thought. When an intelligent being becomes insane, it is because a change has taken place in the nervous centres of his brain. When insanity is only a temporary effect, and passes away, the memory cells which contain the mental images in the ideal form as molecular activities, have regained sufficient strength to make their contents perceptible to Sentient Personality—the inner man—and can therefore provide the Ego with rational intelligent thought.

In viewing the evolution of man all rests in the fact that the Laws of Nature which produced all, give expression to the mind of God. Further that the evolution of the mental structure of man, as a process of sensations, was so ordered of God, to enable us to see how the human soul is developed by the vital force to which our earth gave birth in giving birth to the human sensations to which an individual is subject during his earthly life. These will embody in our immortal race all the changes man has experienced since he became man, for human sensations thus viewed, are Immortal Units.

CHAPTER III.

A SHORT ACCOUNT OF THE MECHANICAL PROCESS AT WORK IN DEVELOPING CONSCIOUS STATES BY THE HUMAN NERVOUS STRUCTURE.

WE are fully persuaded that our sun has given birth to the life of our planet in inducing sensation, which is life, a form of force ever in motion, attracting what sustains and repelling what weakens it. It is just one of the many forces in nature that manifest their presence in attracting and repelling. Life in this form is no exception; it is just a force acting through an organic tissue which it strives to maintain by attracting what gratifies the tissues' natural affinity, and repelling what offends it. Further, that the highest form of this force manifests itself through the human organism. Having formed such a conception indicated, I naturally look to the human brain as the point where the most complicated vital force manifests itself. I find there life making its activities felt by using the white fibres of the brain as conducting rods to unite cell to cell. By adopting this course, life can most effectually sustain and increase itself in acting through the medium of the human form.

The human form having created this highly endowed form of vitality, it develops and sustains it by enabling it to come in contact with the surrounding medium, so as to act and react on that medium in such a way as, in many cases, to put the forces of nature under the control of man as servants acting in obedience to him. Such activities are made very apparent in the Telephone and the Telegraph, but most of all in what Electricity is made to do in obedience to man. Electricity is a form of force into which almost every other force can be converted, and made to do many things man desires to have done, through the agency of inorganic matter. So marvellously as this have the vital forces of intellectual life stored up in the brain of man enabled humanity to fulfil the work first intrusted to man by his God, viz. "to replenish the earth and subdue it," Gen. i. 28. The means which enable man to accomplish the work assigned him by his God are to be found in the white fibres, the conducting rods that bring the intellectual forces of humanity stored up in the living human brain into contact with its surrounding medium.

The Brain, being the crowning edifice of the nervous system, to it I will shortly direct your attention. As it is in the cerebral brain that the activity of the nervous system culminates, it is with it specially I shall take to do. The office performed by cerebral activity is to develop the intellectual forces of humanity. Such intellectual forces in a series of conscious states form individual human units, animated by the energy of self-conservation, who survive death as the souls of the individuals who have formed the human race on earth since man became man. However, it is the action taking place in the brain through the agency of the nervous system which I specially refer to in this chapter, because all forms of sensations are attracted by the intellectual forces lodged in the brain, and to know something of the brain is necessary. So I shall shortly allude to it. The brain, as formerly stated, is composed of two hemispheres united by a series of white fibres. In the very centre between the two hemispheres the axis cylinder runs along, and in a way divides the hemispheres. The axis cylinder evidently is the fundamental of all the uniting fibres, and seems to represent the true nervous elements underlying every phenomenon of both hemispheres. This axis cylinder which evidently is the fundamental form of all uniting fibres, is surrounded as with a muff, forming a sheath composed of the network of the uniting fibres. This sheath varies in thickness as it is observed in the centre or the peripheral region of the system, between this sheath formed of the network of connecting fibres and the axis cylinder there is a highly refracting phosphoric fatty fluid substance called the myeline. Now this myeline, a highly refracting substance, seems to form an isolating body between the axis cylinder and the network of uniting fibres that form the sheath. The uniting fibres, as a whole, are called "Neuroglia," and constitute the mass of the white cerebral substances of both hemispheres. As is to be expected, these white fibres play a most important part in the brain organism, forming a web of extreme delicacy, in the midst of which the nervous cells are embedded and enveloped. For these connecting fibres form the counterpart of all sensibility. The brain is an organ formed of the hemispheres, the lobes of these hemispheres being composed of masses of grey matter irregularly distributed. In the very centre of each lobe is placed the optic thalames, surrounded as Dr. Luys has shown by the corpus striatum. This ganglion of grey matter, as a whole, is called the optic thalames, and forms a most important part of the cerebral brain. The hemispheres are also composed of the cerebral convolutions, which form layers of grey substance folded one upon the other. The sole object of this folding is to secure increase of space.

Before proceeding, I would again draw the reader's attention to the position of the brain, because to understand this clearly is a very important matter. There are the two lobes or hemispheres, with the axis cylinder running along the centre between both, enveloped with its muff formed of the network of uniting fibres, yet separated from the network by the myeline, which is the highly refracting substance. In the very centre of each lobe is the optic thalamus, composed of the corpus striatum and the opti-striata, into which the commissural fibres enter. Then the convolutions of the cerebral, formed of the layers one above another, in appearance well known to all, comprize the brain. I will now state shortly the different functions these groups of nervous elements perform.

The cortex or convolutions of each hemisphere, in a general way, are formed of three layers of cells imbedded in a network of the uniting fibres called the Neuroglia. The deeper layers are formed of what we may call very large cells. The next or middle layers are of smaller cells and of various sizes. The upper layers are composed of small cells. The function of the lowest layer, which has the largest cells, is apparently that of carrying out a voluntary impulse, which may be interpreted as the command of the vital force setting the machinery in motion to execute its desire.

For so it is. The function of the middle or centre layer of medium and smaller sized cells is that of storing up intelligence, whereas the function of the upper layer of small cells is that of giving expression to sensibility proper, and is where all outward impressions are, as it were, photographed in the form that these outward impressions present as human conceptions. As such, they are interpreted by Sentient Personality. Further, the upper layer forms the base of thought in supplying the medium that Intellectual Conception can manifest their presence through, and forming images perceived as ideal conceptions by Sentient Personality. The process at work seems to be this. When the impression is first made on the upper layer of the small cells which is participated in by Sentient Personality, it is in that case retained for a certain period of time on the upper layer, which is in such close connection with the middle layer, whose function is to absorbe the impression as an intellectual conception, just as it was perceived in being participated in by Sentient Personality. At a future time, it will re-appear as the activity of thought when again participated in by Sentient Personality. This is the source from which thought springs, whereas the forces employed to give expression to desire are stored up in the underlying layer of large cells. Remember these three layers of cells, just referred to, form the convolutions of the cerebral contex. It thus comes to pass that the cerebral convolutions, with their three layers of cells, have a three-fold office to perform. First, the upper layer, where human conceptions as mental images appear and when these are participated in by Sentient Personality, they are humanized and absorbed as ideas by the second layer, to reappear as thought. The third layer of large cells give expression to desires that the previous impression created.

The cerebral convolutions, as it were, impress the optic thalamus, which are of an oval form, of reddish colour, and have a double function to perform. First, they transmit all sense impressions which come from the outward world. To do this is the work done by the part called the optic thalamus, which receives and condenses all sense impressions in its own plaxuses before being carried on by the connecting fibres and lodged in the cerebral contex. For, in this central part of the optic thalamus, all sense impressions are conveyed, and apparently transformed into what we might call the intellctual units or elements of human ideas before,—we shall say,—they are photographed as intellectual conceptions on the upper layer cells of the cerebral contex, which we shall agree to call the "sensitive plate" provided to receive them, and present them as the human conceptions of the outward world to Sentient Personality. This the Ego, it may be, lives and vibrates in the vicinity of the axis cylinder which divides the hemispheres. Be that as it may, Sentient Personality, if effected by the intelligence received from the outward world, react accordingly, and does so through the corpus striatum, which forms part of the optic thalamus. For the function of the corpus striatum is that of carrying out the desire of Sentient Personality by appealing to the bodily organism to make these desires known to the outward world. Such is the twofold office referred to which the optic thalamus performs. First, it converges and conveys outward impressions to the sensitive plate—upper layer of cells—prepared to receive them. Secondly, it carries out the commands of Sentient Personality by showing the effect that the impressions conveyed had produced on the Ego. Such is the action and reaction which the intelligence conveyed from the outer world has produced on Sentient Personality. Or, say, an object made up of many parts has been transformed into a subjective state in the conception having been participated in by Sentient Personality passing through the human organism. Now the active agent employed to carry out all is the Neuroglia; that is, the uniting fibres forming the white substance of each hemisphere. And, remember, the fundamental form of the Neuroglia is to be found in the axis cylinder.

The bodily organism is enveloped by a network of these fibres which give expression to vitality, and in functioning, transform physical phenomena or impressions into the vitality of nerve vibration. Nervous vibration and sensation proper are co-existents, and point to the inference that sensation, as life, has built itself up in and of the nervous structure in giving expression to its own form of force. It may be that structure is the equivalent of the resistance vitality may have met with in its ceaseless movements. Anyhow, the vital force of the nervous system does give expression to human intelligence, its correlative, the vitality that creates the Ego, the human soul of sensation, for its ceaseless activity survives death, whose personality is held together by the attractive force of its intelligence acting in harmony to secure that end. Animated by the immortal sentiment hope generates in the—" I live and hope to live." When this end is attained, and the disembodied Ego realises it is so, that Ego will find itself animated by hope consolidated into the immortal conception of "I live and hope to live." For the sentiment of hope consolidated thus secures the eternal life of the soul not united to Christ in belief.

The bodily organism is enveloped in a network of nerve fibre, whose function is to transform physical phenomena into nerve vibration, and the power to develop intelligence rests in the integrity of the network. A network continuous throughout the system, and which culminates in the cerebral brain. The cerebral brain, the Seat of Intelligence, manifests its special form of force by attracting all forms of sensibility into its plaxuses. The eye, the ear, the nose, the mouth, and the tactile, are the special organs of sensibility developed to transform and to transfer their own forms of nervous vibration, first to the optic thalamus, which has, in like manner, a place prepared for each of these forms of nervous vibration. There they are condensed before the impressions they carry are lodged in the cerebral brain. Once lodged there, each impression vibrates in unison with the optic thalamus. The result arising from the optic thalamus and the cortex plaxuses being united by the same impressions is, that they now vibrate in unison. They are united by the white fibres which carry impressions. To these impressions the white fibres perform the office of conducting rods. To understand the operation I have been pointing out more fully, I would direct the reader's attention to plates 5 and 6 in Dr. Luys' volume—"The Brain and its Function." In plate 5, page 31, you will see the arrangement carefully pointed out by the centre figures 7, 8, 9, 10. In these the senses of sight, hearing, smell, and the general sense of sensation, are condensed in the optic thalamus before being lodged in the cerebral contex. Observe that the 8th and 9th condensing mediums are much the largest. That such are the largest is no theory, but a fact, proved by scientific investigation. Such scientific investigation is wonderfully helped forward by the method of study adopted by Dr. Luys in placing his thin brain sections in position, photographing them, and by this means making the form visible to the naked eye. The points 8 and 9 referred to as much larger is easily accounted for by the fact that these are the points in connection with general sensation and the optic centre. The action taking place in the latter may be illustrated thus. A human impression transmitted from the eye is conveyed at point 8, plate 5, where it is humanized, in giving expression to the human form of this group of intellectual combinations. The term *humanized* is intended to indicate a human conception or idea. For example, the conception formed by a human being of natural scenery is totally different from the conception formed of it by a dog or a horse, and this difference is mainly due to the formation of the eye and nervous structure in what takes place at point 8 in the optic thalamus.

The luminous impression conveyed by the eye fibres is absorbed at point 8, shaped into a human ideal conception, and photographed on the sensitive plate prepared for it on the upper layer of the cerebral plaxus, whose function it is to give expression to sensibility. This layer of cells is called by Dr. Luys the "Sensorium Commune." Take note, before the impression thus transmitted, humanized, and photographed, can become an intellectual conception united in every part, it must have been participated in by Sentient Personality perceiving the impression as such and such. It is in the Ego—Sentient Personality—participating in an impression that secures for it an ideal existence as the memory of our intellectual conception united by the law of association. Such ideas are absorbed by the middle layer composed of the memory cells. The function of these cells is to absorb intellectual combinations that have been participated in by the Ego, and at a future time reproduce the conception as thought, which, as such, is again photographed on the upper layer of cells, called the "Sensorium Commune." When all the senses have been engaged in conveying impressions, the action that takes place is quite the same, except that all the centres marked in the plates referred to—7, 8, 9, 10—are simultaneously engaged in a converging and humanizing process, before what we have agreed to call photographing the impression on the Sensorium Commune. But, remember, the idea must be participated in by the Ego, else it would have no existence. The process is what St. Paul would call being " seized by the inner man," as the process of creating him. For so it is.

It is through the agency of the uniting fibres that the optic thalamus and the " Sensorium Commune," (the upper layer of cells) vibrate in unison. The case is this. The uniting fibres which converge in the optic thalamus, and carry the impressions to be photographed by the agency of nerve force on the "Sensorium Commune," are the medium through which the upper layer of cells is united with the optic thalamus, and vibrates in unison as one instrument. (It may be these two points are kept vibrating in unison, while the impression is participated in by the Ego.) Being united by the converging fibres thus, the cortex substance and the optic thalamus form one instrument. For the conception conveyed in the intellectual combination has in each centre a habitation. The centres are united by the converging fibres, which play such a prominent part. You see from what I have said, that the only open gate between the external world and the Psycho-intellectual activity stored up in the cortical substance, is through the optic thalamus, where the objective impressions are humanized before being lodged in the cortex as intellectual combinations through the operation I shall more fully describe as I proceed.

Each sensorial centre has a special point localised and endowed by its own form of nerve force, which is the special form of sensibility that each sense gives expression to in the optic thalamus and the cortical brain. These substances are united by the converging fibres at the birth of the human being, and it is the richness or poorness of the soil of these special forces referred to that determines the natural predisposition of the human being. For example, the foci, say, of sight, develop their own form of sensation, having a point localised for their use in the optic thalamus and the cortex substance. When these points are richly endowed with their own form of vitality, the individual has a soil ready prepared which will amplify and perfect the impression received just in proportion to the richness and degree of the vitality placed at their disposal. The same is true of all sensorial centres. For each being specially endowed with its own form of vital force, will act in like manner. In this way is the secret unveiled which accounts for one individual being so much more highly gifted than another, even in the same family.

From a double induction mentioned by Dr. Luys, it is made clear that the optic thalamus is the essential central region which forms the bond of union between the nervous elements of the central cerebral system. It is shown that through the tissue of the optic thalamus, pass all forms of nervous currents—that is, *vibratory sensibility*. These radiate from the external world, as well as the vibrations coming from vegetable life through the ganglion formed of the cells in the bowels conducted by their nervous fibres. In the secret chambers of the optic thalamus all these vibrations of nervous force are diffused, and make a halt before darting out in all directions, in a humanized form, as food for the activities of the special forms of the vibratory sensibility stored up in the cortical substance. This substance only lives and works because animated by these stimulating excitations.

One thing I wish to be clearly understood is, that it is by passing through the special sensorial centres—the foci of each being so clearly described, pointed out, and proved, as such and such, by the method of study adopted by Dr. Luys—that all sensations—that is, nervous vibrations—pass on to the Psycho-intellectual region of the cortical cortex. These vibrate in unison with the special foci of their own forms of force in the optic thalamus. Further, the function which these parts of the optic thalamus have to perform is that of transmitting humanized sensorial impressions, consequently all the sensorial impressions pass through it.

Now, it comes to pass, that the other part of the optic thalamus I have to explain, called the corpus striatum, which embraces the optic thalamus I have referred to, has a totally different function. Its function is that of carrying out the will or desire of Sentient Personality, Soul, or Ego (built up of and held as the vital energy of self-conservation), giving expression to voluntary, as well as sometimes happens to involuntary impulses, by setting the bodily organism in motion to carry out the desire of Sentient Personality.

To try to make this part more easily understood, I will state a few general facts which enter into the subject matter. With this object in view, let it be remembered that nerve-force is sensibility striving to maintain its vitality. That it is this form of force that creates the nervous cells in storing up special forms of sensibility as nerve-force, capable of reacting in the presence of the surrounding medium. When the medium strikes the cord of any form of sensibility which has been heretofore stored up in a cell, that cell is called into activity. Now, it is in being in this way called into activity that the automatic form of nerve current rests. A nerve cell, charged with a special form of sensibility, as nerve force, by reacting in presence of its medium, creates a course of action that may only cease when the forces exhaust themselves. Such is the automatic activity of the organisms, and in them we have forces ever ready to start into motion in the presence of their medium. When we further realize that the whole nervous system, united in all its parts, is the result of all forms of sensibility striving to live their own life, then we can comprehend the unity at work. We perceive what these united forces, animated by one sentiment, viz., that of maintaining their vitality, have to excite them when the newly-born infant is plunged into a cold atmosphere. Then the profound affinities become simultaneously affected by the excitation from the external world in the infant, at birth, being plunged into a cold atmosphere. It is in consequence of this that the nervous system, in its united action, striving to maintain its vitality, creates Sentient Personality, the Soul, Ego, the immortal part of the infant. Thus, then, the immortal unit, of what we may call the self-conservative form of organic energy, has started into activity, which, in creating a conscious state, shall never cease, but continue to live its own life all through eternity.

The human form, in giving birth to the Soul, as Sentient Personality, creates the vital form of force which henceforth regulates its activities, and gives that activity definite expression in being its life, its vitality. For it is Sentient Personality, in creating the vitality of the infant, that infuses the activity of life into its cells. Observe, Intelligence—the equivalent of conscious states—rises from impressions having been participated in by Sentient Personality perceiving the impression as such. The infant at birth would perceive the cold as pain or discomfort. Once an impression has become united thus with Sentient Personality, in forming an intellectual unit, that unit becomes a moving power in the Psycho activities, and is stored up as such in the cells prepared to receive it. This unit is ready to start into activity if excited by the surrounding medium. Such is the processs by which our Intelligence is created and developed. Intelligence thus created, as the fruit of impressions, is to be guided by Sentient Personality—the moving power which directs the forces stored up in the portion of the optic thalamus called the corpus striatum, the function of which I proceed to explain. From what I have said, it will be seen that the action which governs the forces of the corpus striatum, comes from within, guided and directed by impressions made on Sentient Personality. This form of activity, in its highest function, is governed by intelligence and regulated by motives. It is, indeed, the form of force which gives expression to the desires of the individual, in completing the circle that the outward impressions, carried by the optic thalamus to the Psycho-intellectual cells, began.

The corpus striatum is the complement of the optic thalamus, which occupies the central regions of both hemispheres, the natural poles around which all the nervous elements gravitate. The fact is, that the optic thalamus, as it were, forms the crown of the posterior column of the spinal axis. Whereas, the corpus striatum is situated on the intero-lateral column It is, therefore, a point of interest to remark that the same relations that exist in the whole spinal cord are here clearly represented. In the spinal cord, the region of the sensitive or excito-motor, is posterior, and the motor region, anterior. In the brain, the same arrangement exists as to relation and neighbourhood. Indeed, the optic thalamus is the region where the sensorial impressions are humanized, and press inward to the cerebral cortex — that is, the Sensorium Commune — where they are seized by the Ego. Whereas, the corpus striatum is the place of halt and reinforcement of the motor stimulants that proceed outward from the cerebral cortex, giving expression to the impression made on Sentient Personality by the intelligence received from without and passed in through the optic thalamus. In the brain, we thus find the same automatic arrangement presented where the phenomenon of sensation occurs, and where the motor stimuli are elaborated as that which represent similar phenomena in the spinal cord proper.

Take note, the corpus striata are situated in front of the optic thalami, and gradually diminish in their backward course. As a consequence of the anatomical arrangement of the corpus striatum and the optic thalamus, the converging fibres which carry impressions to the optic thalamus before they arrive at their destination in the convolutions of the cerebral cortex, have to pass through a more or less considerable thickness of the corpus striatum, and traverse it from one side to the other.

The colour column of the corpus striatum is the same wherever it is observed. It is reddish, flabby, and composed of special anatomical elements, and it is studded with an infinite whitish serpentine fibre, which represents the end of the motor fibres of the spinal cord. In this locality, also, there is a mass of yellowish matter, which plays an important part as a centre of radiation for nerve force, related as it is with the cerebellar peduncles called the yellow nucleus, which also play a very important part as a centre of radiation for nerve force. One point of special interest is this, that the numerous elements that enter into the anatomic constitution of the corpus striatum are divided into two groups. One of these groups may be considered as a system of efferent fibres, the other as a system of afferent fibres. To have a clear conception of the following important point, note, that the efferent group represent those radiating from the convolutions of the cerebral, whereas the afferent fibres represent the cerebellar element, being the arrangement of of the corpus striatum. The elements of the first group, on account of their origin and termination, are called cortica-striata. For, remember, they radiate from the Psycho-intellectual activities. When these fibres arrive at the frontier of the optic thalamus and the corpus striatum, they are immediately refracted from below upwards in the form of spiroid lines and are disposed of in the different cell territories of the corpus striatum with which they are specially connected. These fibres, properly speaking, represent the bond of union that indicate voluntary movement. I do not wish to convey what is known as free-will in that term, but force guided by motive.

They proceed from the cerebral convolution, to the different cell territories of the corpus striatum, where they are reinforced, destined to be condensed and changed into articulate sound or gesture, &c., that is, into the form of motor force required to carry out the desire of the individual—Sentient Personality. These elements thus become united with the spinal cord which acts as directed in accordance with the mandate of the Ego.

It has been proved by many that there are in the cerebral convolutions independent centres united with the different parts of the muscular system. A union of this kind must be effected through the spinal cord. From what has been made apparent by many experiments—especially those by Luys—it may be considered as proved scientifically that the different groups of cortico-striata fibres have each an independent point of origin, as the medium through which desire or voluntary effort is manifested. The energy that enables these efforts to be carried out flows into the corpus striatum from the cerebellar through the peduncles and represents the yellow nucleus of the corpus striatum. This flow of energy in an indirect way comes from the active elements of the cerebellar. Fibres of the cerebellum region taper away insensibly, and embrace white spinal fibres which expand in the corresponding region of the corpus striatum. They must be a phenomena of much importance, when we know that through the unceasing active foci of nerve radiation, charged with cerebellar motor influences, they overflow into the corpus striatum. The cerebellar elements in this way become intimately associated with vital phenomena, and like a current of electricity, charge its cells, being connected with all our efferent motor acts, and giving to our movements their regularity, their force, and their continuity.

Thus, then, the cerebellar energy silently disposes itself through all the conscious and unconscious actions of the organism. This force seems indispensable for the carrying out of every motor act whatever. Such an important part as this does the energy of the special elements of the cerebellum play in its relation to the corpus striatum. The cerebellum—little or after Brain—which plays such an important part, is "placed behind the convolution hemisphere, and is connected from beneath with a detached branch of the great stem," and above with the convolution through the corpus striatum. The white fibres through which this connection is manifested are the rods or conductors made use of by the nerve current. This current is the living force by which our conscious and unconscious movements are performed. The flow of conscious movements along these fibres proceed from the cortex of the cerebral brain' and express themselves in the form of voluntary movements, which indicate the desires of Sentient Personality made known to contemporaries. For vital force is of this material form. These efferent fibres, which proceed from the cortex striatum, and produce the marvellous results of all our movements, are called the cerebellar peduncles, and are grouped in an isolated form of fascicles in a spiroid fashion, after having traversed the pins, are lodged in the special point which stands related to their forms of movements in the spinal axis. However, these nerves or conducting rods which unite the spinal cord and the corpus striatum at their point of origin in the corpus striatum, are not distinctly isolated, but when they finally emerge from the corpus straitum, they appear as three demicones, one enclosing the other. They have been much reinforced by the yellow nucleus of the corpus striatum. Thus strengthened, they pass on a level with the mendulla to the opposite side of the spinal cord, and are lodged in various parts of it. All the forces stored up in the spinal cord are arranged like a series of electric machines ready to start into motion, on the arrival of the special form of force stored up in each of the fascicle, such being the expression of the automatic form of nerve force ever ready to start into activity in the presence of its medium, that is in the presence of the active form of force which these fascicles of the spinal cord contain. Indeed, this is true of all fascicles reacting in harmony with their medium.

Observe, the forms of force which proceed from and reside in the corpus striatum have infused into them the forms of force proceeding from the cerebral, cerebellar, and the spinal cord. Further, observe, that it is through these varied forms of force that the circle is finally formed which originates in the sense impression from without, carried on through the optic thalamus to be lodged in the cerebral cortex. This circle, when completed, gives expression to the human form of intelligence in thought and action. The last part of the circle, which indicates motor action proceeding from the cortical substance, makes its first halt in the corpus striatum in its descending course where so many different forms of force mingle. They halt in the corpus striatum, doubtless to be reinforced and moulded before darting on in the form of force with which they stand related to the spinal cord. Remember, these rods which unite the spinal cord and the cortex convolutions, effect that union through the intervention of the corpus striatum, and we know that the forces stored up in the corpus striatum obey the mandate of the Ego in carrying out the desire of the individual. It comes to pass that, when these rods that effect this union emerge from their point of origin in the corpus straitum, they are not distinctly isolated, but appear as three demicones. The one embraces the other, and is much reinforced by the yellow nucleus of the corpus striatum. Now, the corpus striatum is the point of halt and reinforcement on its outward mission in completing the circle that gives expression to the effect produced on Sentient Personality, by the tidings from the outward world which originated the circle carried through the optic thalamus to the cortex convolutions. This being so, assuredly in our present state of knowledge we are justified in assuming that the threefold rod which issues from the corpus striatum in the three demicones, one enclosed in the other, much reinforced by the element of the corpus striatum on their way to the spinal cord is the condition whereby the effect produced on Sentient Personality is made known to the world without. They may be viewed as representing three different mental states, namely, Feeling, Intellect, and Will. These may combine and act in harmony as one united whole in giving expression to the highest form of the mental force called Volition. In consequence, it adopts a course of action which nearest of all conforms to what is called "the Freedom of the Will"—that is, guided by motives to choose the line of conduct with deliberation—a mental state into which Discrimination, Similarity, and Memory enter. They must enter, because on this threefold cord hangs the Human Intellect, with the marvellous power to develop which it possesses. For example, note the great gulf that lies between the power to discriminate the points that differ and the points that agree, possessed by some of our most eminent men of science in comparison with the discriminating intellectual power of a savage, or even of an ordinary individual. The fact is, the men of science, in their own special subjects, see points of agreement and points of difference wholly hid from the ordinary observer. And yet it is the same laws that are at work in all cases. For each class is drawing its conclusions from the discriminating power which Memory supplies. In the Intellect of the race rests the human understanding of the race, the activity which the threefold nerve-fibre, issuing from the corpus striatum, I infer, gives expression to.

Of the threefold cord of Intellect, Feeling, and Will, is man's intelligence formed. On these grouped forces rests man's activity as an immortal unit, capable of an eternal form of progressive development. With us Intellect is the first cause, Feeling the moving current, Will the guiding power. Thus, then, in our present state of probation, it is of much importance to comprehend with clearness how much of the future development of the race depends on making the contemporary race conversant with the laws on which rests the development of the material Soul or Ego to which our planet has given birth, in giving birth to the individuals of the human race. The diffusion of such knowledge must come through the agency of the spinal cord, in talking, in writing, in printing, &c. Indeed, in diffusing knowledge through all the mechanical processes open to the race on all sides, the forces required to accomplish all are locked up in the fascicles of the spinal cord, that receives its mandate through the corpus striatum.

Now, the point which should be known and understood by all is that the activity passing through the spinal cord completes the circle that gives expression to the reaction of the Ego, that is, the organism striving to retain its vitality by securing a pleasure and repelling a pain. For example, supposing something to have happened in the physical world which caused the individual pleasure. The physical condition involved would, by pressing through the organism, be transformed into the intellectual form of vital energy— nerve current passing on through the optic thalamus to the Sensorium Commune (the upper layers of the convolution cells), where the phenomenon carried from the physical world transformed into an intellectual conception formed of the elements of the idea affect the Ego or Sentient Personality pleasantly, and is the action which completes the half circle the physical world gave birth to. The other half of this circle is formed when Sentient Personality, acting through the corpus striatum, applies to the world to have the pleasure continued or renewed, which completes the circle. What takes place is this. The physical phenomenon, by means of the vitality of the human body, was transformed into life current, and as such conveyed a human conception which was participated in by Sentient Personality (and in being so participated in, it became part of the Ego), which reacted on the physical world through the nerve forces of the organism.

As all the physical phenomena transformed into human conception carry with them the pleasure or pain with which they are charged or associated, the effect produced on Sentient Personality depends on whether the phenomenon carries a pleasure or a pain. If painfully effected, the circle will be completed in the reaction of Sentient Personality to repel the pain: if pleasantly, by an effect to retain the pleasure. This circle completed transforms dead matter into the abiding human form of living force that builds up the Soul or Ego—the immortal human form of force developing conscious states on our planet by, we shall say, the agency of our sun. That the vital force of our planet has been developed by the agency of the sun is apparently certain. It is also true that during the period life has existed, the sun has ministered toward all the forms of vital force found thereon, even the most complicated of all, namely, that found at work in the human brain, represented by its nerve cells embedded in its wonderful net-work of nervous fibres, with its two hemispheres. The elements of these are strictly associated in being united by the white fibres that serve as conducting rods, these fibres being the means whereby the brain as a whole may be said to vibrate in unison under the influence of a strong emotion, and communicating its phase of vibration to the organism, in the expression of joy or sorrow, as the case may be, which in the brain agitates Sentient Personality. For the ceaseless vital movement at work as a whole is the vitality of the Soul or Ego, namely Sentient Personality, that living force once developed ever in motion, therefore ever capable of feeling. And to feel, or to be capable of feeling, is to live.

These strong emotions manifest the active energy in moving along the white fibres that unite both hemispheres. In doing so, they pass through the axis cylinder, which is the fundamental fibre surrounded by its sheath of connecting firbes, and the highly refracting substance the Myeline, interposing between the axis cylinder and the sheath fibre wall of uniting tissue. Through these conditions all life currents must pass in uniting both hemispheres. Therefore, the vital action taking place here must play a most important part when viewed from the light thrown on Life and its Laws by modern research which so clearly defines the part the nervous system plays as a whole. We have in this highly refracting substance referred to, an element which can transmit to the fundamental fibre all forms of vibration as life current placed in the very centre of the brain and surrounding the axis cylinder. The axis cylinder doubtless is transformed in being built up of every form of individual intelligence stored up in both hemispheres, yet it stands isolated from them by the Myeline. In this arrangement have we not conditions most likely to form the point from which

Sentient Personality reacts. And it comes to pass that Sentient Personality only lives and acts in the organism while animated by impressions from the physical world conveyed through the medium of our senses. Observe, the vital force of the axis cylinder might react on the physical world by applying directly to the corpus striatum. It would thus set the organism in motion by giving expression to the form of action determined on. By these the white cerebral activity would be thrown into agitation by the feeling and vibrating human personality (we shall agree to say resides in the axis cylinder), and in this way the corpus striatum, through its different fibres, would appeal to the forces stored up in the lower cells of the cortex convolution for their aid, and to the other fibres through the medulla to the fascicles in the spinal cord to carry into execution the behest of the Ego which we assume lives and vibrates in the axis cylinder and its vicinity. That the arrangement in the surrounded axis cylinder must play a most important part in intelligent life is certain, when viewed from the standpoint of the part played by the nervous system as a whole. The axis cylinder stands in the very centre of the nervous structure where the most complicated action takes place.

For, I would again repeat, we have the fundamental fibre running along the centre where the two hemispheres are united, yet isolated from both by a highly refracting substance capable of transmitting all phases of life current, therefore all forms of intelligence. Now, on either side, we have the hemispheres, with their wonderfully complicated arrangement, which receive the physical disturbance vitalized by passing through the senses, and humanized by passing through the optic thalamus, photographed on the upper cells of the cortex convolutions as the impressions which outward things, as well as thought, make on the human brain, and as such are seized by Sentient Personality. Now we have to find a place for the human soul to act from, in the organism which creates it. To postulate the place most likely, is assuredly in the truly vital forces vibrating in the vicinity of the axis cylinder, if not in the cylinder itself. A cylinder which stands in the centre of the points where these double impressions are being made at the same time on the cerebral cortex transmitted by the optic thalamus right and left: impressions which have to be seized by Sentient Personality before they can become the intellectual conception of an ideal form. The most reasonable point to suppose this action taking place in, is assuredly the axis cylinder, or its vicinity as the abode of the soul created of the intellectual units—that is the states of consciousness—it seizes in the point most highly endowed with vitality. Such must be so as the cylinder is the fundamental fibre of the nervous structure; and we are understood to be supposing that the impressions are what we agree to call photographed on either side of it by nerve force impressions which have to be seized by the Ego or Sentient Personality. The thought to which these impressions give birth reappears in the same position. The activity which thought springs from is this. When a physical impression, transformed into an ideal form, arrives from the outward world on the Sensorium Commune, while it is being participated in by Sentient Personality, it becomes absorbed by the second or middle layer of cells ready to reappear at a future time as thought, possibly modified considerably. It is when we comprehend all these vital forces of nervous activity at work in the centre region where intelligence is developed, that we begin to comprehend what is included and implied in Immortality, which is the vitality of Sentient

Personality, ever in motion, whose action does not cease when the organism dies, but continues to live as its Ego by absorbing energy to form conscious states.

The vital forces passing along the human nervous structure possess the power of transforming physical phenomena into the human form of life current, but before these become intellectual conceptions the impressions have to be participated in by Sentient Personality seizing them, and by the act of so doing, it retains the impression for a longer or shorter period in the web of nervous fibres which embrace those upper cells, and vibrate in unison with the optic thalamus. In this arrangement I infer that Sentient Personality vibrating in the centre forces which confront the impression right and left, and in seizing the impression so acts, as to retain the phenomenon on the nervous web as long as it is being participated in by the Ego. For during that time the now contrasted forces, right and left, are as it were held in equilibrium by the action of Sentient Personality. It is in the power Sentient Personality possesses, as the truly vital force, to seize and interpret, that Intelligence rests. The case being so, accounts for the development of the Ego as the vital energy of self-conservation which acts and re-acts in the human form by seizing and interpreting the human forms of intelligence transmitted.

Again I repeat, the action and reaction explained is the basis on which human intelligence rests. It being so, I think all must allow that the most probable point for the Ego to act from must be in the centre region between the two hemispheres—that is the vital forces in and around the axis cylinder formed of the fundamental fibre which the uniting fibres of both hemispheres minister to, yet separated from both by the highly refracting Myeline.

The case might be put thus. Sentient Personality, by seizing the impressions on the Sensorium Commune, holds that phenomenon in its place during the time it is being participated in by the Ego, whose action is in harmony with the effect produced, causing a pleasure or a pain perceived either to be present or remote. Thus far man is an automatic machine, ever seizing a pleasure or repelling a pain. But viewed as an intelligent being, capable of perceiving far-reached consequences, and being guided by motives, he is a rational being.

Doubtless the human nervous system, endowed with its marvellous capacity, is a production of the forces of nature transformed into the organic energy as the correlative of the conscious states the individual organisms of that race was subject to during natural life. These organic forces are rendered immortal in having built up the spiritual bodies of the members of our race. An individual nervous structure thus created, if its own conscious state is the medium vitality strives to maintain in seizing a pleasure and repelling a pain; using this system to develop Intelligence, which is lodged in the brain, and greatly increases man's responsibility as an immortal unit, who as such has to take into account the fact that a revelation has been given to our race, which takes to do with that race in the state of existence which each member of it as an individual unit enters at death.

It is a revelation that defines the laws that govern that state of existence. That condition concerns us all more than anything that can happen to us in this world. This being so, the individual formed of the vital force I have referred to, has to take into account this after state of its existence in choosing the course it will adopt. While animated with the desire to secure the highest attainable pleasure, and to avoid the after consequences pain would cause.

Bearing in mind, that in the immortal state there can be no concealment, as every conscious state whatsoever is a unit of the Ego, inseparable therefrom, as all was achieved through the agency of the human nervous structure, which embraces the body, retains a trace of all, and forms a net-work of nervous fibres connected and continuous throughout with the net-work of the same substance that embrace both hemispheres. The hemispheres are divided by the fundamental fibre, the axis cylinder, that runs along the centre. This system, while tenanted by Sentient Personality, supplies the condition on which life-force develops human intelligence. For what constitutes a living organism is an organism capable of feeling. Therefore, while the human organism retains Sentient Personality, which it creates of the continuous stream of sensation, it is capable of feeling, and consequently is a living organism, having the power to impart vitality to the force passing along its nervous structure. For immediately a physical excitation impinges upon the organism and is participated in by Sentient Personality, it becomes a vitalized unit, united to that organism, and is thus capable of making itself felt as an intellectual unit—say, an idea formed of its elements—solidified as a conscious state in becoming one of the conceptions of which the Ego is formed. It is not the nervous structure that is thus vital, but the forces passing along that structure. Vitality is the moving current ever in motion. Thus, then, the physical excitation passing along the nervous fibres is vitalized while in motion, because it is in a condition capable of being felt. And if the physical excitation is accompanied by an equivalent of pleasure or pain, it is bound to be felt. For, in that case, it will affect the natural affinity of Sentient Personality, which will react accordingly. Thus, then, the living organism, by imparting this power to be felt to the physical excitation that impinges on it, bridges the gulf wherein consciousness resides. Consciousness, in the abstract, is the developed equivalent of the vital force which we say was created by the sun's absence, felt as a privation, and his presence a gratification, as the effect produced on the stored up rays of light he had some time left behind him in some very special condition on our planet. Conditions so surrounded, were rendered capable of feeling, therefore, vitalized. This is a form of force which shows its natural affinity in the presence of what strengthens or weakens, by automatically attracting the first and repelling the last. This natural affinity, in the course of ages, has developed for its use the human nervous structure, to use it as its support, and thereby develop individual forms of human intelligence. A form of intelligence which possesses such marvellous possibilities, both in this world and the next.

Vital force, once produced, is endowed with the property of transforming physical excitations into life currents, because life is sensitive and ever in motion, attracting what strengthens and repelling what weakens. It is vitality creating this automatic current and imparting it to the forces that impinge on it which transforms dead matter into a living form.

The nucleus of intelligence is developed when physical excitations are transformed into life current by Sentient Personality, the moving force of the organism, perceiving the physical excitement to be the cause that affects it—that is, perceiving the action of known objects that affect vitality pleasantly or painfully. To perceive these conditions and guide our actions accordingly is intelligence regulating the activity of Life. It is alike the cause and conditions that transform physical phenomena into intellectual conceptions. Or we may put the case thus. Sentient Personality, the active force of the organism, by perceiving the physical object as such that gratifies it, develops an intellectual conception. For a physical excitation has been thus changed into an ideal form capable of being felt as the cause that excited the Ego's natural affinities in causing it pleasure. Of course, the same is true of pain.

It is in life or nervous current carrying with it the physical phenomenon in the conception, impression, or image perceived, that operates in creating the condition that has quickened into human intelligence. Let us look at the subject from the marvellous arrangement of the sensibility that created the cerebral cells, and that enables them to enter into relation with their surrounding medium. We see from this point, in the vibration of sound, waves affecting atmospheric air, these waves, in assuming the vibration that vital force has prepared by their aid for their acceptance on entering the ear, have vitality imparted to them. For these sound waves have passed into a condition possible to be felt. Atmospheric air being affected in a certain form develops the equivalent of sound. Immediately these waves impinge on the ear of the organism, they become sound or life units. Thus far they are in a condition to be felt—that is, have been vitalized because made capable of being felt. You will observe it is the net-work of nervous fibres that embraces the living organism that produces vibration capable of being felt, by transforming physical force into its own form of force, viz., that of life current. The function of life current is to feel and perceive the objects that affect vitality pleasantly or painfully, so as to avoid the one and attract the other. Knowing and choosing so lays the foundation of intelligence.

The human form of intelligence is created through the human organism so wonderfully endowed by the special forms of life-force stored up in its sensorial centres. Each of these sensorial centres is affected pleasantly by some physical phenomena and painfully by others. For example, the ear is charmed by harmony and pained by discord. The eye is gratified when we emerge from a dark place and always greets sunlight with pleasure. Now, as the automatic action of life is to create a current that attracts pleasure and repels pain—that is, what strengthens or weakens life. Such is the function of vitality, whereas to perceive the cause that affects vitality either way, and act accordingly, gives expression to the function of intelligence. That is, vitality in functioning, repels a pain and attracts a pleasure. Intelligence, in functioning, perceives the cause that affects vitality either pleasantly or painfully, and regulates its action accordingly. These conditions as they develop, produce human intelligence in building up the human brain (of which I have said so much), and the organism. Each sensorial centre in transforming a physical excitation into a vital current, transmits the condition of the phenomena. Pain, a vital phenomenon is the histological equivalent of the organism in conflict with the surrounding medium. Pleasure, a vital phenomenon, is the physiological equivalent of the organism gratified by the surrounding medium—the expression of these vital phenomena, as such, mark the distinction between the lowest organism and the very highest. The human is merely marked by infinite degrees. But the fact that pain is proved to be the physiological sensibility of the nervous elements raised to an extra physiological pitch is of much importance, as it proves that the vital phenomenon of pain is not merely sensibility, but that a certain tension of it is a necessary condition as the phenomenon that marks the *reacting* vital force. Pain, being excessive nervous vibration, is neutralized when this condition is changed. It is so that chloroform just freezes the nervous elements of the Sensorium Commune, so that the painful vibrations caused by the operations cannot communicate their phase of vibration to it, and thereby affect Sentient Personality. Moral pain is no exception, but is the brain made to vibrate in excess through the effect produced by intellectual conception being perceived by human reason as adverse consequences pending, or present.

Shortly, vitality, wherever a brain exists, is being sensitive to pleasure and pain, and acting automatically creates a current that attracts what gratifies because it increases vitality and repels what pains because it lowers vitality. The first increases the sum total of life; the last diminishes it. All living organisms in possession of a brain come to perceive the physical world that surrounds them by that world affecting the organism either pleasantly or painfully. Whereas intelligence is developed in perceiving the cause these sensations arise from, their vitality create a current that attracts the phenomenon of the physical medium to which the pleasure is attached and repels the phenomenon that pain is attached to. This takes place when we say a physical cause is transformed into a mental state, by the force that perceives so as to interpret the nature of the physical cause that affects it. I think we are justified in inferring that the nervous structure has been developed by the forces carrying these phenomena leaving traces behind them to serve as conducting rods for the activities of life. As in the advancing series of life the more complicated the brain structure becomes, the more complicated and varied are the physical phenomena perceived to be which cause pleasure and pain when viewed from the material base, which Dr. Luy's proves mind to have, in his book "The Brain and its Function." The inference that follows is that the base mind rests in, is a production of the physical phenomena that have caused the individual's pleasure and pain. To perceive these physical phenomena which have an ideal habitation in the brain, in the effect they have, or will produce, is human intelligence viewed in the abstract, giving expression to the automatic activity of the human brain.

The immortal part,—the created human personality,— Soul or Ego, are the multiplying forms given birth to by the social organism of our race during every period of its existence. Created thus of sensations is the individual soul of the current of life ever in motion, moving along the human nervous structure. Observe, it is not the growth of structure I at present refer to. It is the growth of the vital current expressing itself in conscious states moving along the nervous structure which the organism and its environments create and sustain during natural life in developing the soul, held together as human personality. What takes place when the human organism dies, is that the soul it created sustains its activities in its body of organic energy, by absorbing energy, to form conscious states which it returns in functioning.

Of such is the human personality, soul, or Ego. For every sensation the individual experienced is the equivalent of a form of organic energy, the soul in its disembodied state is capable of developing, and may liberate in functioning. Thus then, every sensation is the counterpart of a special form of organic energy developed in passing through a human nervous structure, capable of being reproduced as thought by the disembodied soul. Such is the energy that forms Sentient Personality, the Human Soul, the Immortal part. For the Ego in the human form is formed of organic energy, which, in being capable of forming the previous conscious states, embodies the life history of that individual in the current of life ever in motion—immortal, because the equivalent of sensations which the intellectual conception of thought rise from. Souls which embody their life history are units capable of communicating with their kind, represent the highest form of vitality our planet has produced. Immortal human units can combine and communicate in the state of existence *Life* enters into when it quits the body at death, as the immortal human units our race has given birth to. A race divided into two sections by Our Lord: the one section indicates the natural man, which Our Lord defines as that which is born of the flesh is flesh; the other section which have a spiritual nature imparted to them through their union with Christ, which our Lord defined as born of the spirit is spirit: thus clearly does Evolution illuminate Christianity. The first section, viewed in the light of modern research, indicates the material nature of the Immortal Ego; the other, the spiritual nature, union with Christ confers. The first is the seed of man to which our earth has given birth, read in the light revelation imparts, illuminated by modern research, which unfolds the nature and office that the human nervous system performs. Its activity is a marvellous construction, and culminates in the cerebral brain, which can be finally reduced to three principal forms of activity. For it is permissible to infer, the first—Sensibility, which enables the cerebral cells to enter into relationship with their surrounding medium. The second—Organic Phosphoresence, which confers on cerebral life the property of storing up in itself and retaining for a time the sensorial vibrations which excites it. The third—Automatic, the aptitude the nerve cells possess of reacting in presence of the surrounding medium when once impressed by it. For all cerebral activity can be so explained.

It is well known that, in the inorganic world, phosphorescent bodies retain for a longer or shorter time traces of the luminous vibration which have been impinged on them. This being so, that organic phosphorescent bodies would so act in the brain, by absorbing and retaining human conceptions in that form, is apparently the true condition of work. However, I define the same condition taking place in the term when I say such impressions are photographed on the Sensorium Commune. As I think the term photographed will convey a clear conception of an impression made and retained to a certain class than would be conveyed by using the other term. Though, without a doubt, the true condition is that organic phoshorescence stores up in the brain the impression impinging on it, which has been participated in by the Ego. An Ego formed of the individual sum total of conscious states grouped together as the soul liberated at death, leaves in the brain duplicate forms of every sensation to which it was subject.

CHAPTER IV.

THE LIFE-SUSTAINING PROPERTY OF THE BLOOD.

ALTHOUGH the nervous structure is so marvellously endowed, it is wholly dependent on the circulation of the blood to sustain its vitality. Vitality creates the enduring form of human intelligence in creating Sentient Personality, soul, or Ego — the correlative of the conscious states that the organism gives expression to in functioning. All act in and through the nervous system which creates all. The system is sustained through the following conditions. First, it is sustained by the circulating blood. Secondly, by the Ego or Sentient Personality participating in the intellectual conceptions formed in and given expression to by the nervous structure. Thirdly, by the nervous structure being surrounded by a physical medium, which supplies the phenomena transformed by it into the life current of intellectual conceptions, when participated in by human personality in developing the Ego. These three conditions are essential to sustain the life of the nervous system. Viewed thus, the life of the system is dependent on the Ego, participating in its movements, on the nutrition supplied by the blood, and the physical environment that embraces it. Shortly, the nervous system only continues a life-giving form of force so long as it can provide the Ego it creates with physical excitation from the objective world and is nourished by the blood.

These are facts that observation, resting on experiments, have proved.

After referring to the circulation of the blood, I shall show that it has been proved that death takes place when the optic thalamus, which is the only open gate from the external world, has become so diseased as not to be able to transmit impressions from the physical world to Sentient Personality.

The red corpuscles that make the blood red are so minute that 4 or 5 thousand may be placed on the head of a common pin. It is said that in a drop from the point of a needle there are about 300,000. These little bodies make the blood appear red in giving it its colour. We cannot think, speak, move, laugh, or do anything whatsoever, but it is calculated that 20,000,000 of these red corpuscles perish. Now these corpuscles are formed of the juices that have been secreted from one's food. After it has been digested by the stomach, it passes out and is absorbed by little vessels called lacteals, which suck up the fluid part of digested food, called the chyle. The chyle thus sucked up passes on into the blood and nourishes our bodies. The regular process through which the blood passes is this. First, the blood passes from the heart to the lungs, and again from the lungs to the heart. It is now red with the oxygen these little bodies have absorbed in the lungs, where the blood is spread out through the capillaries which lie in the walls of the air cells of the lungs. It is said they would cover a space of 300 yards long by 100 yards wide. Spread out thus, the blood becomes red by the oxygen it absorbs in the lungs, which oxygen we inhale in breathing. Thus, then, the juices of our food, so saturated with the oxygen, provides the nutrition for our bodies in the little red corpuscles of the blood being pumped out of the left side of the heart into the great artery. From it all the arteries over the body are supplied with the health-giving red blood from the lungs. All arteries have three coats or walls. The middle coat of each artery is elastic, and so can expand and retract. All arteries end in capillaries, which have only one very thin wall and it is through this very thin wall that the juices of the food to nourish the body pass. Shortly, the circulation of the blood, by which the organism receives its nutrition, is affected in this way. The heart is situated in the chest, and is almost surrounded by the lungs. It may be called a hollow muscle, divided into four cavities, each of which may contain from 4 to 5 ounces of blood. The walls of the left cavity are most powerful, because they have most work to do. For from the purified blood poured out of the left side all the organism is nourished. The heart pumps this pure blood which it gets from the lungs on through the large artery into every one of the numerous small arteries, and through them into the hair-like tubers of the capillaries, with their thin wall of one coat, into the most minute parts of the body. In this way does the force-pump of the heart inject its blood, so as to feed the organism by the juices saturated with oxygen passing through the capillaries. When the body is fed in this fashion, the half circle originated by the heart is completed. The other half circle does its work, removing the waste of the system which has been burned up by the oyygen in nourishing the body. It next passes through the capillaries, and as such is carried by them into the veins, and by these veins back to the right side of the heart. Through the right side the blood goes on to the lungs to get purified by absorbing oxygen. This completes the circle that began by carrying nutrition to the organism, and ends by removing the waste that the organism causes by functioning. The waste is finally removed from the system in forms of water, carbonic acid, and ammonia, through the lungs, the pores of the skin, and the kidneys.

The facts to be borne in mind in connection with the blood are these. The juices of the food when digested by the stomach are sucked up by little vessels and conveyed to the heart, on by it to the lungs again. From the lungs they pass to the heart, red with the oxygen absorbed in the lungs. This red blood pumped out of the left side of the heart is conveyed to every part of the body in three walled elastic arteries, which all end in very small capillaries which have only one wall. Through these the juices for the nutrition of the body pass, and also the waste caused by functioning. But when the waste enters the capillaries, they are enlarged and so arranged that the waste passes off into the veins. It is now black or purple by the waste that it contains. So laden, the blood is conveyed back by the new set of vessels—the veins—on by the heart through the lungs to get purified and saturated with oxygen ready to begin anew the half circle through the arteries. The other half, you know, is completed by the veins carrying the polluted blood back to the heart. Yes, in many cases it is morally and physically polluted in functioning as the medium that gives expression to the thoughts.

The nervous system, of which I have said so much, is plunged into the very centre of this nutritious element which the blood carries with it everywhere, and pierces the most minute parts of the body by the aid of the millions of arteries in their elastic coats. In this arrangement the nervous system finds itself surrounded with the force and nutrition it requires to carry on its work. For it is bathed on every side, being surrounded with the force and nutrition that the blood carries to enable the nervous structure to repair its waste and renew its activities. The waste is often burned up by the oxygen which gave to the blood its red colour in passing through a process of oxidation as it returns to the heart through the veins black and charged with poisonous matter on to the lungs, which discharge the impurities as carbonic acid, water, and animals, and inhale a new oxygen, which dyes the blood red; and as a stream of nature's purest current, is sent back on its life-sustaining journey, where millions of these little red corpuscles perish every moment. But they perish only to reappear in another form. They provide the liberated organic energy that builds up human personality, and supply the working force of the organism. Secondly, they repair the waste of the system, and remove its poisonous material. It may be that some form of this waste will at another stage of our immortal existence reappear as the fruit that defines the nature of the waste, either as moral purity or moral impurity.

In taking this view of the matter, our red corpuscles, in perishing, have reappeared in forms; one form of which—as conscious states—is immortal in providing the medium that we individually may live as the units of Sentient Personality who form the human species. This is the equivalent of the organic energy spent in a process of combustion, whereby intellectual combinations were formed which were participated in by the Ego. For a large portion of the energy liberated in the brain is used up in the ceaseless activity which surrounds and includes Sentient Personality.

Remember, the process comprising the Ego is immortal,

because such organic energy is spent in forming conscious states, as Ego, that do not cease activity on the death of the body, but continue active as a human soul. The consciousness of each such unit is the separate form of intelligence, the aggregate of which goes to make up the human race. Ego, in its disembodied state, sustains itself by absorbing energy to form conscious states — energy thus returns in functioning.

As the Christian records teach that each Ego is to be clothed in its resurrection body, we Christians believe God able to accomplish even this. Therefore, let us strive to anticipate the law at work. For it must be accomplished in obedience to law. We do know molecules, such as carbonic acid, &c., forming in the human organism, liberate energy, part of which is used in forming the intellectual conception Sentient Personality participates in, and thus builds up the soul, the equivalent of such energy. This being so, we may safely infer Ego will get clothed in its resurrection body by the molecules formed during the earthly life of that Ego in liberating the energy used up in forming that Ego of consciousness. On the resurrection morn, guided by the law that regulates such conditions, these molecules will be led to the habitation of the soul they thus stand related to, and will expand and embrace it, in providing its resurrection body. Thus the final end decreed of God is secured. It began when the sun's rays parted the carbon and oxygen on the green leaf of the plant, and as already remarked, molecules so parted, at some future time, we shall infer, unite in the human organism, and in so doing, liberate energy which gives expression to conscious states in forming Ego. Molecules so related to the soul will, I infer, be led to its habitation and expand and embrace it, thus providing its resurrection body. For, assuredly, such is the final union of molecules so liberated and reunited. This, then, is what the nervous system leads to, and depends on the circulation of the blood for its life; whereas, human intelligence depends on the nervous system for its growth and development. It creates the individual Ego—an Ego that lives and is developed by the agency of the nervous structure, surrounded by its environments, sustained by the blood, and has a life of its own. In viewing the whole operation from the stand-point I have stated, very much is included in the fact that though the nervous structure is dependent on the circulation of the blood for its nutrition, it has the power of regulating the circulation in a great measure. The nervous system lies embedded in the circulating blood, so that when an emotion thrills Sentient Personality, that emotion is the activity through which the nervous system is thrown into a state of agitation, and in consequence makes a double demand on the supply of the blood for nutrition by using up the supply that surrounded it. This quickens the circulation by demanding a fresh supply, to which the heart responds by increasing its action in pumping out artery blood, and taking in the waste vein blood to be purified in the lungs.

Viewed thus, it is the action originated by the impression made on Sentient Personality that regulates the circulating blood, as the conditions that effect the Ego either pleasantly or painfully. The process at work is that the elastic coat of the artery is agitated by the active forces passing through the nervous structure. They possess power to control these forces in regulating the circulation by the elastic middle coat in expanding or contracting. When the nervous structure, animated by a strong emotion, makes a demand on the arteries, they expand and swell out with fresh blood.

When the appeal ceases, they assume their usual size. As may be expected, many are the fatal symptoms developed in the brain which leads to insanity, by the blood being made to circulate too freely in the brain, spurred on by the nervous system, animated by the emotions of grief, sorrow, or disappointment. I will have cause to refer to this further on. At present, the point to be kept in mind is that the nervous system in every part of the body is surrounded by the circulating blood which provides it with nutrition, and can exercise considerable control in regulating its functioning power. For it is in functioning that the nervous structure uses up the elements brought to it by the blood, on which it depends for its activity, its power, and its life. This is a life that, in functioning, creates and builds up the Ego of forms of human intelligence. If the nervous structure could supply the waste of its system from without, it would be independent of the blood, for then it would absorb the elements it required from the forces that surround it. If this were possible, the organism could dispense with much of the material at present forming it.

A point of much importance is that the brain, in functioning, uses up five times as much blood as all the other parts of the body put together does. This proves how very much work the brain does in functioning, because it is the seat of intelligence. The brain also uses up its own tissue, which has to be renewed, else the brain would become bankrupt and cease to do its special work, viz., that of developing intelligence. But this is provided against in the nervous structure being plunged into the midst of the humid atmosphere of the blood, where it extracts from its vivifying medium the material to renew its waste. For every cerebral cell in functioning, wastes its *phosphorizing material.* This is not only true, but it has been proved at what proportion the waste goes on when the brain is doing mental work, by the quantity of sulphates and phosphates passed in the urine. The ingenious course adopted by Byasson proved this. He estimated the exact quantity of these two elements which entered into his diet, and also the quantity extracted from the urine when not doing mental work. He renewed his mental work, his diet remaining the same, and found the sulphates and phosphates discharged in the urine had increased considerably. This experiment fully proves that cerebral work does generate a proportionate measurable quantity in the two elements discharged. Such is very notably put in contrast with the fact that the temperature of the brain also rises when mental work is being done. For in the midst of the vivid flow of mental work the amount of work may so far be measured by the elements discharged and the heat liberated. However, if the circulation of the blood ceases for one moment, the whole machinery collapses and death is the result. This proves how wholly dependent on the blood the life of the system both physically and mentally is.

The blood in its ceaseless activity provides the vivifying stimulation that causes the nervous cells to feel, to stand erect, and to co-ordinate. In the purely sensitive region, where Sentient Personality may be said to dwell, the vivifying action of the blood, taken along with the impressions coming from the physical world, keeps the cells and fibres always active and give the conscious idea of the objective world that surrounds us in building up the Ego during natural life. Whereas, in the motor regions, the energy conveyed in the blood liberated by combustion enables the nerve force to accumulate, and provides a store so condensed as to enable it to start into activity immediately an appeal is made to it, as well as to sustain the activity for a considerable time. In this way the circulating blood enables the nervous elements to recruit their strength and renew their working power. Work done by our Immortal race is doubtless measurable in the heat liberated and in the number of the red corpuscles used up, when such conditions come to be viewed from the standpoint of immortality which most of all concerns each human being individually, as such must regulate his capacity in Spirit land.

If the process of oxidation going on in the tissue being burned up and renewed, was taking place in the physical world, we may safely infer light and heat would be developed, at anyrate in the vicinity of the brain where such a large quantity of blood is used in building up and renewing the tissue. But, in that case, the waste is removed and discharged in sulphates and phosphates, &c.

It may be said of the nerve cells that they play a passive part towards the circulating blood that feeds them, until they get invigorated by it. Then their position changes, and they continue to appeal to it so as to compel it to circulate most freely in the midst of the most active groups. These groups, therefore, cease to be subject to the circulation, and become dominant so far as to regulate the blood supply, by drawing it away to the special cell groups incessantly active. It is to the brain, where the circulation is so much quickened by emotions, that we must look as causing many mental maladies. The great power that moral affections possess in drawing an excess of blood to the brain will be thus seen, and the sad consequences arising therefrom, because all the cells through which the moral element co-ordinates would be kept in perpetual erethism in consequence of trouble or grief from any cause. This is a phenomenon of Sentient Personality which so acts on these cells as to keep them ever in a state of erethism and therefore ever evoking a new supply of blood. This is an action which, when carried to excess, causes the cells to use up their own material in a larger degree than eventually they will have the power to evoke from the blood. For excessive activity, unaccompanied by rest, impairs the cell's own structure as a functioning unit, and eventually ends in deranging the mental power altogether, and leads to insanity by deranging the machinery that forms mental conceptions of the rational order. The case is the blood being too freely evoked by the nerve fibres, and the cells being ever kept in erethism, tends to impair the structure if not permitted time to repair its waste by repose during a period of inactivity. And this period of inactivity is exceedingly difficult to secure while the cause of the moral trouble continues; and, indeed, after it ceases, these cells and nerve fibres, giving expression to the moral trouble, will eventually resume their activity on the least possible cause where the strain has been of too long duration. This proves a very difficult matter to deal with. It is also so where prolonged mental work has abnormally affected the delicate tissue and cells of the brain, by the appeal to the blood being too frequently and continously evoked, in being too urgently solicited and thereby supplied. This may lead to insanity, and will certainly lead to other ills, say at the expense of the digestive organs, or other parts of the system which would act on the quality or supply of the blood, and in many ways affect the integrity of the organism, on which the normal condition of mental life depends, during the term of our earthly life while the Ego is being developed.

The great restorer of the healthy activity of the cerebral brain is profound peaceful sleep. Then the system, in a great measure, ceases from activity and has its waste repaired in rest and repose by the blood circulating slowly through the brain, and nourishing every cell and tissue in its course. For the circulation is very slow through the brain during peaceful sleep. In fact, the slowness of the circulation is the cause of sleep. The brain gets weary, ceases to evoke much blood, the circulation gets slow, and sleep is the natural result. It has been observed in cases in which wounds caused an opening in the skull, that in profound " peaceful sleep the brain remains almost immovable and becomes smaller," and that on awakening its volume increases and so does the circulation. This is also true of the circulation and size of the brain in the case of vivid dreams.

There is no longer any doubt of the mental structure being of a material form. The loss of brain substance can so far be measured as a secretion from the brain during mental work ; further, the heat developed is perceptible and measurable by thermo-electric apparatus. Also, the increase is marked in a special locality as the place where the heat is developed.

Lombard of Boston observed that the head varies in temperature very rapidly though very slightly with every cause that attracts the attention. The sight of a person, emotion, or interesting reading aloud raises the temperature of the head and the head alone. Schiff has even entered the cranium, using exceedingly sensitive instruments, and so ascertained the degree of temperature that the cerebral substance attained at the moment when it was affected by the impression conveyed to it by an external excitation transformed into a conscious unit. Note, such is the work of the recording action of the nervous system, when the record is participated in by Sentient Personality, then the soul is in process of construction; for conscious state and soul formation are correlatives. Schiff further localized such disturbances by marking out in the brain the special point where such and such kind of sensorial impressions occurred, proved by the degree of heat evolved on the arrival of the transformed physical impressions into the abiding form of a living unit, going to form the Ego. He also found that the points where such heat was liberated were the points where it had previously been proved by experiment that the sensorial impressions were lodged.

All that has been said goes to prove that sustained intellectual work is secured at the loss of the material forming the cells which appear in heat and the waste substance of the venous blood. Thus, then, the brain may be said to become bankrupt by using up its material in heat and energy when insanity caused by over mental work, worry, or disappointment, takes place.

It is very certain when the cerebral brain uses up its reserve material during activity, this waste must be replaced by the nutrition of the blood during rest and sleep at regular intervals. When the brain does not secure these health-sustaining conditions, distressing consequences occur, and our asylums receive an increase of patients. However, it is generally allowed that worry, anxiety, and disappointment add much more largely to the number than excess of mental work does where worry is absent.

Doubtless, the most fatal of all causes are those

arising from the excessive use of alcholic liquor. It increases the circulating blood in the brain so rapidly as to burn up the tissue in such a way that it leaves what remains in a rotten unhealthy state.

It is made clearly plain in what has been said that the life of the nervous system is dependent on the circulating blood, which, however, is regulated to a considerable degree by the action of the brain in the impressions made there on the Ego—the vital force living and moving in the nervous structure, but especially active in the cerebral brain. When a strong emotion is agitating the structure, the emotion may cause the nerve system to drain away more blood than the heart can freely supply, and thus disarrange the whole supply of circulating blood, and leave many parts of the body without due nourishment.

But though the nervous system is dependent for its life on the blood, it is likewise dependent on the Ego it creates, to be kept in the state of efficiency that enables the Ego to participate in the external excitation, which that nervous structure transforms and transmits into intellectual forms of energy. Such energy is the equivalent of human reason. For, as already stated, when the optic thalamus gets too diseased to transmit physical impressions, death in a very limited time is the result.

As it is of much importance clearly to understand these two points, I again repeat, that to sustain the life of the nervous system, two conditions are necessary—first, the circulation of the blood; and secondly, that physical excitations be transmitted through the optic thalamus (the only open gate whereby they can be transmitted), and be participated in by Sentient Personality.

The life of the organism depends on physical impressions being participated in by the Ego, which must pass through the optic thalamus. What would happen if the optic thalamus became so diseased as not to permit the external excitation to pass? Would not consciousness cease, and with it, life? A case before referred to where this took place proves this. A young woman lost the use of all her senses in the course of three years, so that she retained no sensation whatsoever. She could not hear, see, smell, or feel, and shortly afterwards died. On the state of her brain being examined, it was found that the optic thalamus of each hemisphere, and they alone, were attacked by a fungus which progressively had destroyed their substance.

Thus, then, the life of the nervous system depends on the integrity of the optic thalamus as well as the circulation of the blood. For it only continues to live while the life current carrying image from the physical world which must pass through the optic thalamus is as such participated in by Sentient Personality. When the nervous system ceases to secure that condition, it becomes a useless encumbrance to the Ego that it created, and by the Ego taking the form of a disembodied spirit, is cast aside as a useless thing, because it is not capable of transforming physical excitations into life currents of an intellectual form, whereby the Ego can secure a pleasure or repel a pain. For vitality is always true to its nature, and will thrust aside whatever does not serve its purpose. But the point that concerns us is, that the action of this form of life does not cease when the visible form of the human nervous system ceases to live, and the natural death of the organism taken place. Then vitality, the energy of self-conservation developed by the human organism, continues to act as the soul, so created to absorb energy in forming conscious states, and in this way sustains its vitality.

Such is the immortal part in its ceaseless activity to which earth gave birth in the intellectual process going on in the human brain during the earthly life of the individual. Activity there is sustained by the nutrition of the blood, which will doubtless at death provide for its activities by appealing directly to the forces of nature to sustain them, and so continue to live on as an individual human soul—the highest form of life developed by our planet—in producing the condition on which depends the energy of self-conservation, the equivalent of conscious states.

In regard to the formation of the energy of self-conservation, let it ever be kept in mind that the heat liberated, and the phosphorised matter discharged in giving expression to intellectual or emotional work, is a form of phosphorised matter that must stand related in a special way to the resurrection body of that Ego—an Ego which does not cease its activity on the death of the body, but goes to form one of such units as make up the social system of our race. For the vital force of our planet has built up the immortal forms of our social system of intellectual being which will and must endure. The marvellous intelligence embodied in such a race has sprung from causes so simple as vitality being capable of perceiving precise forms of physical and moral excitation that affect either pleasantly or painfully. For assuredly this is the base of intelligence which has quickened into the gigantic form of human understanding.

It thus becomes apparent that the laws destined to produce all, were inherent in vitality, manifesting the design originated by God our maker and creator of all. These conditions might have led up to the happiness of the whole human race being the point aimed at by each individual, had not the process been frustrated by the self-regarding interest of the individual taking the lead in seeking his own good only.

However, to live the intelligent life that the vivifying blood enables the nervous structure to live, is to perceive the physical excitation which affects that organism either pleasantly or painfully, and to react on these physical excitations accordingly. This is the germ in which human intelligence rests, and is so developed as to enable man to possess the powers he has over the forces of nature which so marvellously extends our intelligent grasp thereof, as to obscure from our vision the simple operation of the vital laws in which intelligence rests, and make nature as perceived through man such a mystery, because human intelligence had attained such a gigantic form before science unfolded what life was, and when and how intelligence spring in being developed from the simple cause I indicate.

The story of the Ego is simply this. The human organism and its environment in developing sensation creates Sentient Personality, which, when once created, lives its own life—an intelligent unit which can reason, generalize, and infer, so as to perceive the consequences attached to different modes of action wherein rests its responsibility, a responsibility where every thought and action evoke from the blood the energy on which it depends, thus regulating the circulation of the blood and transforming its forces into the immortal vital currents which will proclaim their own history. Viewing the Ego from this point, we can comprehend the large supply of vital force it will evoke from the blood when a strong wave of feeling is moving the nervous system. For the vital force evoked is equivalent in volume to the strength of the sentiment at work. And, I think, we may assume when the Ego quits the body at death, that energy evoked from the blood as the equivalent of consciousness, including the strongest emotions will in equal value be capable of being evoked by the Ego from the surrounding medium to be discharged by that Ego in functioning back into its original medium, as the action and the reaction giving expression to the Intelligent life and work of the Ego in its new phase of existence. We would thus have the Ego living a life of its own, as the vital force which transformed the phenomena of physical units into its own form of vital force, namely, intellectual conception, and the works that spring therefrom.

Thus, then, human personality is the vital force which does not cease its action on the death of the human organism, but continues its activity in living its own life by absorbing the energy it requires from its surrounding medium and discharging it to that medium in functioning—an action equivalent to the intelligent life of the human Ego in its disembodied state. Energy, the vivifying power of the circulating blood, provided the Ego with force to form conscious states during its period of formation.

CHAPTER V.

MEMORY AND ITS LAWS.

I HAVE given a short account of the nervous system and its activity and the circulating blood. In treating memory and its laws, I may have to refer to both, and certainly will have to refer to the nerves' current created by impressions made on the organism by its environments. Impressions carried along the nervous structure to the brain, to be participated in by Sentient Personality, form a current which completes its circle of life-created energy, when the impression made on Sentient Personality by the physical excitement it carries from the objective world, sets the organism in motion from within, in giving expression to the effect produced on the Ego. The blood completes its circle in vivifying the current of life when it has nourished the nervous structure and removed the waste contracted by the working power of the structure.

The first point to be noted is the power which the nervous structure possesses of retaining a record of the impressions that once affected it, and was participated in by the Ego or Sentient Personality. This property is the condition that forms the base and facilitates the growth of memory. We all know that the retina may continue to vibrate the image long after the excitation had ceased. To demonstrate this, let any one stare for five minutes at a bright gas or lamp flame, then close his eyes. After a minute he will find the image of the flame vibrating brightly on the retina. This proves that the duration of the impression continues after the objective cause has been removed. Further, that the light rays forming the image have been stored up in the eye and continue to vibrate the image there, has been proved by those who have long occupied themselves with the microscope in histology. It sometimes happens that after working for hours, if the eyes be shut, an image appears with great distinctness on the retina. We also know that after a long railway journey we sometimes hear the rattling of the carriages for hours afterwards. The power which the ear has of retaining impressions of music is sometimes very disagreeable. The gustatory organs also seem capable of retaining traces of agreeable or disagreeable impressions. Memory of a nice thing makes the mouth water, and the memory of a disagreeable thing causes one to vomit. So much for the memory of the senses. Now, what of the memory of the spinal cord? For its action conforms to acquired habits, such as dancing, swimming, skating, writing, playing on an instrument, and all co-ordinated motion which has not been received by heredity. For the organism is as it is by acquired habit. It is the result of education manifested through the power inherent in the spinal cord to retain first impressions which are the result of traces left in the organism by habit acquired during the lifetime of the individual, arrangements accomplished through the power which the spinal cord possesses of retaining impressions of the records which have sent special sections of it into motion. All depends on the hereditary power of the nervous structure to retain first impressions which vibrate in us like echoes of the past, so that the automatic power of the organism is stimulated to do and to react just as we wish to skate, to dance, to write, and so on. An organism so trained faithfully reproduces the former activity which, by education, has been acquired, and in this way explains the phenomena of the automatic activity of the system.

The fact is, that to retain a record of former impressions is a property of the nervous element diffused, among all agglomerations of cell-groups which become the special foci of the records that once affected them. As part of the nervous system, these special foci are diffused through the organism, and find in the arrangement of the cerebral brain the condition which unites all. Also, through the arrangement of the cerebral brain much of the spare energy of the system is controlled in being used up in the activities most pleasant to the Ego (that is Sentient Personality). This may take the form of skating, or riding, or running; of talking, or preaching, or serving the Redeemer and glorifying Him in deeds of charity and love. Remember, it is into the cerebral brain that all which is recorded on the peripheral plexuses of the system flows, the cerebral being the great reservoir for the peripheral plexuses. Further, it is through the flow of these recorded impressions in the long gone by ages that the cerebral brain has been formed and gradually built up. For the genesis of memory rests in the property which the nervous element possesses of retaining and reproducing the records that impinge on it, records which organic phosphorescence always presents in cell and tissue. This being so, the genesis of memory must be found in the nervous elements. These elements are the unconscious agents that manifest our psycho-intellectual life, working in silence at the operation, which they accomplish in common. A series of stored-up impressions in cerebral life acts simul-

F

taneously to produce the phenomena of memory, and separately gives off reminiscences just as illuminated bodies give off the luminous waves stored up in their substance.

The natural activity of the fundamental property of the nervous elements seen from this point does the work of storing up the phenomena and reproducing them as memories automatically. For what these foci store up they reproduce. The memory of the special senses are the records of former impressions stored up in their peripheral plexuses. Such impressions in being absorbed by the special senses, become the forms of organic phosphorescence to which each special sense gives birth. The eye stores up images of rays of light, the ear, images of sound-waves, &c., all such being *elements* retained as records. When such elements become recorded in the brain, they are moulded into ideas —the intellectual conceptions of which our mental powers are formed. The case is this, in passing through the moulding forces of the human organism and brain, such records are moulded into definite forms, as the " Elements " of which mind builds up "Ideas" just as chemical combinations are built up of their atoms. However, viewed as the genesis of memory, the elements of the cerebral substance are the silent unconscious agents which provide the genesis of intelligence, being associated together by their marvellous properties, so as to produce one harmonious effect. These elements are sustained by the process which the record of past phenomena has built up in these minute organisms, and they are surrounded by a network of fibres specially related to each.

For the marvellous network of fibres and cells in the cerebral brain, which act simultaneously to produce the phenomena of human memory, are capable of giving off reminiscences as ideal conceptions. This is the common heritage of the social organism of our race, whereby man communicates with man through the organs of speech, writing, &c.

I may just note, in passing, that the properties referred to of the cerebral tissue and cell only live and act so long as they are kept in vigour by impressions passing on to them from the peripheral, and are associated with the vital phenomena of the organism.

The memory, looked at so, is seen to be a necessary consequence of the fundamental property of the nervous elements acting through the regular process of cerebral activity: and may be looked at from the point of its genesis, its evolution, and the various phases it passes through in the life of the individual, when the human Ego, the immortal form of its own phase of energy, is being built up as consciousness.

Take note, the brain is the reservoir where the conscious states of every individual is recorded and forms the structural unit of that individual's social, moral, and family history. These records may be transmitted through inheritance, helping to form the brains of children, and moulding their capacities for right or wrong, for good or evil. For the forces that go to build up the Ego are the forces that build up the individual brain. Memory is the name given to the records of these forces, the units retained in the brain which give off reminiscences. Intelligence springs from the power the nervous elements have of recording, retaining, and reproducing impressions. This power is necessarily associated with life, which in a progressive form necessitates the organism to record and retain the impressions as such and such, which affected it either pleasantly or painfully.

For this twofold action is the expression of the vital force of our planet and leads up to the higher forms of intelligence. Having the property of discerning this—that is, of perceiving the source from which pleasure or pain comes—is life in the advanced form which the complex brain and nervous structure gives expression to functioning, always accompanied with a perception or notion of the objects that might affect the subject either pleasantly or painfully. Having this perception is the genesis of intelligence, the simple acting cause that transforms an objective unit into the subjective state. To do this is the inherent action of life-force wherever vitality has built up for itself a brain of any complexity, else life could not repell pain and retain pleasure. This is the law that sustains the force we call vital. A vital organism without a brain is an organism without consciousness. When vital force increases in complexity, so as to produce an organism with a brain, that organism acquires the faculty of perceiving objects as such that increase or diminish its power. To do this is the inherent law of progressive vitality, and includes the condition that transforms an objective existence into a subjective state; making such an intellectual "Element" capable of being combined with other such elements, the processes described are the conditions which create the elements with which human intelligence builds its Ideas, for elements, so understood, are the atoms of which Ideal conceptions are built. However complicated these conceptions are—the complication is to be found in the variety of such elements combining to form the Intellectual Idea.

The case may be put thus. The vital force, spontaneously developed in its progressive form, has the property or faculty of storing up the objective impressions that impinge upon it as records of such impressions, and reproduce them in functioning. To act thus is the nature of the force which, in developing, enables the vitality of its organism in recording the impressions that impinge upon it—to perceive them as subjective " Elements " when reproduced by the nerve-cell in functioning. Records vibrating in the organism so transformed may come to be perceived by the Ego of organism as a source of strength or weakness to it. Conditions so simple as these are the mystery that transforms an object into a subjective conscious state — the element of intelligence — a mystery made so much of in our day.

However, the simple fact is that the process that includes memory in the cerebral brain may be looked at according to its laws as foci of stored up records giving off similar impressions in vibrating these records as the elements of Ideas. That being so, the special senses in the peripheral region of the system must transmit the recorded impressions of their plexus on the one hand, and on the other, the brain must be in a suitable condition to receive and record transmitted impressions. For it is from the peripheral regions that the central region receives the records destined to set the cerebral in motion and serve as its daily food. When an external excitation is recorded in any part of the organism, the nervous plexuses of that part assume a state of erethism, and retain in themselves the records of the physical excitation which impinges upon them, and like phosphorescence, gleams as persistent impressions, they become without our knowledge a store of latent peripheral reminiscences, so as in a way to keep the central region in a state of persistent vibratory sympathy, and thus vivify and maintain its activity. For the connection between the peripheral and central regions of the system is so real, that when the peripheral fails, the functioning power of the central region is impaired and interrupted.

That the sensorial impressions may produce the desired effect on the cerebral "Sensorium," it is required that the sensorial of the peripheral region be in a special state of sensibility and peculiar erethism. This condition enables them to retain for a time and transmit the record, a process which has to be repeated again and again before the structure of memory is so well-formed as to be sufficient for its work. Everybody knows that it is by having the same impressions repeated again and again that the memory is trained to retain the details of the subject dealt with. We forget, and require to renew the process, so as to make sure of retaining the knowledge of the subject which we desire to know well, in order to be capable of applying the ideas we gather to illustrate our own views; or, it may be to apply old ideas to explain and illustrate the new condition which we perceive. Though a pretty good knowledge of the subject has been acquired to do this, we have again and again to refer to the books we use to revive details, as the process of building up the structure of memory, both in the peripheral and centre region which is to serve in securing the object we have in view.

But we must never lose sight of the nature of the base vital activity has provided for its work, whereby the process of building up the structure of memory is secured. That is as to whether the organism is affected pleasantly or painfully by the recorded phenomena; a condition which is the genesis of the nervous structure itself, as well as the condition that endows the structure when formed with the power to record, to transmit, and reproduce physical causes transformed into intellectual "elements" which vitality can use to repell pain and attract pleasure. For the latent activity formed by the nervous system coming into play transmits to the "Sensorium" not only the announcement of the arrival of the external excitation, but also the special emotion of pleasure and pain related to each excitation. "For every memory slumbering within us, from the very moment it was perceived, was stored up with a special co-efficient which recalls to us the joy, the pain, or even the indifference of the peripheral plexuses at the moment the record was incorporated with them, and when it began to live a life of its own."

That the memory of corporal chastisement, so vivid in young animals in training, is the principal condition that secures the effect desired is true. That man, in so far, is no exception, is also true. "For pain endured by him is a most effectual warning to avoid faults where there can be no escape from the pain such would assuredly lead to. Inversely, the records that give us most joy are the deepest rooted memories in us, forming groups of external impressions which perpetuate themselves with the greatest tenacity." These two opposing series of stored-up records of the co-efficiency of pleasure and pain are the natural pivots around which human activities gravitate to generate the desires that induce human action, and the cause of every emotion that slumbers within us. "The indifference we experience is the border line of either group, and may be said to mark the rise and fall of these contrasted emotions around which the vital activity of the human form gravitates in choosing the course each one will pursue in fighting the battle of life." Something has been said of what the genesis and transmission of the persistent sensorial impressions are when begotten in the peripheral region.

How they are received in the plexuses of the Sensorium, and the reaction they beget, is the next point to touch on. "Thus, then, the connection between the external sense and the Sensorium is so complete and intimate, that as soon as an impression impinges upon the former, the central region enters into immediate union therewith, for the nature of the case is that a nervous condition of similar pitch has been developed which harmonizes the one part with the other." When the primordial impression is of sufficient intensity, then the plexuses of the Sensorium are sympathetically associated by adopting a similar phase of erethism. In this the whole moulding process of the human brain play their part in developing the energies proper to the sensorial. Such a process is rightly called the womb, where external excitations are incarnated in being transformed into a mental element fit for intellectual work—elements which perpetuate themselves in persistent vibrations, just as a phosphoric gleam does in the external world. For such is the mystery proper to the nervous elements in persisting to vibrate the records that impinge upon them (so manifest on the retina in its case of persistent impressions) and repeated in the centre region where the character these records acquire, depends entirely on the moulding of the processes which serve to maintain them. Always bear in mind that these intellectual elements, formed of external impressions, include the emotion we have experienced at their birth, and that such remain alive, capable of thrilling us with their own emotion ever afterwards. "Now these elements penetrate into the recesses of cerebral life when sufficiently alive and often enough repeated, and in this way they become the memories of ancient emotions that have thrilled us." Such then are the phenomena of memory shocks capable of reproducing their ideal combination of elements so as to be seized by Sentient Personality just as at first because the reproduction is similar. That is the vibratory echo of the past which accompanies the vibrating element—the idea—the equivalent of the intellectual units. Remember, it was the joys and sorrows that were included in the genesis of Intellectual Elements at their birth in the peripheral plexuses that form the series of emotion related to each. When a strong emotion is present, that emotion modifies the elements which are being lodged in the memory cells of the brain ready to resume the functioning form which they possess. In reproducing the group of former memories to which such forms give expression, through impressing their forms of emotion on the network of nerve fibres and cells that impresses the upper layers of the cerebral convolutions—that is the Sensorium, it follows that the grouped forms of memories which build up the human brain have in the immortal human race the structural phenomena of every condition through which that race has passed or shall pass.

"In the case of the young child, it is because his sensibility has been impressed in a special manner that he expresses his inward sentiment, and in time recognizes external objects, and names them — remembering what he has heard, seen, and felt." Through the persistence of the acoustic impressions and retina images, such groups of memories become the reminiscences which enable him to speak and apply to each object its proper name. In time, by somewhat similar processes, he learns to trace written characters which represent the symbol of absent objects. Further, in reading aloud, he recognizes such sounds as the equivalent of the written characters that he or others may trace. However, at the bottom of all, there is always the intellectual elements which build themselves up as the Ideas, elements and combinations which have been formed and fashioned by the human brain and organism which vibrate as a faithful echo of first impressions. " Endowed thus, man in time becomes capable of expressing the emotions and thoughts that pass through his mind, having learned that each word, or combination of words, expresses an external object, a thought, or a sentiment, for memory groups being always a source of strength in knowledge possessed, form the basis of language, the inexhaustible store of generalized conceptions that provides man with the means through which he can express his feelings and what he thinks to his kind."

A thing of great importance in viewing mental states from this point, is that the mental elements that unite in forming intellectual combinations or ideas, when understood as their kind, are always the same, however different the language, written form, sound, or character, may be that conveys the Idea. For example, a dog will be the mental element called up in any language in representing this animal to all the race. In like manner, in the mental structure of every man of intelligence, there is a somewhat similar intellectual combination of elements to record the idea which would be called up by such a conception as this, "A nation is not more certainly made discontented by bad government than it is made contented by good government." However varied the language or written character that gave expression to this conception might be, the cause that leads to this similarity is simply the fact that each intellectual element is a production of the human race, surrounded by its environments, formed and fashioned in having passed through the human organism, and moulded by the marvellous properties of the human brain. By this means, the conditions that surround the human organism, both social and physical, are transformed into Intellectual Elements and combinations of such elements capable of giving expression to human conceptions of the ideal form. Such forms of Energy are human in their birth, but immortal in their duration, because of such the human Ego (the immortal human soul) is formed.

Formed in this way are the bricks which the vitality of our race creates and employs. It has produced the human nervous structure, by which vitality can form and fashion conditions that endure. It provides for itself in the souls of our race an enduring form of vital force. However, it is because nature is one, and the human organism is one, that the mental elements forming Ideas have a uniformity of structure common to the human race as a whole, however varied the language of that race may be. The conditions to which language gives expression are the mental elements that the human organism, surrounded by a social and physical medium as its environments, has created—conditions common to the race. Therefore the mental elements are the heritage of that race, because each member of the race could be taught to reproduce every one of those elements. All follow, as a consequence rising from the processes that combine in creating mental Elements—grouped Memories as Ideas common to the race.

In viewing mental elements moulded thus as forms of vital force created by the human organism and its environment, it would be of some interest to refer to the phenomena of unconscious impressions that get lodgment in the cerebral. " The process is somewhat as follows. Social or physical impressions impinging upon our special senses, and causing the required state of erethism, get moulded thereby into elements in passing on through the optic thalamus to get lodged in the plexuses of the cerebral cortex, where each sense has a special locality prepared for its reception. Such unconsciously formed elements get lodged without our knowledge in the cerebral cortex. They silently accumulate, and are ready to start from their obscurity when affected by an exciting enough cause. "Doubtless, it is aided by such stores that new factors sometimes come to enlighten our judgment with new ideas when the unexplained side of a question left in suspense, is made quite clear" when looked into at another time.

The different groups of sensorial impressions have each a special territory of distribution in different regions of the sensorium. As might be expected in the human brain, there is great inequalty in these groupings in different individuals. One has one sensorial grouping most highly endowed, and another has another most highly endowed, and so on. Now, it goes without saying, that it is in consequence of these inequalities that one individual has special aptitudes for the reception of different kinds of sensorial impressions, and another for others. For example, when the optic cerebral regions are enriched with well endowed nerve-cells, the individual will have clear conceptions of the external world by perceiving objects with their colour and relations. Another, well endowed in the acoustic region, would have a predisposition for musical harmony, and so on. Further, in such psycho-intellectual activities, we may safely infer that the elements of moral, religious, and social relations have each their special locality for distribution more or less unequally endowed in each individual.

Where psycho-intellectual grouping of any forms are

well endowed, these special forms of impressibility will leave more enduring records, more vivid reminiscences, and from such factors rich stores of fertilizing material is stored up even at birth. It is because the conditions are so, that memories connected with such and such stores of mental energies vary so much in different individuals, nature favouring one more than another. The study of the brain proves that there are regions destined to receive and elaborate the sensorial impressions independently. " The study of the cortex also proves that functional dispersion of impressions is in this way continuous throughout. The continuity secured in the nervous tissue of the cortex which is continuous through all its extent, is the condition that secures complete functional unity." For it comes to pass, " when simultaneous impressions of optic, olfactory, acoustic nerves, &c., are recorded at the same moment, and get localised in their appointed foci at one time, the series of sense impressions thus created will represent a definite group of impressions in their elements being united by the mysterious band developed in having been simultaneously participated in by Sentient Personality," and as such live together in being mentally united one with the other. So that henceforth to perceive one of these impressions, the others, guided by the law of association, will be called up one by one till the series is completed. For Ideal conceptions so created are thus united. Elements created thus in forming ideas build up the Ego, and provide an individual mental structure of an immortal form in creating the human soul. A combination of vital elements united as Ideas in this way is the immortal form of vital energy, "*Sustained by its own activities,*" which survives the death of the body, and comprises the individual immortal units of the race.

It is certain from this point of view that the individual soul or life must begin with the birth of the child, and grow with the intellectual development of that child, the general faculty of memory being provided in the organic phosphorescence of the cell, which absorbs, records, and reproduces them in functioning. " Memory groupings, however complex, therefore, are the reflexes of the histological properties of the cells reproducing the records stored up in them, which is the means by which the idea reveals itself in functioning," the birth of the infant being the date at which its soul, which is immortal, begins to be created. Thus, then, it stands to reason that the nervous elements would be liable to present great modification when viewed at the different periods of the development of the human being. In young children, the cerebral cells have special histological characters. At birth, the cells are virgin from the dynamic point of view in not having records stored up, because no energy has been spent in storing up vital force as mental elements. " The cerebral cells of the young child are greyish, flabby, flexible. At that age the sensorial excitations that affect it find the cells almost in a state of vacuum, ready prepared through the law of inherited transmission to receive all records and retain them, so that, in the first years of life, the cerebral substance is in the perpetual exercise of organic development, new mental elements being perpetually added to the old ones." In providing the basis of memory capable of developing intelligence, as well as the character, through the predisposition of inherited tendencies of certain groups, the state of the brain is at an early state so that it retains all the impresssions that assail it, just as a prepared photographic plate seizes the images and retain those that impinge upon it. This process takes effect in course of time, and the child remembers objects and individuals that surround it, and recognises each as the effect of the persistence of the impressions reproduced by the activities of the brain. By this means the child gets to perceive the value of sounds always the same, applied to the same object. They reproduce in its cerebral the mental elements as the idea which these sounds typify. In this way the child gets to know the objects and persons that it often sees and hears named. So that little by little the process of constructing a human brain goes on in building up the Individual Ego.

As the region of the intellectual activity makes more and more use of the records that come from the surrounding world, progress is rapid. Without trouble in this happy age, the child retains what he sees, hears, tastes, &c. Everything being thus a vivid impression to him, the sensorial impressions received at the same time constituting a natural family among themselves, are a great resource in the education of the child's intellect. These conditions all through life play a very formidable part in Intellectual Development. Such Intellectual Development goes on rapidly up to the years of maturity, say about forty, when the brain gets stocked with memory grouping, and its power of retention fails considerably. Then the labour of getting acquainted with new subjects is very great indeed.

Enough has been said to indicate the growth and development of the memory grouping of the mental structure in the processes that differentiate the individual brain in forming the organic Ego and creating the human soul, which does and must endure.

In dealing with memory grouping, as this chapter does, it would not be complete did I not refer to the importance attached to the Education of the Intellect, and to the method of cultivating its faculties, a method which greatly centres in the fact that sensorial impressions received at the same time constitute a natural family among themselves. To get a clear conception of the method referred to is so very important, that all should strive to do so, because in memory groupings which differ, yet have points of agreement, the one suggests the other, independent of the details that lead up to the observed agreement, so as to become the counterpart of each other. For example, there is a certain form of acute rheumatic disease which indicates effusion in the joints. This disease also affects the heart in giving rise to heart disease, so that the two mental ideas included in these conceptions are henceforth an intellectual grouping of two united memories where the one suggests the other. Such is the nature of the law that regulates associated memories. For when it is known that one suffers from an old affection of the heart, the mind at once suggests the presence of acute cardiac rheumatic affection also. It is the law that regulates associated memories acting in this way that affects all. For instance, a series of Ideas, including scientific principles, become recorded in the brain. Such grouped memories may be artificially evoked by appealing to the first of the series, which has the germ in it which leads to the inference with the details left out.

To make clear what follows dealing with the intellectual groupings in memory series, which Christianity develops, I will once again refer to the processes whereby the records from the external world are transformed into mental elements of an intellectual form as Ideas in passing through the humanizing moulding process of the human organism, and being participated in by Sentient Personality.

Such are the conditions that create the groupings of memory and the human soul—the last the permanent form of human vitality with which Christianity takes to do. With this understood, my wish simply is to explain the working of the system by which objective facts get transformed into the memory grouping of Ideas. To do this, I will take a few Ideas from the 1st chapter of Ephesians, and must therefore refer the reader to that portion of the Christian Records. This is an Epistle addressed to believers, and principally concerns them. The rendering in the following paragraph of this chapter is given as an example to show how truth revealed gets transformed through the conceptions conveyed in printed signs into the human brain, so as to become the elements of the ideal combinations of the memory grouping which comprise Christian intelligence in the printed signs passing through the humanizing process into the brain prepared to receive them, and reappearing in what follows as memory grouping functioning the contents.

In referring to the blessing God the Father of Jesus Christ has conferred on the converted, called " spiritual blessings in heavenly places in Christ," such are the conditions that take to do with the spiritual world from which the Lord came, and into which He entered after His resurrection and His ascension. The kingdom all converted, Christians enter at death in vitality, " being absent from the body and present with the Lord," a kingdom where the inhabitants are animated by the Law that generates Love, springing from the consciousness that they are accepted in the Beloved. This is the condition realized that converted individuals anticipate while in the body, and from such anticipation springs " the Faith that worketh by Love," a sentiment that more or less animates every Converted Believer.

G

The explanation of the reference made to predestination must be sought for in the Laws of the Inheritance, which modify and regulate the capacity of the individual brain, as well as the surroundings to which the birth of each child expose him. For none can choose their own parents. However, such knotty points become considerably more intelligible by the explanation given in the 10th verse, which unfolds the final end God has in view regarding our race.

For a race animated by that self-regarding instinct where each strives to secure his own ends, having little regard for his neighbour's good ; yet for a race so selfish as this, God's design is "that in the dispensation of the fulness of time, he might gather together in one all things in Christ, both which are in heaven and which are on earth, even in him"—the Redeemer, the Son of God, the Saviour of the world. The Divine Intelligence prepared for this end from the beginning, for so it was decreed of God, and so it must be fulfilled. However much suffering a bad life may lead to while the Uttermost Farthing is being paid, the life is purified in being made "perfect through suffering." For such must be the law of the Decree working through retribution which leads to sanctification and purity ; because (as the Revised Version has it) all things must be summed up in Christ—which must be that the race is to find an abiding place in Christ and strength to overcome in Him. That it will be well with our race in Christ at the end is certain. And well may we Christians, who know the sentiment Adoption begets, say so. Though well aware this sentiment can only be begotten during our life on earth, yet God must have much good in store for a race who are to be summed up in His Son. But I do not for one moment infer that the unconverted can ever have the benefits conferred on them that are conferred on the converted, who on earth are brought into vital union with Christ in having a new sense developed at conversion, which sometimes so overwhelms the individual with a sense of God's presence, as ever afterwards to have in the memory grouping a consciousness of the joy thus imparted, which proves how little the world has to give compared with it.

One notable fact seen from our present standpoint is that all comes through the intervention of our senses, absorbing and transforming the intelligence conveyed in the Christian Records, through the agency of sound waves or written characters, into the vital forms of force that human personality can grasp and comprehend, so as to form a vital union with the Redeemer in the point of space His risen body now Inhabits. You perceive it is the subject grasping the object through the intervention of the moulding process of the human organism, which enables Sentient Personality to participate in the tidings conveyed, so as to create memory groupings of the intelligence imparted full of joy and gladness, henceforth to be remembered as a special personal experience which the glad tidings conveyed in the Gospel impart. A Gospel accepted in Faith, where the centre figure is Christ, the objective existence on which all rests, is and must be invisible. These conditions cannot be repeated under other and different circumstances. When the Ego ceases to be clothed with the body, the garments of humanity that developed it, the unconverted cannot participate in the glad tidings of the Gospel after death. They must remain a separate creation, where, doubtless, the law of expediency which animates that section now, will find that law then of such a nature that the final good of the whole race will be sought as the best means to secure the individual's good, so that Christ, the God of the whole earth, the Developing Intelligence thereof, and the giver of strength to overcome all adverse tendencies, may be glorified, by enabling the race more and more to increase in intelligence and in happiness.

It is evident from verses 11 and 12, that the converted section are so because it was the purpose of God's decree that they should be "to the praise of his glory," as those "who first trusted in Christ."

However, I have dwelt too long over the first part of the chapter, as my object in choosing it was principally what is stated in verses 13 and 14, to illustrate more fully the subject in hand, "Memory and its Laws," by stating how the memory groupings which Christianity begets come to be formed and henceforth assert themselves. This understood, you will note in the 13th verse the conditions required to develop memory groupings strictly in conformity to these laws. First, we have the tidings conveyed in the word of truth; secondly, accepting the Gospel thereby; thirdly, the memory grouping formed in being sealed with the holy spirit of promise. This is a series which, as might be expected, fully harmonizes with the laws governing memory imbedded in the human brain, which develops and grows by such groups being added to it, and thereby producing the experimental evidence in the "earnest" or pledge of the believer's inheritance until the redemption of his purchased possession (14th verse). For the experimental evidence of the inheritance is to be found in the functioning power of these grouped memories, which have linked to them the sentiment that accompanied them at their birth as the earnest (or pledge) until the redemption of the purchased possessions "unto the praise of Christ's glory."

First, the structure is laid in the knowledge which the intellectual conceptions convey in "the word of truth"; second, by accepting the conditions offered in the word of truth, namely, the vicarious sacrifice or deliverance by substitution; third, in the functioning processes which acceptance begets in developing joy and gladness. Joy, in conformity to the laws of memory, will always accompany the thoughts that include all this, because the joy is begotten by these thoughts and included in these memory structures, which give expression to all in functioning. Such memory groupings, kept in activity by functioning, radiate joy and gladness, and appeal to the individual, and on through him to the Saviour. Memory groupings, similarly created, become day by day added thereto in the individual taking possession of promise after promise and making them his own. These promises, scattered all over the scriptures, new and old, God has made to His people. Just take as an illustration of the growth and development of such groupings—Isaiah xliii. 1-4—which speaks of the comfort, consolation, and strength imparted to any one making this promise his own. The scriptures are full of such promises, which, in being transferred into the human brain, become memory groupings as seals of Adoption possessed by the believer as the pledge of the future that awaits him in the purchased possession provided. These conditions enable him to triumph, animated by the strength of the "Infinite." The human brain, so stocked, includes all this, because "all the promises of God in Christ are yea, and in him Amen"—(2 Cor. i. 20)—so that in being united to Christ in Adoption, all the promises of God become the believer's purchased possession, and as such ought to be taken possession of, so as to form memory groupings which will ever be radiating their contents. In dealing with this subject, we are taking to do with conditions which have a physical base as surely as the reflected rays of light have, which reveal to the eye the world that surrounds us by forming a connection between the eye and the objects. In the process we have the external objects transformed in the promises into memory groupings radiating their own form of vital force as the intellectual elements forming the ideas which the promises contain.

Ideas, on being seized by human personality, are reflected outwards through space to the Reedemer, telling their own tales in proclaiming the believer the adopted child of God, united to Christ by substitution, and so forming a unit of the church called our Lord's body, which embraces the human soul developed by the vital energy which the human organism provided. In the present case the energies forming intellectual combination radiating from the believer's brain pass on through space to find their equivalent in the person of our Lord. These intellectually formed Ideas, the duplicate of memory groupings, pass through the space between just as other forms of Energy do, in uniting the Subject with the Object, just as one man communicates with another through the medium of sound waves, the vibrations being reproduced in finding a soil prepared for them. There is always the sender, the receiver, and the medium, and the conditions that unite our Lord with His people, and form His body (the church of the first-born) are no exception. There is the sender in the transformed promises into memory groupings from the human brain, the receiver in the person of our Lord, the medium, the luminiferous ether, which I hold to be the base of all substance and fills space. Therefore it must be some form of this ether or energy which builds up the human soul, the Ego that wings its flight to the abode of the Redeemer immediately it quits the body at death. Of such a material nature as this are the connections and conditions which constitute Christ and His body the Church. These conditions are represented in the last verses of the chapter as " His body, the fulness of Him that filleth all in all "—Eph. i. 23.

This is a condition which in so far will embrace the human race when all things are gathered together into one in Christ. This will be, however, in two sections so very different as to be called in the Scriptures the lost and the saved. The saved are the church of the first-born, and are co-existent with the Redeemer in having His sentiment imparted to them while on earth where they have honoured Him. The energy of the mental grouping forming the souls being purified and strengthened, and thereby in having been brought into vital affinity with their Lord, is in so far one in nature through the favour conferred in substitution. Such is the class addressed by Paul in the following verses of the chapter. For St. Paul, in hearing of their faith in Christ and love to the brethren (a mark of their adoption) gave thanks and prayed that the God of our Lord Jesus Christ, the Father of Glory, would give them the spirit of wisdom and revelation in the knowledge of Him, the eyes of their understandings being enlightened, that they and all such might know the mysteries that follow—verses 15-23. To secure this, the terms of contract conveyed in the "spirit of Wisdom and Revelation," must be that the individual addressed would have the brain stored in building up the soul or organ of mind with what is revealed of the kingdom of God, and he must be animated by the sentiment which union to Christ begets, so as to live and rejoice in the glorious prospect in store for Christ and His people the members of His body, who, through the gate of death, enter His presence, where there is fulness of joy and pleasures for evermore. They are children of the covenant, not doubting and questioning the truth of these things, but believing and rejoicing that, though they are in the world, they are yet not of the world, therefore constituted so as to be able to live above the world—in being in possession of all—children of the covenant and heirs of the promises.

With all this stored up in the individual brain, and understanding them as the Ideas included in the wisdom and revelation referred to, the second or next stage is safe for the believer to enter on ; the eyes of his understanding are enlightened so as to be able to comprehend and understand the mysteries revealed when read in the light modern science provides—enlightenment that can be employed to illustrate how the mysteries revealed are to be accomplished through the agency of nature viewed as one ; in its laws being employed by the human Intellect to accomplish what has yet to be fulfilled of God's revealed word. For the human Intellect endowed man with the faculty of Imagination, which confers on him the power to comprehend and deduce the conditions that will secure the end he desires to accomplish.

Now let these conditions, "the terms of contract," be applied as the means decreed to accomplish what is revealed of man and his destiny. Let us suppose the Christian, fully persuaded that the prayer of Faith is a working power that generates energy capable of securing the fulfilment of the end he desires. From this stand-point try to comprehend the intelligence conveyed in the following verses of the first chapter of Eph. 17-23. It will thereby be seen that what accomplishes all is the power of God in Christ transferred to the believer so as to put "nature, which is one," absolutely under the control of the believer, so that the forces required to secure this end can be accumulated thereby. From this view of nature, note what is said regarding the resurrection of our Lord, as accomplished by the working of God's mighty power in Him, when He raised our Lord from the dead. The means that secured this end were that Christ (the Son of God) was capable of accumulating the form of force (the equivalent of the grouping of memory), that in functioning, secured His resurrection, and the equivalence of the laws at work in the decrees of God. Observe, Christ never doubted but that His resurrection would be accomplished. He believed, and in believing, accumulated the forces that accomplished it. The process employed to explain the mystery is simplicity itself, when we accept the fact that "Nature is One," and may be stated thus. The Redeemer's human soul (the correlative of vitality), as the organ of mind created by His conscious states on earth, quitted the body at death, went to preach to the spirits in prison—(1 Pet. iii. 19). On the morning of the third day, He quitted that abode to take His place in His human body as its organ of mind, over which He had complete control, capable of evaporating the body at will so as to transform it into a subtle fluid whereby He could pass through doors and walls, yet continue to be the person Christ. His ascension was accomplished by this means. He overcame the force of gravitation as the cloud seen by His disciples received Him. For the human and the divine of our Redeemer was there. "Who," in scripture language, "is now at God's right hand, far above principality and power, &c."—(20-23

verse). He was possessed of a human nature, generated just as ours is, through the united action of the nervous elements, surrounded by its environment, building up the individual cerebral brain. For in these varied forces, united by a special process of co-ordinated units, acting through the phenomena of memory, we have in each and all of us the vital force that builds itself up as the organ of mind in that inner personality, seizing every conscious state on its arrival as a sense impression. Remember, it was through these sensorial impressions having been so often repeated as to create for themselves individual centres of force in the cerebral brain, by the original impression being recorded in a way that can be reproduced in the network of the upper layer of the cerebral convolutions; that these records come to have their own habitation, so that when their activities are called into play, they present the phenomena which first acted in forming them, and are thereby participated in as thought by Sentient Personality. The records of the memory groupings of the past uniting itself with the life of the present, influence that life in many ways by the experience which the memory of the past begets in helping to guide the course we pursue in the present. But the point we are concerned with at present is that the activities of memory groupings are conditions on which memory rests. For, when any of these centres disappear, the memory of them disappears also, and Sentient Personality is, as it were, no longer confronted with the memory records of thought which it can seize in building itself up. These groups are the incident which stands thus related to the Ego during the earthly life of its development.

From what has been said, it seems evident that the genesis of the moral element takes its rise from intellectual development. "We remember the causes of our pleasures and pains, and know that our race is similarly affected by similar causes. Our sympathies are called into play to induce us to strive to alleviate their pains and increase their pleasures." The activities of this form of sympathy the social organism in its highest phase begets and calls humanity. "But the mental element forming the moral combinations of memory, apart from the influence infused into it through the operations of the religious sentiment, is with many so very weak as to be of little benefit to our kind." For the moral action of the individuals forming the social organism is so much guided by personal expedience— that is, what is viewed as most beneficial to the individual's self, is often so grossly selfish as not to be worthy of being called a moral action, even though pain has been thereby relieved. Notwithstanding the strong tie of kinship, the associated memories of pleasure and pain might beget, if human sympathy was more highly developed in uniting the race as the organic growth which our earth has produced and endowed with the immortality which its vitality begets, a race, as a whole, united through the process embraced in associated memories. For such memories, viewed in the fullest sense of the word, are the self-conscious states that build the Ego, and so form these associated memories which may be reproduced to unfold its history. It is these associated memories that we strive to evoke by uniting a certain memory with a visible object, a knot on the handkerchief, so placed as to arrest our attention, and thereby cause the memory we had associated with it to leap out of its hiding place in the brain, and record itself to the Ego as the root of the memory wanted. As before stated, the law which regulates these associated memories acts very powerfully in developing intelligence; indeed, intelligence itself rests on such laws. For associated memories give birth to new ideas in giving expression to cause and consequence. One highly gifted in this way is called a great natural genius, an original thinker, and so on. The gift rests in the inherited capacity of uniting cause and consequence with rapidity, so as to give the rational explanation which underlies the new idea, and so make these conditions intelligible to one's contemporaries. They are similarly constituted, and endowed with a human nervous structure, the activities of which act in harmony, and consist of the truly physiological process to which the nervous system gives birth, and maintains as the base on which all human intelligence rests; so that when local memories decay, memory fails with them, because the Ego is only in course of development during natural life, and cannot act an independent part until liberated from the organism, when that organism ceases to reproduce the memories of which it is formed, and hold intact as the equivalent of an individual soul—a soul immortal in its activity.

The rational explanation of all this takes its rise from the vital energy slumbering in the nervous system united as one whole, on the one side, in the circumstances that give birth to Sentient Personality on the birth of the child; and on the other side in the activity to which Sentient Personality gives birth in functioning sustained through natural causes. For the activities of this truly vital force—the vitality of the organism—is the origin of all associated memories, and finds its own origin in the human nervous system surrounded by an environment. It is a system endowed by inheritance with the form of vital force which gives to Sentient Personality birth and continuity in providing the base that develops and creates the Ego, through which it acts during its earthly history.

Take note, a living organism is an organism capable of feeling, and such is the human nervous system united as one whole. It serves as the medium through which Sentient Personality and the physical medium that surround the nervous structure, act and react on each other—an action and reaction which is sustained and transmitted through the power inherent in the co-ordinated nervous structure united as a whole in an organism capable of feeling. It is therefore a living organism, because vitality slumbers within it. This being so, it serves in its organic life as the intermediate form of vital force which separates Sentient Personality from the physical world that surrounds it, yet it provides the means by which the Ego and that world can act and react in being brought into the harmony of mutual relationship. Sentient Personality is undergoing a process of growth and development which only ends on the death of the bodily organism; because then the evolution and growth of the Ego end in the activities of its changed condition in so far as its earthly history is concerned, for its structural unity as a whole, evolved under special conditions, has been completed. Its capacity, its energy, and its power, are to be found in the structure which its conscious states give it in functioning. Thus created, Sentient Personality is embodied in a human form and held intact in the series of conscious states that form the individual life.

The forces which comprise each individual sense—the eye, the ear, and so on—are the developers of their own form of vitality, for the activities of these forces do not cease on the death of the organism, but by absorbing energy from the surrounding medium, continue to act as the Ego or

Sentient Personality. Though the nervous structure now dead was the origin of that Ego's birth and development—when being created thus—its reaction on the physical medium through its nervous structure was always determined as to whether the Ego was pleasantly or painfully affected by the physical medium. It thus comes to pass that the vital force slumbering in the human nervous structure is the medium through which the physical and vital forces act and react on each other in forming the Ego during the earthly life of the individual. On the death of the individual, the Ego or Sentient Personality comes into direct action with a physical medium of its own form, which certainly must be very different from the physical medium that surrounds us.

The human nervous structure is only the intermediate link which vitality has built up of its one form of force, in paving the way for developing the uniformity of action and stability of thought that eventually leads up to creating the Egos of former generations. This structure is transmitted by the law of inheritance to serve as a support between vitality and the physical medium that surrounds it, and enables vitality to act on that medium and develop its own forms of Intelligence in memory grouping, which that medium supplies, called the objective world. The structural units building the memory cells are composed of the vital form of force which builds itself up into the nervous structure. When these cells decay, they limit the growth and development of the Ego; because the Ego is in course of development, which only ceases on the death of the body. When the Ego is liberated, it is capable of acting an independent part as an individual unit created by our race.

The quotations I give are chiefly from Dr. Maudsley's work, many of whose Ideas I have adopted to illustrate my subject.

CHAPTER VI.

VITAL ENERGY IN ITS AUTOMATIC FORM.

IN giving an account of the machinery that develops the human soul, and clothes it during the earthly history of its life, it will be well to examine at some length the automatic activity of the system before entering on higher subjects. The stored up motor power condensed in the nervous structure which we use in voluntary motion, and which also provides the motive power of vegetable life, are simply stored up units of vital energy of a special form. When viewed in the form of automatic activity, they may be called forms of electricity transformed into the vital energy stored up in the nervous system. The electricity stored up in the electric fish, to be used as a weapon of defence, is such a form of vitalised electricity slumbering within the fish, ready for that purpose, developed by the species as a weapon of defence. The automatic activity of such stores of latent energy give expression to our emotions and desires, by completing the circle which recorded physical excitation began. The new property which the automatic activity of the system manifests, is the spontaneous action of recorded forms of sensations previously stored up in these plexuses. When such groups are agitated, they continue to act automatically. Thus, then, the automatic activities of these groups are simply the forms of Histological sensibility stored up in them, to which they give expression in an uninterrupted current as long as the movement lasts. They may be called the memory in exercise of these groupings, the histological form being the grouping of the activity in functioning, giving expression to its memory—that is, giving expression to what it can do and has done before.

The automatic forms of vital energy viewed as giving expression to the memory of the special grouping, become the fundamental elements of cerebral activity, which will be explained as we proceed. Histologically the automatic forms of vital energy must be viewed as the form of activity that builds the structure and acts through it, and in so doing gives expression to its own form of vital energy. The action emanating from the spinal cord clearly proves this. For experiments show that every segment of the cord viewed separately performs its own function. Though distinctly isolated, they can give rise to co-ordinated activities, and as long as the blood continues to feed the cells, they can store up new forces after every discharge, continuing to act as before in producing nerve force, and performing their established habits. It has been proved by exciting the spinal cord after death, that the hands will perform the movement of defence with as much regularity as if the brain was directing it. This occurs even though the head be separated from the body. The structure was originated by the directing brain, but as a structure once formed it can dispense with its dictation thus far.

The automatic action of the medulla oblongata, the region of the vital knot, performs its life-long function to heart and respiratory muscles without our knowledge or intervention. Automatically it does its life work in functioning a vitalised form of energy. But the automatic form of vital energy plays the most remarkable part in regulating the division of labour in the human nervous system, so as to dispense with the intervention of Sentient Personality as far as possible. Because when the action which has sprung from directing Intelligence can be performed without the intervention of Sentient Personality as the automatic activity of the vital energy of specially formed groups or memories, Sentient Personality, which is the primary source of all such actions, would be left free to carry out its higher vital function of originating new forms of intelligence. For example, when we are being trained to perform a simple form of handcraft, say knitting, the closest attention of the Ego is required during the process of learning. Once the habit is acquired, the automatic forms of the vital energy stored up in these groups perform their function so well as to dispense with the directing brain, in so far as to leave Sentient Personality free to originate new structures and educate them, so as to increase the potential energy to a yet higher point of efficiency in the division of labour and so minister towards perfecting the nervous structure. Each group comes into play on the slightest excitation : so marked is this that it often happens we lift a piece of work, and only discover we have it in our hand after having begun to do the work. The grouping which typifies local memory had its energy liberated in taking up the piece of work, and performed its part most satisfactorily, and doing so led towards perfecting the organism for its work. We thus see the astonishing part the vital energy of the automatic form performs without the intervention of conscious will. However, it is when entering physiologically on the study of the cerebral activity that the marvellous part which the automatic activity performs is seen to perfection, in the infinite number of forms it is capable of giving expression to.

H

Before entering on it, I would again direct my reader's attention to these few simple facts. First, Histological Sensibility is giving expression to a special group of structural units in functioning. Second, Automatic Activity may simply be called repeating in functioning the form of the original structural unit. To adduce an extreme example: the horns of a stag have been developed in functioning as a weapon of defence in the bygone history of the species. We may say the automatic vital energy is seen in its very lowest form in the white corpuscle of the blood, and the masses of platoplasm formed of the same substance, the organic form of automatic activity, at any rate in its progressive form, secretes at the expense of its substance. The structural form thereby possesses power to radiate or eject in an intermittent current to a distance the vital forces which they have accumulated. The action of defence performed by electric fish is such; also the force we employ in fighting to defend ourselves. All such forces are accumulated in the tissue and are projected to a distance as forms of an intermittent current of vital energy.

As human beings, we store up records in our brain as the phenomena of the objective world and the acts of the social organism that surrounds us. Now, it is through the power of the automatic activity in the form of (say) voluntary excitation that we give expression to how the phenomenon has affected us individually. The nervous system, being the reservoir where the phenomenon of the automatic activity is perfected, amplifies each structure by giving its own substance, and places at the disposal of the structure its conducting fibres to radiate such automatic activities to a distance. The fact is, automatic activity follows step by step in the development of the nervous apparatus with which it is connected. But how strangely different is the automatic action going on in the ganglion of a few cells in the bladder, the wells of vessels, or the intestine coils, carrying on their appointed work of regulating vegetable life, where a complete separation seems to characterize the automatic rhythm of their action, compared with what takes place in the complicated action when they enter the brain. For in the brain complete subordination takes place in the distribution of the living forces of nervous activity. In this way the optic thalamus transmits the sensitive impressions to the point where it is participated in by Sentient Personality. The effect produced on Sentient Personality is wafted to the corpus striatum, which transmits the form of motive power that originates special forms of automatic action giving the expression of Conscious Will, *e.g.* that of attaching our signature to a document, and assuredly writing one's name, is an automatic form of acquired activity. How strangely different is the work done by the automatic force of the few ganglions of cells where sensibility and automatic action are vaguely fused into one form, for the purpose of sustaining vegetable life, compared with writing our name.

Yet the difference rests in the complicated action of the human brain and nervous system. I explain automatic activity as the action of a structural unit functioning. This action is precisely similar all through the organism, only in the brain the action is so complicated that it is difficult to distinguish the separate units brought into play. Take such an example as this: when a sudden emotion thrills us, say the network of nervous elements in the upper layer of the cortical cells that have been inhabited by the impression, it is bound to be participated in by Sentient Personality, because a shock of the vital nature of pleasure or pain agitates every organ of the body. Let us suppose that the thrill was caused by music in a gay assembly. The music gratified the Ear, the gay assembly pleased the Eye. The persons in that group, the music of that tune, would have formed a structural unit in the brain capable of reproducing in automatic activity on the sensorium, the spectacle as at first perceived; and so appeal to Sentient Personality at a future time, in the automatic activity of the structure as the memory grouping of the spectacle. And not only so, but the tune being heard, or even one of the individuals of the group seen, or the incident being talked of, might be enough to rouse the automatic activities of the former group with which the music and the person stood related in such a way as again to present the record, and appeal to Sentient Personality just as at first. Such are the changes that may take place within us through the operations of the automatic activity going on in the complicated forces of the human brain. It is the union effected in creating those structures which come into existence simultaneously as conscious units, that causes these structures thus formed by their automatic forces to give expression to the conditions that created them, in uniting these conditions with the Ego or Sentient Personality as a durable memory. Further, such conditions have become an immortal memory in having formed a unit of a human soul, which is the immortal part of man.

The mysterious union that unites the countless number of units formed as I have indicated, is most clearly seen in the fact that one group causes another group to start up, that is to assert itself by assuming the automatic action of its form of force, and by so doing representing an intelligent impression which is seized by Sentient Personality, being an ideal conception. You will observe all that is necessary to create one of these groups is that the impressions are presented simultaneously, and so participated in by Ego. The intermingling of the automatic groups is so regulated by the law of their being, as to originate the automatic activity of each other, which as Intellectual Conceptions appeals to Sentient Personality as such—the cause probably being that of a communicated motion, through the tie of a contemporaneous impression. For it so happens that when our experience is that of an excitation being participated in as an ideal entity by ourselves, " that is by Sentient Personality," we also find that through the mysterious bond of association the idea causes another to spring up. All this happens without any conscious participation of the will.

The phenomena of these automatic structures, the associated units of former memories succeeding a recent impression, repeat themselves at every moment of cerebral activity. So blind are we, that we suppose we think of a subject, whereas the truth is, that it is the ideas presenting themselves in automatic units of vital energy that takes place within us, and providing us with the subject matter of thought, vital energy being the current ever in motion to which feeling in a general way is attached. But vital energy in the human brain takes the form of the feeling that represents intellectual conceptions as ideas in the special form of a memory grouping peculiar to each conception. With the organized brain so endowed, and animated by these ideal forms of vital energy, it is enough for us to come fortunately upon one external subject, to think of another which has either directly or indirectly been associated together on a previous occasion. It is from the structural forms of memory that all spring. Such structural memories are simply the expression of a vitalised object, in having been participated in by the Ego as an intellectual conception. This process creates the idea which afterwards manifests its vitality through its organs or structure. It is through this process that the vitality of Intellect stores up the intelligent conceptions it has created as its structural forms of memory. To do so is the equivalent of the units that conscious life builds itself up in, and gives expression to in functioning. For (consciousness) the developing Ego is thus related to the brain and the organism that creates it. Feeling, as life, represents vitality that builds the structure of memory. To feel or perceive such forms of motion gives expression to the forces at work histologically. Always bear in mind that a living organism is capable of feeling, and such capacity distinguishes a living from a dead organism. Further, viewing memory as the structural form of intelligence, which perception or feeling has created, we find the rational basis of reading in calling up those intellectual forms and interpreting them. The intellectual forms are the signs which the printed pages present in the ideas which they typify. These written characters rouse in their place in the brain the ideas, and form the automatic groupings of memory. For it is such a process going on within us that makes the printed pages intelligent to us. But let us come upon a new idea, say a technical expression, we do not understand—immediately the intelligent rhythm is snapped. We have to find out what that sign means, and by so doing we build the structural units of a durable memory, which henceforth will be called up by the printed sign as the idea it represents in the human brain, giving expression to its automatic grouping. In future, this new sign, as an ideal conception, will be participated in by Sentient Personality, and the intelligent reading of the page will be pursued without a necessary break. The brain supplies the signs called up by the printed page in quick succession. The printed signs are simply an easy mode of conveyance to enable one mind to communicate and appeal to another. The secret of all is to be found in the wonderful structural formation of the human brain to which the law of inheritance gives birth, in providing the child with the marvellous capacities to which the human organism gives expression in its nervous structure. The nervous structure may be called a form of potential energy which the vital force of our planet has created as its support, and through which it acts and reacts. In conversation, ideas follow each other, and evoke one another in quite an automatic fashion. We often think of a thing outside of the subject talked of without wishing it, and sometimes get drawn away from the real subject through this intrusion.

The automatic forces of thought are of such a nature that where the character of an orator is known, we may be pretty sure of the lines of the automatic forces at work. In his case, they will lead him to give expression to his favourite thoughts as the automatic forms which have been kept in persistent erethism. Further, it is well known that certain examiners give the same ideas in new forms again and again. The logic related to this in the automatic activity of the cerebral brain is of such a real form, that those interested in passing examinations strive to forecast the ideas that will be suggested, as the fruit springing from the automatic forces likely to be liberated in preparing the examination paper. It often happens that a wonderfully good forecast is made. Every one knows that it is enough with some individuals to start certain topics of conversation, to know what the result will be, for the individual will give expression to his favourite subject in the usual strain of ideas which the automatic forces evoked on such occasions.

The phenomena of common sense has no other meaning or basis than that of the automatic forms of thought of a species of diffused generalizations repeated by similarly situated individuals in an identical manner, giving expression to the wisest course to be adopted under the circumstances. This process corresponds to the notions held of expediency giving expression to the ideal conception in the term common sense. Structural units conforming to their notion of common sense, are developed out of cause and consequence uniting in such a way as to indicate the most natural course to follow, which has been generated by the sequence of events common to the community. The secret of all rests in the vital action that alike animates all, and induces all to pursue a pleasure and repel a pain. Complication arises from the different notions that various individuals have of what will give pleasure. What constitutes a pleasure to one may not give pleasure to another in the same situation. So it comes to pass, that the law that regulates the social organism in its notion of "common sense," steps in and so far regulates the action arising from the varied notions of what gives pleasure and causes pain, having a due regard for the good of the community at large.

Ancient history proves that in similar circumstances the social organism acts very much alike. The proof of this is to be found in every page of history, whether tragic or comic. We find the same graphic ideas serving the same end, and applicable to every epoch. They appeal to the reader of our day just as they did to the reader in the age in which they were written. This, and much more, proves how human brains act in a similar manner in the presence of similar external excitations. One thing is very certain, that a social community, animated by one sentiment, will, when taken as individuals, act very much alike; for in such a case their pleasures and pains arise from similar circumstances, and as human beings, they give expression to these in like manner.

It was the automatic action springing from the similarity of conditions that our Lord's promise indicated when He strengthened His disciples by urging them "to take no thought beforehand what they should speak, neither to premeditate, but whatsoever should be given them in that hour to speak when delivered up to the councils, beaten in the synagogues, and brought before rulers and kings for His sake for a testimony against them." Because it was not them as individuals that spoke, but the Holy Ghost.—Mark xiii. 9-11. They were inspired through the influence of revealed truth, and strengthened by the teaching of our Lord. In this way the Holy Ghost inspires and enlightens in all ages. This is a source of intelligence which will supply suitable answers, no adversary can gainsay or resist, for those that hold fast to Christ are in vital union with the source from which all revelation comes to our race. The Holy Spirit is the influence that is at work in the rich and life-inspiring promises the Christian Records contain, which by their influence mould the brain, the organ of mind, into harmony with their teaching. By the very same processes, the full assurance of some great good being in store for any one would mould that individual's brain or mental life. In both cases, the effect is exactly similar; the object and the nature of the good in store being the only difference, though it is the stream of divine love ever in motion, revealing more and more of God's character in Christ to our race, that is the sum total.

Those animated by the Holy Ghost, and kept in active union with the Lord, are animated by a similar emotional state, and in consequence, will react in an appropriate manner. If this happy emotional state had been attained and kept up by all our Lord's followers, the action and influence of the Christian church would have been harmonious, under whatever latitude, and at whatever period of human history we viewed it—the harmony would have been complete. One joy, one sorrow, one enthusiasm, one aversion, would have animated and inspired the link established between the Redeemer and His church on earth, where His presence was ever a felt power in the joy it imparted.

Thus, then, the automatic expression of love to our Lord would be the reaction to which this condition gives birth. It would, in fact, be the reflex action of the cerebral brain of Christendom vibrating in unison with the redeemed in glory. All may be said to rest in the human brain reacting in the presence of its medium. The medium is the Redeemer provided by God, the source from which all Christian action springs, and which gives expression to the vibrating medium which love to Christ begets in vitalising the energy that united both.

That the emotions of pleasure and pain are the source of all action in the human brain is evident, and may be evoked, as every theatre-goer will prove when he adds his bravo and tears to those of his neighbour, when his emotions are simultaneously evoked. Further, the fact may be proved on every hand, that the automatic action of the human brain works according to laws, and may be excited so involuntarily that we may calculate with certainty the action which certain emotions will give expression to, just as we see bodies, electrified in a certain way, act at a distance on their neighbouring bodies, and modify the electric forces latent in them. The process is similar whereby the automatic forces stored up in the human brain act on other human brains, either through the medium of speech, written form, gesture, &c. It causes the same ideas, accompanied by their special pleasures or pains, to start into vibration or visibility on the network of their neighbour's brain, and they are participated in by Sentient Personality and manifest the ideas present, the same forms of force having been automatically evoked. By this means the distance, in time and space, is bridged, and a Shakespeare can liberate the same forces in the individual's brain of to-day as his written and spoken words did in his own day.

Now it is so, that between those that hear and those that speak, there is a union formed through the physical medium by the forces that are liberated in the human brain, and which act in harmony. Further, the art of persuasion has no other explanation than that of exciting the ideas to which former pleasures or prejudice were linked. It is by this act that one may excite unexpected sentiment, and often disarm another's judgment. The fact is, that in the reflex action to which I am referring, into which consciousness must enter, we have the highest nervous centres functioning the conditions we call knowledge. Dr. Maudsley very aptly terms these conditions "reason made substance." This is explained as "incorporated knowledge." For, as he says, "what are these purely bodily operations at bottom, but processes which, when they take place consciously, we describe as feeling, retention, or memory, apprehension, judgment, belief, or will." Dr. Maudsley goes on to give a very graphic explanation of the automatic action to which the term judgment is applied. His words are, "An agile person, who is accustomed to cross a busy street, quickly darting in and out among the vehicles with which it is crowded, performs a dozen acts of judgment in as many seconds on each occasion without being conscious of them. Let him deliberate about the several decisions which he makes, and he will most likely be knocked down and run over. For the relation of his quick and apt movements are not to the conscious Ego, of which they are well-nigh independent in direct aim as in function, but essentially to the preservation and maintenance of the organic Ego, the mind having little to do with such movement." The author goes on to say, "it will probably be a long time yet before the full meaning of this physiological fact is realised, and the conception applied to the bodily operations of the same kind which, because they are illuminated by consciousness, are deemed to mark a new order of being, and called mental; and before, therefore, clear and exact notions are obtained of what the body can do by itself, and of the part which consciousness truly plays in mental function." Notwithstanding his adverse foreboding that these facts will not be generally accepted soon, my own judgment is that the dawn is fast approaching when they will universally be accepted, and the part consciousness truly takes in mental functioning be clearly recognised and made apparent to all. The general acceptance of these conceptions is much hindered, because the immortality of the soul seems to many to be incompatible with the material views which these facts indicate. But let it be realized that consciousness in its functioning property is in its very nature indestructible, and as such forms the individual soul, then the dread of accepting the fact that consciousness has a material base will cease. Any man will perceive how such views affect future destiny, and will thereby strive to live a just, good, and righteous life, so that the moral element in the race will be greatly strengthened through accepting the truths modern science advances in the doctrine of materialism. Moral action will be viewed from the point of contact referred to by our Lord in the words of "as ye judge ye shall be judged," and the necessity of having the moral activity developed through a good structural foundation laid in infancy, in youth, and in manhood, so as to guard the individual from consequences which might mar his eternal destiny, will be a necessity recognised by all. For by the moral structure, early and carefully laid in the organic Ego, the automatic action thereby established would guard and protect the individual from taking an adverse moral course. And such is the machinery at the disposal of wise parents in the training they adopt towards their children, that the result is almost certain to ensure a good moral life, by inducing moral action as the result of the habitual course of action developed in building up the organic Ego.

Viewed from this point, the automatic action of the organism supplies us with the rational explanation involved in the promise God gives to parents, "Train up a child in the way he should go, and when he is old he will not depart from it."—Prov. xxii. 6. Such teaching by the parents lives and acts in the nervous structure of the child prominent among the forces which build up its organic Ego, the immortally combined atoms which are to form part of its resurrection body. For the brain so built up is incorporated knowledge, and immortality is indeed—Reason made substance. The structure formed grows with the brain—a process of unconscious growth to which the organic Ego is subject in various ways. It is a form of growth totally different from that employed in forming the soul. For the individual soul is formed by the forces combined and united in giving expression to consciousness which creates Sentient Personality, Ego, or soul.

Remember, it is through the medium of the automatic action of the human brain that great orators move their audiences, by commanding to spring into visibility the Ideas to which he well knows the memories of emotion and enthusiasm are attached. In so doing, as long as this mental state lasts, the orator has great power, and may lead his audience to immortal glory, or eternal death, in forming the structure that may hereafter mould the course of action they will adopt during their earthly life. By the same power how many authors have led their readers to perform the noblest as well as the most degraded acts. Further, in the former case, it is a joy to such authors to reflect on the good fruit left in their written pages. In the latter case, the memory of what is left written leads to pain and remorse, for at death such memories form part of the soul of both author and reader, and as such must continue to live. Note, all is effected through the operation of the general law through which emotion is communicated; also, that our Duty is measured by our Power.

The automatic activity of the human mind—say the organic Ego—is often roused indirectly by using words of double meaning, which calls out the desired emotions, and leaves the guilty author thereof free, though he may have ruined his dupe. In some cases he may appeal to a court of law as the injured person, because falsely accused. Those who handle such double meanings with art, can by a look, a word, a tone, a gesture, or by underlining a word, rouse in the mind of another a series of ideas, with their emotions attached, totally different from what the words indicate and directly imply. The allusion in the brain is perceived by Sentient Personality, and links itself with the associated memory suggested by the implied tone or gesture; and the corresponding emotion is omitted from the brain of incorporated knowledge, in reason made substance, which forms the organic Ego of the structural grouping of human Ideas.

When viewing the automatic action of the brain, we must remember that the roots of our memory, let them be ever so closely associated in ideal conceptions, retain the emotions that accompanied them. Further, they are not dependent on excitations from the external world, but reveal themselves as foci of old memories which kindle associated groups. It thus happens that automatic force feeds itself, maintains itself, develops itself, by the meditation and reflection supplied by the brain as the store of previously accumulated Ideas. These intellectual activities of the organic Ego provide the medium whereby we can fence and direct our future actions, and so protect ourselves from being taken advantage of, by those who have acted a false part previously to secure an indirect end, as well as to induce us to accept unhesitatingly the simple pledge of one we have always found trustworthy. For in this, and in many other ways, does the brain, well supplied with clear and distinct ideas, the correlatives of reason and reflection, guide us from trouble and lead us in the right course during life's brief day.

The guard reflection provides, all have need of before coming to an important decision. It is supplied by the old memories of automatic forces taking possession of the subject matter involved, and in the effort induced by the decision causing new ideas, unexpected thoughts, unforseen probabilities, to appear, in the latent energies at work rising and speaking in their own language as formed ideas, seized and comprehended by Sentient Personality, which in this way forms a set of structural units that aid the growth and development of the organic Ego.

In sleep these elements repose and feed, to awaken full of revived energy—for "wisdom comes in the morning." The automatic forces at work that provide the material of reflection, concentrate round circles of new ideas to intermingle with and modify each other, so as to create entirely new methods of seeing and considering the subject-matter in hand. Observe, it is the securing of a pleasure or the repelling of a pain to Sentient Personality that is desired. Each element in its own way is personally interested in the issue. For the desire of pleasure is the motive everywhere at work in animating action. It is, indeed, the life base so stated that ministers toward a general uniformity of action.

One strange feature which sometimes take place in the automatic activity of the brain when the mental powers have been taxed beyond their strength, is that the process continues to go on (say in solving a mathematical problem) where Sentient Personality seems to be standing as it were aside, looking on at the work, quite unable to retard it when it is developed in excess. The fact is that sometimes the automatic forces become so invigorated, that the individual has little or no choice in the subject that takes possession of the mental powers. For that subject will speak in its own language so loudly as to render close attention to any other matter impossible till the forces exhaust themselves. The strange feature is that the individual is often powerless afterwards to state the subject so freely scattered. A few thoughts on the subject, so freely dispersed by the intellect a short time before, is all the fruit that can be gathered in.

Perhaps the most remarkable part of all played by the wonderful automatic activity bound up in the physical elements of the organic Ego, is their fundamental property of causing pleasure or pain. Though these emotions are equivalent to life and death when applied to Sentient Personality, it is so that the Ego (Sentient Personality) has no power of choice, but must suffer the anguish of pain or rejoice in the gush of unexpected pleasure that may agitate the organism, over which the Ego has no control so far as the expression of that present emotion is concerned. Nevertheless, the Ego has gained on the whole in the new experience that it has got to guide its future in choosing the course it will adopt. Thus, then, the most painful experience is not without profit. For though the Ego has no power to choose whether it shall be a throb of pleasure or a shock of pain it may have to bear at any moment of its development, yet it gains by the experience. It learns to act wisely hereafter.

Further, it is from our joys and sorrows that the moral element springs. Man's sympathies are liberated because he has suffered, and would fain save others from the suffering that he shrinks from himself. As the moral element develops, man becomes the more eager to impart to others the joy he has drunk and will further drink. He rejoices in the link he forms by enabling others to drink of the joy he creates. So gifted are the mortals of our race, that by a glance of tenderness, a look of approval, one may communicate to the Ego of another, the sentiment of overflowing joy. Also, one may, by the imperious glance of scorn or contempt, fill a fellow-being with intense pain. It is a consequence inherent in vitality itself that induces love and hate, the equivalent of pleasure and pain. Fundamentally the former emotion feeds on the pleasure love begets, the latter on striving to crush a foe. Both emotions may be said to be inspired not commanded, for both are forces slumbering in the subject—the Ego.

It is in the fact that love is so related to the Ego that we find the key to the automatic activity Christianity begets, which springs from Christ's life and death in His vicarious sacrifice having secured the sinner's discharge. The sinner who realizeth this as true to him is inspired thereby by love, and gives expression to that emotion in the self-sacrificing work of Christian benevolence. While this emotion lasts, the automatic activity of the brain centres round this Ideal conception of Christ, viewed as the Individual Deliverer. For this conception inspires each individual with a similar emotion of Love, the highest pleasure known to us; therefore, when it is fully realized the life-long struggle of the organism will be to secure and retain this, the highest phase of pleasure. For such is the inspiration our Lord imparts to all united to Him through his vicarious sacrifice. When fully understood, and viewed in the light of present knowledge, the source of Christian action becomes so plain, that even a child who runs may read. Then it will be seen that Christianity infuses life into the organism by infusing the highest phase of pleasure known to us, namely "love," and therefore induces the automatic activities that love begets, one form of which is that of being willing to suffer, so that the loved One may be thereby exalted and glorified. In this way the automatic action of the organic

Ego to sustain this source of pleasure should find expression in the self-sacrificing work of Christian benevolence as its life-work on earth. The law of the organic Ego in its automatic action thus stated, was the force at work animating the early Christian Church that endured so much persecution. They endured persecution because they did not doubt but believed, and continued to be animated by the Faith that worketh by Love, the correlative of the automatic activity at work in the Ego, developing the emotion of love. For as long as the emotion of love animates the Ego, it will circulate round the ideal conception to which the emotion of love is attached; because this emotion gratifies the vital forces of which the organic Ego is formed. It is when the emotion of love ceases, that the Christian's self-sacrificing spirit fags and dies. Then worldliness takes the place that love to the Redeemer once occupied. Then the Ego circulates round the Ideal conceptions which omit worldly pleasure, as the spring of its automatic activity, and the Christian becomes more and more worldly-minded accordingly.

The Law or conditions that explain all may be stated thus. The nervous structure is formed of the vital forces that Life has built up for its own use by grasping the phenomena of the physical medium that surrounds it, phenomena which have in the bygone ages affected the living organism either by increasing vitality or retarding it. The nervous structure so formed is surrounded by a social and physical medium. These are the conditions that develop the soul or immortal part in developing consciousness. This is the process that creates the Ego or Sentient Personality. The organic Ego is formed of memory groupings, which give continuity and expression to the immortal

Ego. The grouped memories forming the organic Ego have the pleasures and pains that accompany them attached to them. These are the pivots around which automatic activity circulates, so that when the grouped forces of memory emit the emotion of love, consciousness, the actual Ego, is stimulated to acts of self-denial in striving to increase the joy of the object loved, as the equivalent of that emotion. We love and must serve—we love and must follow. The moving vital force at work, including consciousness, is the force building up the immortal Ego, Sentient Personality, and the organic Ego is formed of vital forces grouped in forms of memory as the vitalised forms of physical units. When these vitalised physical units give out in functioning the emotion of pleasure, the automatic action of the Ego is to follow that lead, and in doing so, the Christian exerts the forces in the work of benevolence. I repeat, it is a fact of much importance, that the logical sequence leading to sentiment and passion develops the moral element in one that has suffered. His sympathies are roused when he sees others suffering, and he gives expression to that emotion in deeds of kindness to relieve the sufferer. Hence, the moral element comes to be developed, and emits its own form of pleasure, which induces moral action as its automatic equivalent in the Ego following this lead of pleasure, and explains the mental operation at work in the proverb—"It is more blessed to give than to receive."

In dreams, the Automatic activity of the cerebral brain is very prominent in the persistent impression emitted. This is the natural sequence of what has been explained in groups of persistent memories being in a state of erethism, and remaining awake while others sleep. They emit persistent ideal conceptions which imprint themselves in such a way by speaking their own language, as to rouse the Ego's attention during sleep. The explanation of the mental condition present in dreams may be found in a strong previous excitation, or some peculiar receptive condition of a special group of cells kept in erethism. They may arise from the fear of consequences involved in an impending calamity. Anyhow, all have their root in unconscious memories and disordered ideas which follow one another in strange forms. Dreams often cause a series of long-forgotten impressions to rise again in a very disorderly manner. They are always part of the store we have accumulated. In dreams of any kind, we must have seen the phenomena in some form. A great number of dreams are more or less united with some strong impression we may have had during a recent waking state—as the pleasures and pains linked to external impressions always accompany them in thought. When such Ideas linked thus occur in dreams, these emotions accompany all the phenomena of the dream. You will thus perceive that pain, attaching itself to a great personal or national calamity, might be so linked to Ideal Conceptions in a group of cells in erethism as to rouse a whole series of neighbouring cells. This might be done in such a methodical manner as to present a graphic conception participated in by the Ego, and convey intelligence of the nature that the individual had been accustomed to accept as a providential warning that an approaching calamity was to be avoided by, we shall say, fleeing for safety to another country. Now, over an individual fully convinced that such an arrangement was a providential warning to take a course that would deliver him from impending trouble, such dreams would have an extraordinarily powerful influence. It is when taking this view of the matter that we can understand the marvellous power Dreams had over the Jewish race. They were accepted by that race as warnings from God. God did sometimes make use of this method in communicating with His people. One special case of this nature, that will suggest itself to all Christians, is that of Joseph being warned in a Dream to flee to Egypt with the little Child Jesus. The rational conceptions fit to explain such an operation are very simple. Let us suppose that the troubled history through which the Jews had passed, had so operated as to induce that race to attach to the subject-matter of certain Dreams a providential warning that they were to flee for safety to a strange country. We may well suppose God to make use of such a belief in Joseph's case through the language of a Dream. The forces liberated in Joseph's brain would produce the desired effect, through the law of Associated Ideas operating in calling into Erethism certain groups of cells, which, in functioning, automatically give expression to the ideas required for this end—ideas which would be so linked with painful memories as to produce a shock of dynamic effect, which impressed the dream so vividly on Joseph's memory as to assure him it was a warning from God. This was so, for God was dealing supernaturally through natural causes. Natural causes, observe, presided over by God in a special manner, accomplished the desired end. The bodily safety of the Redeemer of mankind was secured, that thereby He might live a human life and die the death of a criminal on the cross, arise from the dead, and ascend to His appointed place in "space," to plead the cause of His people, and wait for the Ransomed church of the first-born to partake of His glory. Those who have loved and suffered for His sake must assuredly share in His glory. They loved and must follow; for they loved and did suffer, and will evermore rejoice in their Redeemer and Head.

It is always merely the automatic forces of the nervous elements that regulate and govern the world in thought and emotion during our wakeful mental states. It is this same automatic action persisting in groups of cells while we sleep that speaks in the language of dreams in a most incoherent form, because unaccompanied by the reacting influence which is bound to proceed from the Ego in a wakeful state. The Automatic Language of an abnormal kind is, however, most clearly of all traced to the Phenomena peculiar to Mental Diseases. In all mental disease, the automatic energy of the cerebral cells is more or less the cause of the irresistible impulses which characterize many of the actions of the insane. General delirium manifests the automatic activity at work in the most extraordinary way in showing how Thoughts conflict and associate in the brain, this being the highest form of the force of our activity expressing its form of action in the most abnormal way. In delirium, less vehement where a dominant idea expresses the activity of a certain group of cells pretty constantly in erethism, we find the individual repeating the same ideas, not perceiving them wholly out of harmony with surrounding facts. Such persons may maintain that they are robbed, poisoned, or ruined. You may reason as profoundly as you please, having proof in hand which leaves no doubt of the fact; but all is of no avail, the Dominant idea persists in the automatic activity of the brain being set in a false direction by the objective conditions which they give expression to, in the subjective signs appearing in their place on the brain in such a way that the patient has no power to dispel the delusion. To him it is a reality and no delusion, and therefore they repeat again and again the same phrase as the equivalent of the automatic forms of these groups of cells causing the troubled mind to utter their language only. In the knowledge possessed by experts of these automatic manifestations, we are provided with the explanation of most mental diseases. It may be said that all mental maladies arise from the manifestation of different degrees of erethism in the fundamental properties of the cells apparent in their automatic activity. In many cases this may be traced to the blood too freely evoked by some portion of the brain being kept in perpetual erethism by the effect of bereavement, loss, or grief, of some kind; or in consequence of the effects proceeding from the life the predecessors have lived transmitted by the law of inheritance to their offspring.

In reference to the automatic activity which this chapter takes to do with, Dr. Maudsley very aptly remarks that "the impression which has lost its distinctly conscious character as a sensation has then become a want or need, so that the absence of it is felt as the discomfort of something wanted, it has been so incorporated in our nature, that its removal leaves a sort of rent or wound in our mental being. In like manner, it dulls perceptive consciousness till perception becomes almost or quite automatic. We practice it habitually in regard to familiar objects without consciousness of what we are doing, and experience the greatest difficulty in the world to get outside the path of habit, therefore it is, that bound to the tracks of habit, we fail to perceive new facts that lie close at hand, and miss for years the most obvious discoveries which they suggest. In these habitual perceptions men are scarcely less automatic than are ants and bees in their perceptions and acts. Desire, again, intense as it is in the first instance, becomes automatic by habitual repetition, where it notably happens that the end desired is lost sight of in the means adopted to attain it, that which was means coming to be desired as end; and afterward when prolonged repetition has made this pursuit the habit of a life, even the consciousness of the secondary end disappears, being transformed into a need or necessity of an habitual activity. Thus we see man brought in all the relations to his habitual mental activity to automatic states very like those of the Ants and Bees, and find it, if we attempt the task, almost as difficult a business to move him out of them as it is for these creatures to go outside the range of their machine-like doings, the moral of the whole matter being that most men eventually are little more than machines, whose sayings and doings from day to day may be predicted with as much certainty as the cries and doings of a parrot. Organisation proves itself capable of doing in them that which it does by itself in the ant or bee."

That these graphic words I quote of Dr. Maudsley rest on facts capable of being clearly understood by any one who makes himself acquainted with this branch of science is certainly true, and indicates that mind is a quality of matter. This is clearly evident from the facts that can be deduced from a careful study of the human brain in its functioning capacity. For, observe, habit so rendered is transformed into the structural units forming part of the organic Ego manifesting their own form of force in functioning these habits. This course is adopted by vitality so as best to secure for the organic Ego an equal division of labour among its units in functioning, by economizing the directing power of the immortal Ego in leaving it free to develop the movements that form new structures, and in this way secures the growth and development of organic complexity all through life.

The Christian moral to be deduced from all, illuminated by the light with which modern research, aided by evolution, provides us, is, that habit in its grouped forces could produce a base so strong for the moral element in the organic Ego to act through as would induce the Ego spontaneously to follow a moral course in the automatic forces kept in active functioning vigour. For it is to act thus, automatically, that a Christian organisation should aim at, yes, and prove itself capable of attaining to, if animated by the Inspiration that springs from vital Union with Christ which ensures a Glorious Immortality to each member of the community. So animated, the organisation could not fail to convince the sceptical that Christianity had a divine origin, and was the permanent religion of our race. Further, the automatic actions of the moral element in the organic Ego thus animating a Christian community, are the conditions the Redeemer points to in the moral taught in the Sermon on the Mount. He calls His followers the salt of the earth, and the light of the world, inferring that each member would reflect the glory of God in the exalted religious and moral form His church indicated to all observers. For the automatic activities of the organic Ego so animated would be a convincing evidence to the sceptical world of the power the God Man possessed on earth.

Christ henceforth is to be recognized by all as "the God of the whole earth."—Isa. v. 4-5. He is recognized at present by the Christian church as the Son of God, who has secured for all believers the right to be called the children of God, and as such are to reflect His glory all through eternity. The assurance that the converted believers pass into such a glorious state at death, ought to lead them to dispense with worldly pleasure, and to live the self-denying life of their Lord, Redeemer, and God, during the short time they are on earth — witness-bearers of Jesus of Nazareth, the child of Mary, but the Son of God and Redeemer of our Race—the only God it can ever know.

CHAPTER VII.

PROCESS CREATING AND DEVELOPING IMMORTAL SOUL.

THE vital force inherent in the human form at birth awakens into Consciousness and creates the soul of the first sensation—a soul developed by the series of sensations that follow to which the individual human form gives expression during its earthly life; the fact being that vitality is sensation, a force ever in motion, repelling what weakens and attracting what sustains. Further, it is a property inherent in vitality itself that transforms dead matter into living forms and induces natural selection. The structural units of the organism can be transmitted through the law of generation, so as to preserve its species.

This understood and admitted, the evolution of the human soul follows in the natural sequence of conscious states to which the human brain and organism, surrounded by an environment, gives birth in functioning. Where Reason is rooted in brain and structure, this form of vitality secures for Sentient Personality increase and growth, as well as creates it. In this way "Mind" secures for itself a permanent form in the Immortal indestructible units of the human race as its social organism. Acting in these units, "Mind" in its self-directing force, preserves as the fruit of the organism, in the form of the organism, the human form of Intelligence. It is a form of vital activity ever in motion, therefore Immortal, because capable of feeling, of moving, and of transforming dead matter into living forms. As is often said, it is an organism capable of feeling that constitutes a living organism; and such is consciousness, the activity of Sentient Personality, soul or Ego, the "self-conservative force" that constitutes the human form of vitality of endless duration. It is ever capable of sustaining consciousness by absorbing energy to do so. Indeed, human vitality, once formed, is not dependent on the human body to sustain its vital activity, but sustains itself as a self-conservative unit, capable of transforming dead matter into feeling and movement as conscious states. And such is the vital form of energy which the human organism has created, and at death liberates, in the human form as the soul : the fact being that the vital energy of the self-conservative soul or Ego, on the death of the human body finds that organism an encumbrance, and casts it aside just as we cast aside a useless garment. In both cases the fundamental instinct of self-preservation animates and guides the Ego. For the useless garment no longer served the end required of it, and it was cast aside in consequence ; so is the bodily organism, rigid in death, no longer fitted to serve its purpose of creating feeling or motion by transmitting and recording objective units, either as thought in associated memories, or the external records that are taking place around it. The dead human body is therefore a useless encumbrance to the Sentient Personality, which embodies the truly vital form of energy, now a disembodied soul or Ego. As such, its fundamental instinct of self-conservation casts the dead body aside as a worthless thing, because the soul can only maintain its individual form by doing so.

Observe how true to its instinct the vitality is, that manifests its activity in self-conservation as the force inherent in the human organism. The vitality to which the organism gives an enduring form consists of the capacity consciousness possesses of maintaining itself, in forming conscious states on the death of the body in the human form animated by self-conservation. For such is the Ego created by the human form transforming the forces of nature into the vitality of self-conservation. Observe, the force of self-conservation was not until the human organism created it, though once created, it never ceases to exist as Ego.

When we comprehend with clearness the uniformity of action manifested in the human organism, and the wonderful accumulation of vital activities stored up in the sensorial forms to which the special senses give birth, as a store of vital force animated by one aim, we cease to be surprised that an enduring form of the energy of self-conservation in the human form, such as the soul or Ego embodies, should be produced as the natural sequence of these accumulated vital forces acting in harmony, and animated by their fundamental instinct of self-conservation.

Just consider the wonderful operation going on in the human brain, in its capacity for recording and retaining every external and internal excitation, which has been participated in by Sentient Personality, this same Sentient Personality itself being the result secured through the united action of the vital forms in the stored up forces of the organism acting in harmony. It is human vitality in the united action of harmony uttering its first note, that we have in the startled cry of the new born infant complaining that the vitality of the organism is being attacked, by being plunged into a cold atmosphere. In its own way the child solicits the aid of the sympathising hearts that surround it, though of course wholly unconscious of being so surrounded. It is from the peripheral region of the organism that the first spark springs, which represents the united harmony of that organism in creating and giving expression to Sentient Personality, which is to endure and will henceforth develop the play of the organic machinery which has given birth to its Sentient Personality. The developing process which succeeds and builds up the Ego during its early days is purely the automatic action of the organism manifesting the vital force through the operation of nourishment. The child takes the breast of the nurse automatically. The first visible indication of the reacting form of vital force may be seen in the smile with which eventually the child will welcome the sight of the breast, as the recognized source from which pleasure flows to it. The breast, and the emotion of pleasure to which it ministers, have formed one of the earliest roots of the co-ordinating processes of memory, as a structural unit in the brain of the child. The surrounding condition, accompanied by its emotions of pleasure, is recorded in the brain of that infant, so as to give expression to the record in a sign of pleasure understood and participated in by its kind (represented in the nurse). Such actions as these prove the fact that vitality centres in perceiving what increases or retards its strength or growth.

In the brain we have the structural unit as an associated memory of the history that gives expression to Sentient Personality, and as such is a record co-existent with it. For to create the unit which soul or Ego embodies, is the work of the vital energy inherent in the human organism at birth. The complexity of the developing process taking place in the brain, is co-existent with the forces uniting in building the Ego, the immortal form of vitality which springs from the transformed physical excitations recorded as the organic Ego in the brain, and which carry the emotions that accompany them with them. The first spark of the vitality of Sentient Personality is given expression to in the current that chills the body of the infant, and reacts in consequence, giving out the note of pain, indicating that vitality is attacked by the chill that affects the whole human form. Later on in the history of the Ego's development, the breast of the nurse is recognized as the physical excitation that gives pleasure. Now the child, as the embodied form of vital energy, makes its first selection, and chooses the breast as its source of pleasure.

What I now wish my reader to take special notice of, is the enduring form of this vital current that is ever in motion, created by, and acting through the human organism. It is therefore, bound to assume its form embodying the vital energy of self-conservation in Sentient Personality. This form of vitality, once created is indestructible in itself, and can never be annihilated, but continues to live as the vital force that the human organism created. It is a unit in the human form of vital energy, ever in motion, capable of giving expression to human intelligence by functioning. On the death of the organism, it casts it aside as a garment; but it retains in the embodied activity that conscious states can develop, every iota of the records of the vital energy into which consciousness entered. Then does the self-conservative form of human energy in its disembodied and immortal state contain the life history of the individual that is built up in creating the self-conscious Ego. The Ego sustains itself by absorbing the energy that surrounds it, and restores it, functioning intelligent conceptions — simply a unit of vitality that sustains itself in absorbing its medium, and restoring that medium in functioning.

The fact is, that the structural unit, Sentient Personality, is animated by self-conservation as its fundamental instinct, in going through its order of development, is a vital force ever in motion. The structural unit which will embody in its form of vital energy all the conscious states that the organism has given expression to, is linked together as a continuous series of its life-history. The series is held intact by the mutual attraction inherent in the vitality of self-conservation, soul, or Immortal part. Let us suppose, just by way of illustrating the conditions, that the universal ether does actually build itself up as Sentient Personality of that substance; then we can imagine the operation taking place in such a compact vital unit of living intelligence, held as one whole even on the death of the bodily organism, and consolidating into its own form by the mutual attractions of intelligence, so as to form a bodily organism of the energy generated as nerve current, into which conscious states entered. Remember, a trace of every one of these states is a structural unit capable of reproducing such conscious states, and is to be found in the human brain, in the structural unit of memory. They are the result of the currents I have referred to which agitate the human form. Now, in the consolidating forces such as I indicate, all that would be required to effect what I infer, would be supplied by the energy in erethism, which these structural units could liberate simultaneously, just in the same way as the latent energy is liberated individually, in the co-ordinate action of every-day memories. The energy capable of producing the consolidated form to which I refer may be found in the human nerve-structure culminating in the brain. What is required to evoke it is a strong enough exciting cause. Now, we may assuredly infer a strong enough exciting cause to exist at the moment of death, inherent in the united forces built up of self-consciousness animated by self-conservation. This self-conservation is thrilled to the core by the shock severing the soul from the body. This must take place when vitality asserts its power to exist independently of the body that developed it. To do so is the work of a truly vital unit of disembodied vitality. Observe, the joint action of these forces in consolidating, would be participated in by the whole latent energy of the nervous system when thrown into a state of erethism, therefore, they would glow with the vital energy which each would liberate. They are marked by their own form of vitality, and contain in their grasp the energy of the network of nerve-fibre that envelops the body, and forms the conducting rods whereby physical excitations are transformed and transmitted from the objective world, and recorded as their equivalent in an ideal form in the brain. Such a process would embrace the form of the human body united by its superior ganglion —the brain.

It is very certain these consolidating forces would necessarily bear the human form as the equivalent of the fibrous network that embraces the organism, and which transmits impressions to the brain, the seat of the vital energy of the system. The energy liberated at death would provide the form and substance of Sentient Personality in the brain of that form, animated by the vital force of the Ego continuing its functioning power as active as ever. The developed form of vital force is that living thing working from within, and developing the latent forces of Sentient Personality, animated by self-conservation, the ever-active and ever-enduring vitality, because in its very nature of self-conservation it is indestructible as a self-conscious unit. Such are the developed forces of the vitality that leaped into being on the birth of the child, and on the death of the human being appear as the structural unit recording the earthly history of his life—a life where action originating in consciousness may develop its activity by unconscious acts, afterwards in the play of the automatic activity of the organism. Yet, the unconscious action which first springs from a conscious act, is so united to the conscious act as ever afterwards to form a link in the chain of the indestructible Soul or Ego.

We may have a pretty clear conception of the building up process of this indestructible unit if we follow the developing forces that give expression to the infant's life on earth. We had the first painful structure laid when the child at birth was plunged into a cold atmosphere. And as an early manifestation of the recorded vital energy reacting, we find the child recognizing the breast of its nurse as its source of pleasure. Operations of this nature, of great importance, will soon follow by natural selection developing the latent energy of the senses. But the satisfaction which the milk that the child sucks ministers to in feeding, may be compared to an organic cell which absorbs from the surrounding medium the substance that sustains it. The infant expresses his pleasure at the sight of the breast. He rejoices because he retains a memory of the satisfaction that he experienced in his appetite being satisfied.

As we proceed, this wonderful structural unit, the Ego, that is evolved in the course of our life on earth, is formed purely of sensitive units, multiplied hundreds of times by the intervention of Memory and Intelligence. The Intelligence is derived from the social organism of which it forms part. Sensibility develops with wonderful rapidity through the machinery put at its disposal in the human organism. The different sensorial foci lighten up and are developed in obedience to the action of the forces at work within and without. The child learns to see, to feel, to hear, &c. He remembers the pleasure imparted by the people that surround him, caress him, and minister to his comforts, recognizing them as his sources of pleasure — for it is in recognizing the source of pleasure and pain that the real developing power of the human vital force rests. This process includes the progressive life of the species, in the intelligence that acts and reacts in leading up to new forms of knowledge and understanding. A unit of the living force, embracing the social organism as self-conservation in the form of the child, manifests the simplest properties of its form of life through the machinery which the human body puts at its disposal, by the smile with which it welcomes those who soothe and caress it. The vital force of the human machine is simply recognizing the source of its pleasure, and reacting in consequence through the life-current so originated. An action so simple as this is the force at work, of which it has been said it was impossible to define and bridge the gulf that transformed dead matter into the living organ of self-consciousness. This condition is created, defined, and bridged, if bridge there be, in our planet developing a quality of force which sustains itself by attracting what strengthens and repelling what weakens it, This is a form of force which, in the course of time, developed special senses that lead up to the human form that develops human intelligence; which perceived the cause of such actions, and classed the former as the sensations of pleasure, and the latter as the sensations of pain. Thus, then, in pleasure and its cause, and pain and its cause, the physical forms that are associated with these sensations are grasped as the structural units of human intelligence, which is, as such, transferred into an indestructible form of the physical world in forming a unit of mind. For the vitality of the human organism gives this indestructible form to its units of mind as the equivalent of the work done by the human, living, acting, and thinking organism, surrounded by its medium; the work done being that of forming an enduring structure in the form of an intellectual conception of the physical world, represented as the objective unit that caused Sentient Personality, or was likely to cause it, pleasure or pain. For Sentient Personality is indestructible as the fruit of the vital force animating the human form, and created by that form. Remember, the term living organism is the definition of an organism capable of feeling. As long as the human organism is capable of feeling, it is capable of developing Sentient Personality, by giving expression to a pleasure and its cause, or a pain and its cause, as a form of the physical medium that surrounds it. Viewed from my standpoint, those who caress the child are in the ideal form, transformed into enduring forms of the social medium, thus related with it as the source of a pleasure. The force in the human form we call life, transmits the forms of the physical and social medium that cause a pleasure. The same is equally true of pain, with the difference that pain lowers the vital action. In this way the enduring living force of soul or Ego comes to be developed.

It is the accumulated forces of such intellectual conceptions, derived through the organism and its environments, that the social medium has stored up in the human brain, that provide the base of human intelligence which develops the wonderful capacity that the individual possesses of perceiving the source of a remote pleasure to be desired, and of a remote pain to be avoided. These movements, as the activity of vitality, are as simple in their primary aim as the activity of the simplest organisms in seizing what invigorates and repelling what depresses or weakens. For such is the action of vitality. The complicated action manifested by man arises from the complicated organism he inherits from his kind. Life, which includes a brain, is giving expression to the conscious action of attracting a pleasure and repelling a pain. Intelligent life consists in perceiving the source of a remote pleasure or pain.

The smile with which the child greets those who fondle and caress it, is among the earliest forms of vitality recognising its source of pleasure. Whereas, the first germ of the force which will develop into the moral element is laid in the first link of family affection, for the family affections bind themselves together as the cluster of units that spring from the family circle. The structure built thus becomes the origin of the child's sentiments and emotions. The vitality at work will now be recognised by the name that the child is called. The vital forces at work in that child love those who approach it for the pleasure they have already given it. The child, acting as the grouped structure of Sentient Personality, can recognise those who give him pleasure and pain, and likewise those to whom he is indifferent. The power of recognising objects that are indifferent, rests in the capacity acquired by the brain in developing human intelligence, arising from the accumulated forces transmitted through the law of inheritance. The point of importance to be remarked is that the objects of indifference do not call into activity the primary vital energy of repelling or attracting. This is simply an incident to which the vital energy makes no response. It simply observes it as a phase in human intelligence. Because vitality participates in the impression by seizing it, it becomes a phenomenon of the soul. But let the indifferent object so seized afterwards minister to, or create, a pleasure or pain, and immediately vitality records the phenomenon as the cause ; the object of indifference is no longer an incident, an item of intelligence —it has a life of its own associated with the pleasure or pain it creates. In memory, the vital force of self-conservation attaches a gratitude proportioned to the good or evil influence received. The child loves his parents first, because they contribute more or less to his pleasure and wellbeing. Being constantly in their presence, and seeing them day by day, the impressions so made keep the cells related to such condition in constant vigour. For being present to his eyes is being present on the web of nerve tissue prepared for receiving these impressions, to enable Sentient Personality to group itself in its own structure as the immortal form of intelligence which the child's organism will give expression to. And the centre groupings thereof are those about him in his early life causing him pleasure and pain, and building self-consciousness of the energy of self-conservation.

Later on in life, the organism will be thrilled in all its parts by manhood being set quivering to its very core through the operation of the sentiment of love. In this sentiment, vitality finds its maximum of pleasure realised. As the sentiment in which the life-invigorating activity of the individual culminates, the object which created the sentiment rules supreme as the moving force animating vitality for the time being. But to our race the special point of importance is, that earthly love gives expression to the heavenly sentiment that animates the Redeemed in glory. The sentiment throbbing to the core is similar. The difference alone rests in the object who inspires, and, therefore, becomes the centre around which vitality clusters in striving to serve the object loved. That object is to Christians our Lord Jesus Christ, the God of Humanity, the Son of God, the Saviour of Man. The place longed for is that which the body of our Lord, animated by His human and divinely endowed soul, now occupies in space, for there the Redeemed gravitate at death, animated by the sentiment of the race, therefore earth-like. They love and serve just because of the good things they have got and will get from their Redeemer. Thus, then, vital energy, such as we know it, is ever true to itself in this, that we Christians have in our Lord an object which we love for the good things He has given us and will give us, therefore, human-like, we serve; for such action is assuredly human nature divinely inspired and directed to perform the work assigned it, at this stage of development in the adopted children of God loving and working, thus serving the object loved. For in thought the person of the Redeemer, God, is ever before the eyes of one converted, and animated by the sentiment Redemption gives. You thus see how exactly similar in its way the case is to the child who loves those constantly about him and give him pleasure. For vitality clusters round a pleasure, and the object that originates the pleasure alone constitutes the difference I refer to. But how great is the difference, when we realise that in Christ we have a permanent object stimulating love and returning the sentiment all through eternity as the source from which love flows to and from the Redeemed.

But it is necessary to return to the developing process

of the earth-born soul, fully to understand the forces at work in developing the individual nervous system. For though the nervous system provides the base of all being, the base of human life and action, yet every individual develops in the general structure a special form of his own— a structure rightly defined as the organic Ego.

We have seen that it is the vital forces in the nervous structure of the organism, grouping themselves together as one unit, which start into being in creating Sentient Personality on the birth of the infant. However, the distinctive notion of conscious personality as the living thing acting and moving, grows only by the mutual action of being developed, and developing the individual form of force as the differentiated apparatus of that child's nervous system; which gives it the definite notion of conscious personality in forming and fashioning the forces of its own nervous structure, which is the equivalent of the sensations its surroundings beget. This illustrates the fact that the nervous apparatus itself has to go through a process of development during its period of growth and decay, as the equivalent of the sensations that build themselves into an individual and indestructible form of Sentient Personality, Soul, or Ego.

Sensations are supplied by the machinery of the human form, and are put at the disposal of the developing Ego for its use. Ego—Sentient Personality—creates, in differentiating into individual forms, the nervous system placed at its disposal corresponding to the units of our race in representing the organic Ego of each. The actual Ego, its equivalent, liberated at death, we may point to on all such occasions and say, behold the man, woman, or child known to his contemporaries as the force acting through each individual body and liberated in the human form as its soul.

The growth of these forces in building up conscious personality during the early years of the infant's life are indeed very vague. The plexuses of the brain forces are scarcely formed, but they wait the development of the sensorial apparatus to develop the cerebral activity whereby the infant can distinguish his sensations, and so keep a conscious memory of external impressions. To do so he must see, and hear, and taste, and so on. That is to say, the vital force at work in building up the structural unit of conscious personality, must develop the latent energy stored up in the ganglions forming these special senses as sensorial units, which develop themselves in giving definite expressions to consciousness. For the reflexes of the histological properties of the cerebral cells being the forces at the disposal of vitality are flabby and greyish, and not differentiated in any way into structural groupings of memories, and are, therefore, virgin to any definite external expression which would enable the child to keep a conscious memory thereof. However, through these plastic forces at the disposal of vitality during the first years of life, the cerebral substance is in constant exercise, and develops the grouped elements that are engaged in building up the earliest structural units, that give a definite notion of conscious personality by the child distinguishing his special sensations as such. Through this process going on, the infant begins to comprehend that it is he who is addressed when his name is called. He can walk, talk, and he gets a conscious notion of his own activities. He recognises the things that have pleased his sensitive organism. Now, natural selection takes active form, for among the acquisitions made, he chooses those that gratify him. He sees himself distinct from the external world, and recognises that it is so.

Henceforth the intellectual conceptions involved in subject and object has for the child a definite meaning, though very vague. The plastic cerebral substance in a young child retains every impression that assails it, as passively as a sensitive photographic plate exposed to the light. All such intellectual combinations or mental images in their own way become that child's patrimony, but those that gratify or pain him stand specially related to him as the moving vitality of conscious personality. In time he learns to know that certain words will convey to others the knowledge of his emotions, his pains, his joys, and his sorrows. These abstractions he makes use of, for they save him trouble and serve his purpose. Growing in knowledge so rudimentary as this, he comes to perceive that his name, a single word, an abstraction, will personify all he feels and knows, so he uses the name by which he is called to signify to others that he is talking of himself. He has perceived that this is the name by which he knows himself and by which others know him. In this abstraction the force of the indestructible vital energy forming the soul builds itself up as Sentient Personality, and clusters and grows as the forces personified by the child's name. The name is incorporated in its substance as the abstract which distinguishes these forces as the grouped unit, known as such on earth to its contemporary race. And the name is left to posterity as a patrimony which distinguishes the vitality of indestructible energy now forming his soul or Ego.

The developing process that follows at this early stage is well marked during the interval that takes place before the child perceives that, by substituting "I" and "me," these words supply the abstraction used as his name. But the child speaks as he feels. He saw himself, an object, addressed by a name, and uses that name as the abstraction by which he can approach others, therefore he speaks of himself as James or John, as the one pained or pleased. By observation, it is seen how much labour is required before he was prepared to make this abstraction, and how much more is required before he is able to use the " I " and " me." We by this means see the time it takes to develop the structural forces that embody all that is required to be done in laying the foundation of the organic Ego, by carving out a new structural unit from the forces placed at the disposal of self-consciousness. However, these and all abstractions are the signs ready made and used by the social organism in its intercourse with its kind. They save trouble and are the germs around which intelligence crystallizes. What we have to bear in mind is the incessant labour with which the foundation is made, in developing the individual structure of the organic Ego from the forces placed at the disposal of Sentient Personality in the inherited nervous system, so as to build up the indestructible energy of self-consciousness, animated by self-conservation, through the process I indicated taking place in the child developing the actual Ego which is liberated at death.

It was to give some slight notion of the forces that surround Sentient Personality in the nervous system that I prepared the chapters on Memory Groupings and Automatic Activities. For to all the human nervous structure gives birth, as well as serves as a support during its earthly development. Therefore, it is well to note the process at work in the earliest stages of the young life. The process is continuous all through the life of the organism that sustains it, for such is the natural sequence; and it might be expected when we know it is the physical force we call life that has built up, and is building the nervous system of the human body. Else how can we explain the law of inheritance. It is well marked in the course breeders of stock adopt in choosing the animals possessing the qualities they wish to preserve. This law assuredly holds good in the human nervous structure, as is proved by the painful experience of many in having had deafness and other diseases transmitted from their parents. So well is it recognized that such forms of diseases are transmitted, that the doctor often questions his patients regarding the state of the health of their antecedents. By such enquiries the doctor determines whether the disease is transmitted: say, in the case of inherited deafness, the infant born with a defective auditory organ might only manifest the sentiment in middle life by becoming prematurely deficient in hearing, though the conditions that to this lead were present at birth.

It is well to note that vitality rests in generating the movement that responds to pleasure and pain—the equivalent of attracting what strengthens and repelling what weakens—as these responses embrace Life. When this force was developed, vitality came into existence—was created in obedience to God's decree. Whereas, for the human organism to respond to pleasure and pain confers on the Ego it creates the ceaseless activity Immortality rests on. For the Ego, separated from the body, inspired thus, is endowed with a force ever ready to start into activity in responding to pleasure and pain, as the self-conservative force the human body, surrounded by its environment, creates. Therefore, an Ego so created, is capable of sustaining itself independently of the organism, as the end served in the physical pleasure and pain introduced by the body.

When we suffer physical pain, it is the organism that introduces the pain; when we enjoy the pleasure of health and strength, it is because of the physical joy which the organism imparts that we rejoice. And, in consequence, when the organism shows signs of decay, vitality is affected by that change in being deprived of the full complement of sensations. Because, while the human organism lives, the Ego must participate in its weal or woe. However, we, as Christians, are justified in marking an apparent distinction which sometimes happens in the case of a believer suffering great physical pain emitted from the diseased state of the body, yet, overpowered by intense joy for the time being by our Lord manifesting His indwelling power. Take for instance the joy sometimes animating the early Christian martyrs at the very time their organism was emitting the pain of torture caused by the flaming faggot of which that body formed part. In such cases bodily pain is neutralised by its place and phase of vibration in the brain being taken possession of by the highest, the heavenly phase of joy. For the life of the individual, the Ego is yet the life of the organism; though the sensation of joy imparted has a heavenly origin, notwithstanding, these sensations are emitted by the body because the Ideal Christ of heavenly origin is incorporated in that body as a structural unit which emits its own forms of sensations, namely, heavenly joy. Thus, then, it is only in so far as the ideal Christ is of heavenly origin, that I am justified in saying that the energy of self-consciousness is only subject to rise and fall by bodily sensation; but in thus far that the source is not of earthly kind, I hold I am justified in what I have said.

Otherwise, the Ego must participate in the sensations of the organism by accepting them. When memory groupings decay, they can no longer erect themselves so as to emit in thought the energy of intelligence capable of appealing to Sentient Personality, the Ego, the structure held together as one whole and liberated on the death of the body. In consequence, its development is greatly retarded. Even when the blood continues to provide the substance that feeds, and the forces that vivify, the nervous system itself, in the form of the organic Ego, has begun to decay. But there can be no decay for the actual Ego. It is liberated at death, and is ever capable of motion and sentiment, embodying its life-history, and continuing to grasp a pleasure and repel a pain. It is active as ever with the activity of life and its laws, the activity that creates and sustains itself as soul or Ego. The histological vitality of self-conservation, complete in all its parts, with the special senses created of their own forms of force endowed to perform their appointed work, as the structural units which develop in functioning, conscious states of the world that surrounds, by absorbing energy from the surrounding medium to do so, is the equivalent of the forces which the human organism and its environments created in creating Sentient Personality.

The actual state of matters is that the physical force we call life, animating the body, and surrounded by the physical and social medium of which it forms part, was created in building its own form of nervous structure, the organic Ego, as well as the actual Ego : the latter is the form of force to be disembodied at death. It is then capable of giving expression to its earthly history by developing intelligent conceptions forming that history. Thus, then, the actual Ego is liberated at death in its own form of force, and is the energy that embodies the Ego, forms its support, acts and reacts in obedience to it, as well as develops its history in the images formed of intellectual groupings. These images, when created in the human brain, were perceived as forms of thought, the equivalent of how Sentient Personality perceived the environments of the organism, and reacted in consequence. The actual Ego thus formed is the fruit of vitality slumbering in the nervous system at birth, and preserved through the law of inheritance, surrounded by a social and physical medium. These three factors, in joint alliance, create the Ego, and in doing so, differentiate the nervous structure into the forms of the organic Ego, which also give expression to human personality as the equivalent of the forces that build themselves up as soul or Ego.

There is another way of looking at the subject, viz., viewing the vitality slumbering within the nervous system awakening at birth into the activity of an individual life—as the force called into being by the cold atmosphere of the physical medium causing a thrill of pain to the human organism. Sentient Personality, developed thus, may henceforth be viewed oscillating, as a whole, backward and forward in the moving current when its organism is affected either pleasantly or painfully. In this way the Ego would course through the nervous system; and continue to do so as its truly vital force all through life (and at death course so in the human form), the equivalent of Ego affected either pleasantly or painfully, built up a conscious unit— soul or Ego. Such a unit embodies every conscious state whatsoever, though it only responds to pleasure or pain in oscillatory movement of the complex unit—Sentient Personality—coursing thus. Thus, then, though the Ego seizes every conscious state, it does not oscillate, as a whole, moving backward and forward. This movement is the expression of the purely vital activity inherent in the living Ego, and as such, it responds to pleasure and pain only, where pain may be viewed as the physiological equivalent of the individual sensibility of that Ego in conflict with the surrounding medium. The organism is painfully affected and the Ego resents it. The same is true of pleasure, with this exception, that the movement of the Ego gratified an effort to retain the exciting cause. And we may fairly infer that the individual Ego, liberated at death continues its backward and forward oscillation in response to pleasure and pain in shrinking from pain but invigorated by pleasure. Observe, the two points between which the backward and forward movement is carried on, is, the peripheral of the human body and its brain, whether you view the vitality acting in the human body or acting in the medium that forms the disembodied Ego, namely, the forces of which the human Ego is formed complete in every part—a form of energy as such that survives natural death.

While the Ego is being developed by the operation vitality is subject to in the human organism, we may infer pleasure to be life, the truly vital force ever in motion, subject to be painfully affected by the condition of the physical medium which threatens to annihilate pleasure viewed as life. The resistance thus generated by the opposing forces so related may be sufficient to raise the temperature of the resisting medium—the nervous elements—to the condition we may call white heat, the equivalent of intense pain; a process which, for all we know, may be capable of being measured by the force of resistance met with in the moving forces acting through the nervous structure. Viewing the case thus, what we call either physical or moral pain, would be the human organism so affected by the physical or social medium as to have to encounter the resistance of the vitality of pleasure (life) oscillating in the organism, a resistance which raises the temperature of the resisting medium to the point of pain. The fact is, pain is the expression of the histological sensibility of the nervous elements raised to an extra histological pitch. This being understood, pain is always identical with itself regarding its genesis, and only reveals itself in a different manner according as the nature of the nervous plexus thrown into agitation is different. For example, when light is intense, the sensibility of the retina is developed to excess, and so imparts a similar reverberation exceedingly painful to the Sensorium. It is the same with all the senses when stimulated to excess—which is the equivalent of being sent vibrating at the pitch of pain. For a nerve discharging pain is the element raised to a white heat. It has arrived at a certain period of erethism, a definite phase of vibration, the equivalent of pain. The true phenomenon of this is in reality a vital reaction where a certain tension is pain's necessary condition.

If the nerve is rendered frigid, pain cannot be developed, the tension necessary being absent. The skin of hysterical patients often manifest this frigid state, and may be pinched, pricked, or have burning substances applied, but the patient feels it not, because the nerves are not in a state to take on the vibration equivalent to pain. By producing local frigid anæsthetic, the evolution of pain is prevented by the nerves being chilled. The brain is no exception in its mode of developing pain. For local heating of the cerebral substance co-exists with pain; the fact being that pain is just the expression of the sensibility of living tissue exercised in excess. Chloroform freezes the nerve plexus of the Sensorium by producing anæsthetic therein—just as the skin of an hysterical patient sometimes is—so that the pain of the burning flame attacks in vain. The zones of the brain cells are physically modified, and cannot erect themselves, therefore they cannot be raised to the pitch of pain. Moral pain arises from the sensibility of the intellectual grouping being carried to its maximum intensity. For the moral shock once experienced perpetuates itself in becoming incarnated in the brain—the echo of a former agitation, and the phenomenon of moral grief, each in his own way must feel and suffer from. The degree will vary in intensity in proportion to the delicacy or richness of the nervous tissue of the cerebral. The genealogy of moral pain, which must originate from without, consists in the persistence of the impressions into which, as its base, the incessant participation of the intellect must enter. For the persistent moral sensibilities participated in by the Intellect are the true physiological factors at work that provide the history of moral pain. When the brain plexuses are thrilled to their depth, the impression persists for a shorter or longer period, in vibrating automatically in such a way as to make its emotional phases so felt that the individual can think of nothing else. For the automatic activities vibrating subjective images as the objective condition to which the moral pain is attached, are the activities that keep Sentient Personality in a constant state of vital oscillation, vibrating backward and forward as a whole. This is the equivalent of the moral elements being raised to what may be called a white heat, and kept in that condition of activity or tension, possibly till the forces exhaust themselves.

Such is the rational explanation of the emotion of moral sensibility. The evolution of this depends on bygone memories vibrating in their intellectual activity. Moral pain is developed by a regular process through which man can estimate the loss he would sustain by his affections and dearest hopes being blighted, his fortune lost, his worldly hopes blasted, &c.

All through the evolution of moral pain the vitality of pleasure is being attacked, and may be called the phenomenon of the reaction of pleasure contending with its most deadly enemy. By this process the tension of the nervous structure is raised to the pitch of pain. Pleasure and pain are the contrasted forms of force to which we give the name "vital force," and as such they form the fundamental of the human Ego, Soul, or Sentient Personality, fighting the battle of Life. The Ego strives to nullify pain, its deadly enemy. This is equivalent to saying the Ego is constantly striving to retain pleasure by combatting pain. It would be well if we Christians moved

"Unruffled through earth's war
The eternal calm to gain."

The battle does not end with the death of the body, for the Ego must be quite liable to suffer from the attacks of the memories of the moral pains it has caused others, and the consequences thereof, as a disembodied unit of humanity. Else a part of the individual life-history in these memories would cease and so cause a break in the continuous strain of self-consciousness that forms the Ego. But this break is impossible. On what other ground than that of past memories can the law of retribution rest, which regulates so much the future life of the unsaved portion of our race.

Lest the fact should be doubted, that pain is the correlative of a phase of local heating, tension, or strain of the nerve fibre, it is well to add as a proof of this that the absence of repose for the brain in prolonged intellectual work, or moral emotion generates a local heating of the cerebral substance, which causes aching of the brain. If the activities of the cerebral cells are developed to excess, we have histological sensibility, the equivalent of the erethism of pain. Through the discovery of Cloroform, and in many other ways, medical science has greatly modified the sum-total of pain. By the advance of this science, much of the pain suffered by our race during the period of its earthly development will be nullified. In this way, medical science will lessen the maximum of painful memories the race will carry into the immortal state. An immortal state entered, in this simple way that Sentient Personality, the vitality oscillating in the human organism, will just continue to oscillate in a human form on the death of its organism as an intelligent being, capable of absorbing energy from the surrounding medium and transforming it into forms of thoughts and actions in functioning—an intelligence which, during earthly life, was developed by the organism. The function of the organism was to create the immortal Ego, as the units which embody human intelligence. These units, once created, reproduce forms of intellectual groupings as the work of their normal activities. Activities giving expression to intelligence, developed by the human form, are the activities of our race. The forms are sustained by absorbing the surrounding energy which they return in functioning, and so give expression to normal activity.

Thus, then, human personality finds itself acting as a disembodying form of humanity, before it is aware that it has passed into the immortal state; an individual life coursing through the human form. For then the rhythm of thought is just similar to what used to take place in the body while on earth. The Ego or human personality awakens thus in spirit-land to find itself in the human form capable of, so far, thinking and acting as it did on earth. It has a human form, which you may call material or not, just as you please. For it is the Ego being capable of forming conscious states that sustains its life, by absorbing energy and liberating it as conscious phenomena, such being the natural or normal force of the activity of its life. The case would be somewhat similar to that taking place in the organism which absorbs the energy liberated by the small red corpuscles of the blood in functioning.

The life action of the disembodied human personality, knit together by its special senses, will be complete in every part, and absorb energy direct from its medium to return it in functioning, yet it will be subject to the law that governs the conservation of vital force. If we view the energy vitalised through its relation with the race in forming conscious states as the sum-total of energy, the unconverted section of that race will find conditions under their control, doing what they wished to have done, as the expression of a community, animated by a similar sentiment. Observe, a section of the race, so animated, would be guided by similar aims, and acting for a common end. All may be viewed as the fruit generated by the united action of feeling, of thought, and of intelligence, giving expression to the harmony proceeding from these Egos as the equivalent of united aim and action.

Remember, as regarding earth-born units of our race, the last conscious states that the organism gives expression to end the growth, the development, and the capacity of the Ego as an earth-born unit, which at death becomes the inhabitant of another world. Further, in that world the Intellectual groupings which go to form the Intellect of each individual have linked into them the emotions of their own special phase of pleasure and pain. That living moving form of consciousness, built up of every conscious state to which the bodily organism gave expression, is held together by the mutual attraction inherent in the life-history of the individual. In the light of these facts, how clear the Saviour's teaching becomes, when He said, all "secrets shall be revealed."

Finally, I may sum up all I have said in these few words. The vital energy of disembodied humanity is built up of the oscillatory force ever in motion generated in the action of the accumulated forces at work in the individuals of the race. These forces do not cease their activities on the death of the individual organism, but continue that activity in the form of the body as disembodied spirits. In the united action of the forces generated by the collective human organism, there vibrates Humanity, whether viewed as the forces given expression to in the human body, or as the immortal energy of self-conservation, active as ever, forming the souls of disembodied Humanity. For in each unit the Sentient Personality or Ego of that unit is the vital force coursing through its human form, bound together by its life-history, formed of its serial conscious states. True it is, the Ego, the vital force, starts into independent activity on the death of its body, come when death may ; and henceforth continues to course through the human form, which retains its own special sense as developed by the organism, though in spirit-land separated from that organism.

CHAPTER VIII.

WILL GUIDED BY MOTIVES.

WILL is the force that starts into activity when a pleasure, present or remote, is to be secured, or a pain, present or remote, is to be repelled. Will, assuredly, is an equalizing power, guided by Intelligence, regulated by Deliberation, that adjusts the activity of vital force. For the equalizing power Will possesses is the moving force at work in the human Ego, the energy of self-conservation. Volition in its mode of operation is very interesting and instructive; a force guided by intelligence striving to invigorate vitality by increasing pleasure and repelling pain either present or remote. Thus, then, Will-energy, guided by motives regulated by pleasure and pain, explains the known fact that pleasure increases the vital functioning power of the organism, while pain lowers and hinders it. Pleasure stimulates life's activity, pain hinders it. For the indestructible form of force which operates in building up the differentiated nervous structure, comprising individual human life on earth, has in pleasure a distinct or definite form of power reigning in the organism; which Life or Will strives to maintain in its warfare waged against pain, its opposite or contrasted force, which lowers vital action. Pleasure invigorates—pain depresses. The signs which the social organism has invented "as abstractions" to characterize these opposing forces are—animated, gay, cheerful, &c., contrasted with their opposites —sad, miserable, unhappy, wretched, woe-begone, depressed, dejected. One of these written signs, as an abstract image, will convey to another's mind the state that vital activity manifests, or has manifested, in the individual himself, or in another, at any period of the history of either.

The prostrating effect of privation, severance of ties, shame, remorse, and calamities of all kinds, is well known. Mental depression, which often leads to insanity, is sometimes the cause of premature death. It is also true that death has resulted from excess of joy. And the fact is thus proved that the organism will only serve as the habitation of the human vital force between certain limits. When that limit is reached, human vitality casts aside the organism, because death reigns therein. In that state the immortal Ego has no part.

Now, in the law that regulates pleasure and pain, we have the key to the expression of the feelings. To these the features give the most prompt indication, then the voice, and lastly bodily movements. For example, look at the step and gait of a conqueror, placed in contrast with the conquered. We have the fulness of life Will strives to retain, manifesting itself in face and form, in the erect bearing of the one, and the drooping hopeless attitude of the other. Note the gush of woe often typified in the image called up by the words—" His countenance fell." For pleasure and pain are forms of force as opposed as cold and heat. It is because pleasure increases vitality that the organism so animated stands erect, being full of life. But mark the ebb of life in the drooping form and bent figure, as the answer the organism gives to " I suffer "—" I die."

Further, pleasure and pain, as opposing forces, arrest

and destroy each other. Our contrasted ideas may be viewed as signs marking the boundary line wherein the vital force of the organism may oscillate, as the limit of its moving current in retaining pleasure or repelling pain. Viewed from this point, heat would form an attraction to invigorate and induce Will to strive to retain the influence so long as it imparted pleasure—cold would do the same. Take for instance the cool bracing air of summer, and the warm glow from the fire in a cold night.

Individual life was not till the organism gave it birth; so the natural activity of Will-power regulating individual life will be to maintain the organism as its stay and support — the medium that imparts to vital force its joys, and marks the limit of its moving current, wherein a pleasure may be retained or renewed, and a pain repelled. As a fact of physiological science, we feel only the wounds of our own bodies. The organism is the boundary line marking the limit of the living acting forces which embrace individual life wherein Volition acts.

Darwin in his "Expressions of the Emotions," page 178, gives a graphic description of the life-retarding effect of pain—Volition's most deadly foe. Therefore Volition's act, so as to extend the limit of Pleasure, is to retard the limit of Pain. In giving expression to these effects in reference to Pain, Darwin's words are—"The circulation becomes languid; the face pale; the muscles flaccid; the eyelids droop; the head hangs on the contracted chest; the lips, cheeks, and lower jaw, all sink downwards from their own weight. Hence all the features are lengthened; and the face of a person who hears bad news is said to fall." Adding at page 213 in reference to pleasure—" the whole expression of a man in good spirits is exactly the opposite of that of one suffering from sorrow." Many graphic descriptions are given in Darwin's book which demonstrates pleasure to be life-sustaining, pain, death-threatening forces at work in the human organism. Herein lies the explanation of the laws at work in the energy of self-conservation regulated by Will. It is true, that the mental conflict from which we suffer so much, is the conflict raging between these opposing forces, where wasting vital energy in the fight depresses the mental tone. Conflict includes the pleasure of harmony and the pain of discord—Will striving to secure the pleasure we desire in a war waged against the cause of the opposing feelings; but Conflict thwarts the law that connects pleasure with increase of vital energy. The sting of punishment rests in craving for the things denied us. Craving is the internal conflict that lowers vitality, therefore, when we cease to crave for the thing denied, the sting of punishment ceases, and with it the lowering of vitality from the conflict. In so far the energy of self-conservation is at rest—a rest implied in the wish that the dead one may live in Christ (the Redeemer, God), and so rest in peace.

From what I have said of the energy of self-conservation, including the struggle going on between the opposing vital forces of pleasure and pain, I trust my readers will thereby be prepared to understand the views I advance in Will-energy. For the Ideal conception included in Will gives expression to the action of Vitality proper. Will is the power that starts into activity at any moment, when a pleasure is to be secured and a pain avoided. It is the force directed to the point to secure these ends. An end, when successful, is manifested in the operation of the spreading current that vitality infuses into the route it takes, to secure the pleasure it desires. For such is voluntary effort embracing the fundamental law of our being that connects, whatever the indivdual values as a pleasure, with the increase of vitality and pain with a decrease. Thus, then, Will is shown to be the movement at work in the energy of self-conservation, and may be viewed as the activity of life, manifested in the self-acting impulses of the nerve currents passing through the conducting rods of the nervous system as the vehicles which the ceaseless activities of life make use of for its own benefit. When in a joyful mood, the nervous structure is invigorated, being inhabited by the vitality of pleasure. When one stands erect, saying, in effect, "I can defy all comers," one is full of life and contented, and Will's desire is that the organism may continue so. But let something wound us, and the vital flow is at once cut off—the current is broken and dried up by the smart of pain. The destruction of vitality by the broken current is at once displayed in the face by the loss of vital energy. Will makes an effort to regain the condition by voluntary action ; guided, as such ought to be, by the insight which the intellect places at the disposal of the Will. Such are the forces which the education of Moral Training is to give special form to, by infusing into the moral element the emotion of pleasure. This process is the base that induces Will to act, because actions lead to securing a pleasure. This is the true guide for future conduct. Voluntary action would in that case be the activity associated with the moral structure, ready to start out at any moment, since it is associated with pleasure either present or remote.

To infuse this form of activity into the moral element or structure of its adherents, is what the Christian Church had the power to do, and should have done, long ago. By education, moral action in Christians may become an instinct, starting into activity whenever or whatever the occasion demands. If the Christian community had been educated thus, the nervous structure, long ere now, would have assumed the co-ordinating form for giving expression to the force, as the conscious expression of the Will of the individual working towards the desired end. Voluntary activity, so animated, would have none of the conflict involved in the mental struggle which so often takes place before a difficult moral course is taken, in choosing to suffer pain for the benefit of others. Physical pain might have to be encountered, but mental conflict would have ceased.

However, observe it is the structural base laid in the moral Education that secures the end so stated. And how strong is the base Christianity has the power to develop, in raising its adherents above worldly pleasure, must be apparent to all. As the base rests in the glorious eternal future our Lord has provided for all converted believers, who, "as sinners saved by grace," have the right to enjoy the assurance that realization of belief imparts, and in consequence live above the world. Animated thus, if the command, "love not the world, neither the things of the world," had been obeyed, the co-ordinating function desired would long ago have been developed in Christendom through the Law of inheritance. For inherited structures have a most powerful effect in facilitating the necessary process of moral Education or retarding it. This being so, the possibility of voluntary moral action to have become an instinct long ere now in the Christian community is no ideal conception too exalted to admit of practical application. For apart from Christianity, even in our degenerated age, much may be accomplished when we know that the plastic forces of the young brain puts at the disposal of the educator the powers to infuse into the moral element almost unlimited resources where the emotion of pleasure can be infused into the growing structure, in being so linked to the moral course of action as always to accompany it. And, remember, pleasure, the vital power of the spreading current is Will, stimulating to voluntary action. In other words, the lead that the diffusing vital current ever takes is in the direction of pleasure. This being so, the fact is plain, that through a process of education, aided by the inherited tendency Christianity is capable of infusing into the moral structure, the equivalent of Will-power in the emotion of pleasure it creates. This voluntaryism stands at the parting of the way, ever ready to start into activity when pleasure is to be secured or pain avoided. If such action is not instinct, what is it?

To educate this instinct would become comparatively easy if the social organism of the Christian community was such as to stimulate and not to retard this instinct—say by combining in such a way as to protect the individual form from being unduly taken advantage of either by Christianity's own adherents, or the world at large. The sentiment of justice leading to this is clearly involved in our Lord's teaching by enjoining the "worthy one" at a feast to take the lowest place, leaving the responsibility with the Lord of the feast to raise to the place of honour "the deserving one," as well as to remove the self-sufficient one who, "human like," had usurped the highest place.—Luke xiv. 7-11.

A Christian community possessing this sentiment, and realizing the responsibility referred to which it involved, would protect the individual from being taken undue advantage of, when the voluntary energy of moral action had become an instinct in giving expression to the spontaneous moral power of that structure in functioning. In this way the bad effect which might arise from instinct, we shall say, unwisely directed, would be guarded against by the community. Further, viewing the moral taught by our Lord in the "non-resistance creed" from this point, it is plain that the moral thereof rests in the duty of the mutual responsibility which the individual and the community have to perform to each other. Into this pleasure the activity of the energy of will would enter—the individual rejoicing in thus serving his Lord, and the community rejoicing in protecting such from undue oppression.

As Intellect takes such a prominent part in directing Will Force, it is well to insure a clear conception being formed of the combinations and processes which comprise Intelligence. For it must be clearly understood that the Intellect has sprung from the grouping which vital energy in the course of ages has produced, in perceiving the sources where the pleasures and pains of life spring from. The fact is, that Intelligence is consciousness of differences and consciousness of agreements. This consists in the consciousness of how certain conditions have, in the course of ages, affected the vital action either pleasantly or painfully, surviving in what we justly call knowledge-made substance; illuminated by the consciousness of vital energy perceiving points of agreement amongst a variety of differences, as the points capable of imparting pleasure or causing pain. (Intelligent Will power is following the lead that will insure, or be most likely to insure, the pleasure desired). The perceptive power of Intellect conceived from this point marks the source of vital activity—therefore includes volition as well as provides the force which forms the base of all Intelligence. In the groupings which have stored up the memories of the ideal forms in knowledge-made substance with the effects of the pleasures and pains of past generations induced by and held in the organized brain as the energy of Intellect, is the base or source which enables vitality —or Will Force—to perceive the points of contact when new pleasures may be secured and how new sources of pain may attack and can be neutralised. This explanation proves the whole range of human intelligence to have sprung from the operation at work in sensation or feeling. In having a clear comprehension of this, we find all to arise from feeling, and the conflict between opposing feelings, the forces which leave the grouped forms of memory, embracing human intelligence, clothed in the form of contrasts, which are the contrasted ideas that have sprung from Will viewed as including vital force following the lead of pleasure till checked by the shock of pain. The shock of pain conceived in this manner would leave the grouping or basis of a painful memory as a caution to Will to avoid in the future the conduct that caused it. Whereas, the shock of joy attached to the conception that caused it, will leave the grouped memory of a pleasure to be desired and followed after by Will guided by Intellect adopting a similar course of action in the future.

These grouped memories pre-suppose the ideal form of the physical cause perceived and recognized as such by Intellect, into which Will enters as the active agent which strives to avoid a pain and secure a pleasure. In this explanation we have the discrimating power of the individually trained Intellect doing its allotted work, that of perceiving the points of differences and points of agreement as the fruit of the intellectual groupings of memory, and Will its active agent, ,that vitality leaves to posterity. These general propositions apply with great force to Christendom,
L

which, in the Christian records, has a moral code of fixed laws. All are capable of developing in the community similarity of sentiment, where pain would be inseparable from one course of action, pleasure from another, if Christendom were in a healthy state regulated by the precepts laid down in the Christian records.

Intellect always embraces the forms of speech which the social medium makes use of, to enable man to communicate with his fellow. The forces at work in the law of diffusion follow the lead of pleasure till checked by the thrill of pain which breaks the flow of vitality followed by an effort—Will generating—to regain lost ground. This is an effort which rouses the latent forces of the Intellect so as to illuminate vitality—viewed as Will guided by reason—to perceive points of agreement where new pleasure can be secured. In the human brain animated thus, the current of life flows on, perceiving the sources of its pleasures and pains in the forces that Intelligence places at Will's disposal. Intellect itself is the growth that vitality has produced to act through by increasing the forms of Intelligence that the energy of Will, following the lead of pleasure, can make use of in sustaining the energy of self-conservation. You see by Will power following the lead of pleasure, its spreading current infuses vitality into the Ego, that is the energy of self-conservation, and so sustains it. The power that Intellect confers is that of simply extending the power of visage by extending the range of perceptions wherein the energy of Will, which is the activity of the energy of self-conservation, can secure a pleasure and repel a pain.

Intellectual development is enlargement of the perceptive power, resting in the operation of the law we know as cause and consequence. When a man is more known than his fellows, it is because he sees distinctions where they see none. Those so gifted apply old facts to explain new circumstances. He perceives the points of similarity where known facts will include and explain the newly discovered conditions. The power of visage in this way becomes extended; and also simplified by including totally new conditions under the old law, defined by an abstraction typifying in one word all that is included in one intellectual conception of great magnitude, which makes the conditions intelligent to all acquainted with the subject. This process of acquiring knowledge saves trouble. It binds up the mental structure by adding new forms, and it is the mental operation whereby scientific discoveries are made.

The operation of intelligent will is similar in its action. The vitality of Intelligent Will finds in scientific discoveries a new and vastly extended field of operation open to it, whereby Volition can secure new pleasures and guard against possible new pains. By applying old facts to explain new conditions, Intelligent Will follows the lead of pleasure, ever gathering strength as it goes, until the current is broken by the shock of pain, arising, it may be, from the fear of the consequence which is or may be involved in the line of conduct adopted to secure a pleasure desired. For such in some form are the shocks Intelligent Will is most liable to suffer from. However, where the pleasure desired by Volition is of the nature that requires the stern form of a rigid self-sacrificing course, then until Intelligent Will has succeeded in effecting the co-ordinating process in the mental structure which the diffusing current of this special phase of Volition requires (and if persevered in, will ultimately effect), in that structure in following the lead which Intelligence perceives to be the highest pleasure, the course pursued in perfecting the structure for that end will involve a great mental fight. And of this nature was the struggle endured by St. Paul, and referred to by him in the seventh Chapter of Romans. But observe how different his mental state referred to in Phil. iv., 11-13, is, in its peaceful nature when the co-ordinated process of the mental structure had been affected. This peaceful issue must be apparent to all when the mental states referred to are placed in contrast.

It must always be remembered that intellectual combinations include these sensations of pleasure and pain. Such sensations constitutes the moving current which the intellectual combinations typify as the cause. For all primitive shocks of human feeling are at once intellectual and emotional, therefore every intellectual group has an emotional side, and every emotion its intellectual side. As before said, all is the result of Will-energy perceiving where its pleasures and pains spring from. The emotions infused into the intellectual combination are forms of vitality handed down to posterity by the law of inheritance, which accounts for the emotions of fear, love, and anger, &c., in the association of objects with feelings. When we are angry, the anger is associated with some object—when we love, the love is associated with some object—when we are afraid, the fear is associated with some object. It is through the operation that the Intelligent Will includes, taking cognisance of all in following the lead of pleasure that action is so manifested. The fact is, Intelligent Will only differs from the most rudimentary form of vital action, in the effort to secure a pleasure, in having the extended range of visage which these intellectual combinations—associated by their pleasures and pains—confer on Volition. The Intellectual combinations forming the moral and religious elements have a most powerful influence in determining the course the Intelligence of Will will pursue.

We have in so far followed vital energy from its origin in spontaneous generation to its loftiest form of expression animated by Intelligent Will, where the individual follows the lead of pleasure, and is guided by the enlightened conscience our Lord's teaching unfolds; this induces the loftiest form of Volition to which our race can lay claim.

When it is so that the human form of the energy of self-conservation, Sentient Personality, Soul or Ego, the immortal unit that our planet has produced, when taken collectively are correlative units acting in harmony with their nature, which does and must seek the individual's own happiness as an ultimate end. This explains the action of Intelligent Will, stimulated by self-conservation. This is a form of force sure to lead to oppressing the weak. Being immortal, man carries this sentiment into his immortal habitations with him—however, the question then arises who are the weak? The case being so, have we not a strong enough reason for a God-appointed means of deliverance being provided as the rescue through which a race so animated could be redeemed. For it may be clearly seen that the individual units of a race, animated by this form of Volition, and surrounded as we are, could never affect the deliverance or redemption of the race, when the very actions of the individual life is that of the energy of self-conservation, ever in quest of its own individual pleasure. It is, therefore, utterly selfish, utterly depraved, and utterly spiritually dead too, when viewed from the point that a revelation has been given, unfolding man's chief end to be to glorify God, and Him alone. Viewed thus, apart from the rescue that Christianity provides and the love that deliverance generates, where is the stimulus to come from which will induce the Intelligent Will to seek only God's glory?

For few find life, such as we know it, so desirable as to be thus grateful for it. The truth is, the germ of Original Sin is to be found in man's very nature, who, as a product of nature and an immortal unit, seeks only his own individual happiness. Further, that the oppression and degradation we find in the world is the natural consequence of the utter selfishness which must animate Intelligent Will so animated is true. The human form of Volition being so, provides the strongest possible necessity for a revelation such as the Christian doctrine unfolds ; and also proves such must have been included in the original plan as the process whereby this depraved form of the Intelligent Will was to be renewed, in man's nature being so changed as to find his pleasure in serving and glorifying God in Christ, or Christ as God, as the object of his love, because his Deliverer.

Why man, the developed production of God's laws, was created a depraved being, utterly selfish, does not concern us, though the fact that man is selfish, therefore depraved, does. For all we know, man's destiny may lead to the rescue of the dumb animal creation from death, and the degradation that their instinct naturally leads them to, by imparting immortality of a desirable nature to the highest forms of them, who in consequence would love and serve man as their deliverer, just as man loves and serves God in Christ, his deliverer.

We not only find a revelation given, but the very revelation needed, because it infuses the principle of new obedience into the intelligence which induces Volition in serving God to follow the lead of pleasure. Man following the lead of pleasure in his natural state, is fatal to him. Yet, strange to say, it is following this lead that leads the Christian on to glory: because, inspired by new obedience, which induces following the lead of pleasure in striving to glorify God by adopting the self-sacrificing course that Christ enjoins. For Christianity provides man with the pleasure that springs of love divine and leads to a life of happiness and holiness as the end of the benevolence that induces the form of Volition that will endure.

Yet the action of Intelligent Will is nevertheless the energy of self-conservation guided by motives. For Volition follows the lead of pleasure in following the Redeemer, God, for the good things that He has provided, even willing to suffer the present pain of a self-denying course in prospect of the pleasure that is to follow. Perhaps the case would be more clearly stated by saying man was willing to suffer in serving the object loved.

Finally, viewed in the light of a scientific investigation applicable to our age, Christian Revelation leads to the conclusion that there is an Intelligence at the heart of everything, and that Intelligence is a God of Love. But, as viewed from the converted Christian's standpoint, that Intelligence is seen and felt in the fellowship which union with our Lord imparts to the believer in inspiring the emotion of love divine. Thus, then, the activity of a renewed form of Volition is proved to be the activity of divine life at work as the energy of self-conservation, building up the new man, treading in the old track, namely, that of following the lead of pleasure, changed thus in the individual being animated by love divine, which gives expression to the renewed form of volition in following its lead of pleasure as the sentiment the renewed mind acts from.

CHAPTER IX.

THE SOCIAL ORGANISM—WHAT IS IT? HUMAN IN ITS ORIGIN—IMMORTAL IN ITS DESTINY.

THE social organism forming the human race is the developed units, the human nervous structure, surrounded by its environment, gave birth to in creating Ego of conscious state as the forces Sentient Personality builds itself up of, which include the race. These individual forms of vitality, once created, are Immortal.

Vitality, ever in motion, is oscillatory in its activity and immortal in its destiny. Ego created by the organism and its environments, lives and vibrates a human personality. It is the form of vitality which does not cease its activities on the death of its organism, but continues its oscillatory movement in the form of the body as a disembodied spirit, and while in the body, Ego is the vital energy of the human beings forming our social organism.

This is true of Ego, whether viewed as we find the race on earth or in the immortal state entered into at death. We may put the case thus. The social organism of our race is formed of the children born on earth. All of them at death as individuals pass into their immortal state clothed in human form, which we shall agree to call the "human spiritual organism," developed on earth. They pass through the gate of death into another sphere of existence as the developed intelligent Immortals of our race.

But, observe, it is a race divided into two species, when viewed in the light the Christian Revelation unfolds, called Believers and Unbelievers. Believers are the portion saved by substitution in accepting the forgiveness that the Son of God has provided. Unbelievers are not saved, but are exposed to the consequences that their earthly life may entail. Take note, it is in both cases sections of the social organism of earth-born units we take to do with. This distinction understood, it is well to define what we mean in calling man a social being on earth. It is that he is a unit of a social organism in vital relation to it, acting on it, and being acted upon by it, being inspired therefrom, and breathing its social spirit. He could not live and move, and have his human being separate from it, any more than he could live and move in a vacuum, or than a nerve cell could live detached from its plexus in the brain. As the air is to the breath of the body, which without it would be dead, so is the social organism the life-breath of the mind, which without it could not wake into consciousness.

Further, no one can help assimilating unawares the moral atmosphere of the medium in which he is—he will feel and be as he lives. And so it comes to pass, that persons like thieves have renounced all the obligations of common morality, and yet are still imbued with a sort of honour among themselves—morality, the obligation of which they own. Further, that "persons of an average standard of general morality are sometimes no better than criminal in respect of some special relation of their particular sects, trade, or other social circle, to the rest of the society." This being so, proves how watchful man, an immortal unit so far responsible, ought to be in the choice of his friends, his associates, and his profession; and, above all, ever to be doubly careful to keep far from temptation's way, mindful that the first wrong step is the fatal turning point that may lead to ruin. For true it is, that the way that leads to the grossest immorality becomes easy when the first wrong step taken, comes to be often repeated. To secure a pleasure was the cause, and to retain a pleasure will spur the victim on, it may be, to his eternal ruin. For mind, as the self-conscious unit of the individual life, is the immortal part created by the human organism and its environment—at death issued into Spirit Land. Without these, it could not be, but with them the individual mind is developed an immortal human organ, which shall endure because of its very nature, the energy of self-conservation formed of human intelligence, and as such is liable to suffer from consequences. It is so that our organism is such that we imbibe our surroundings unawares, and carry these impressions into the immortal state. The exercise of function is to give expression to the combined internal and external condition. The unfolding from within of the incidental conditions within and without are the factors at work in functioning, which give expression to human intelligence in forming the organ of mind. Individual mind must possess an organism to give expression to its individual form of energy, and such organ must be human in its form.

Viewing the social organism from the point I am doing, it becomes a very simple matter to perceive how the social feeling in civilized society, can make a person feel obligations not perceived at all by a savage race. The difference rests in the unfolding of the energies which have sprung from the internal and external sources of a civilized social system in giving expression to the action and interaction of such an organism and its environment. For both savage and civilized man feels and responds to the constant presence and influence of the " social medium in which, for which, and by which, he lives," both classes following the lead of pleasure as it springs from their own nature animated by the inspiration the social medium to which they belong imparted to them.

So true is this, that the social units even, forming the civilized medium, have to be trained before they are prepared to accept a new idea, unfolding a truth which a genius of their race may have perceived by possessing a prophet's eye of recognising the effect of cause and consequence from afar.

Nevertheless, a phase of truth which for a century may have been ignored by his contemporaries, often remains so until a new language is formed and learned, springing from the condition that form the abstraction of the new idea, and making it intelligent to them. For new language has often to be formed and learned before new truths are imparted to a civilized race. This being so, new ideas may be said to come into the world still-born. The author of them pays the penalty of being in advance of his age, and yet may have left to the social units of which he formed part, a legacy of great value when they learn to unfold its contents. The unfolding process forms the education for which the genius must wait as one neglected and despised, till the new mental groupings in the race are formed, which unfold all that the new idea—the intellectual combination as an abstraction—contained or held together.

This proves the training that organic mind has to pass through as a progressive intelligence. The struggle that progress, which generates Intelligence, has to pass through, is well marked in the following a passage from a well-known writer:—" The inhabitants of northern and temperate climates make progress by being forced to gain their means of subsistence and comfort by stern struggles with nature, and so develop understanding by combatting and overcoming the laws of nature against which they struggle. They are made more earnest, industrious, practical, and inventive than the inhabitants of tropical regions, where the luxuriance of nature favours indolence and frivolity." Viewed thus, we see the source from whence intelligence is developed in the struggle with nature to which man is exposed by being driven to combat with nature's laws, if they are to endure and develop their own individual phase of intellect. Though man naturally is so prone to struggle, and so longs for the ease that leads to indolence, yet the stern laws of nature compel man to struggle that he may triumph by overcoming. So he rejoices as a conqueror who wins a well-fought battle of which he is justly proud. For, in developing new forms of intelligence, he develops and enriches the race. When educated to understand the nature of the mental images that go to form the abstraction—the intellectual combination —that includes all which in this way in such mental images become part of the automatic activities that give expression to Ego—Sentient Personality. In this way the new ideas become immortalized in passing into the enduring social organism of the race—a race endowed potentially with the intellectual energy of earth. It is Immortal in its nature, though human in its origin and social in its forms.

That man is a social being, is true; but how he became so, may well cause astonishment with his egoistic propensities. For as soon as a society is formed, individual egotism is seriously attacked by being compelled to make concessions for the common good. Through these concessions tribes are formed. When once formed, the tribe egotism struggles and dies hard, while the consolidating process of forming nations is going on. As the work of consolidation advances, the egotistical tendency becomes transferred to the nations as they grow, and in their turn they usurp the places of the weaker nations. So the strongest stands erect in the strength of its own egotism, often ready to declare war whenever an advantage is likely to be secured, heedless of the terrible suffering involved. For instance, how proud an Englishman is of his country and its laws, its Colonies and Indian Empire. Of an Englishman it has been said, his step, tone, and gait indicate his nationality. Yet, all this time, he seems indifferent to the claims such natives of the Indian Empire, who are intelligent enough to discharge such a duty, have to a vote in its legislative council.

"By blood and iron has the moulding work been done in obedience to a stronger impulse than human passion could counteract." Egotism comprises purely personal gratification, and when a society is formed, the individuals forming it must bear and forbear. Tolerance and compromise arise from obligations rendered and received, and a desire to do as we would be done by, will strengthen moral action by enforcing into the social organism the life which pleasure gives. For this is the genius of moral action, that the individual forgoes a personal gratification so as to infuse pleasure into the social organism by an act of self-sacrifice, which thus far increases the pulse of pleasure beating in the soul of the social organism. Pleasure thus transferred by the individual as a free-will offering goes to consolidate the social organism, mitigating its pains, and as such is the life of the organism without which it could not endure.

So as to comprehend the social organism fully, what must be perceived with clearness is the fact that it is composed of the opposing forces of life struggling to secure a pleasure and repel a pain. Such are the forces at work in the contrasted ideas which give expression to passion and sentiment. Assuredly, the forces at work in the social organism are such. Virtue and vice have no meaning as abstracts; but must be placed in contrast to form an intelligent intellectual conception. They typify the opposing forces of the social organism formed of the human race, which as such, has come into existence in giving expression to the egotism, typified in the passions and virtues displayed by the men and women that form the race. Human rivalries, jealousies, ambitions, and the like, have been restrained and utilised in spite of man to serve the common good, and they are really the conditions of social progress.

"Rivalry encites to commercial zeal and activity, self-interest to establish rights of property, ambition to stir men to political and other good works, envy to spur them to make themselves equal to the object of envy, vanity to inspire them so to please, as to gain the approbation of their fellows." The end served, as Vico remarks, is, " vice capable of destroying the human race produces public happiness, the end attained is that the complicated re-action of these personal forces when brought together in the social crucible are constrained to issue in results contributive to the welfare of the whole." The complicated action going on is so constituted and regulated, that for one "to seek private good in the fullest gratification of his passions, the individual must recognise social inter-dependence, and adopt his conduct to the conditions in which he is a social element. Self-love is not despicable, but laudable, since duty to self, if self-perfecting—as true duties to self are—must needs be duties to others." These words typify the moulding process going on in the social organism.

The consolidating forces of the organism provide the intellectual combinations which serve as elements for the contrasted ideas which play such a prominent part in human intelligence ; by giving expression to such abstractions as virtue and vice, right and wrong, good and evil, great and small, rich and poor, happy and miserable, pleasures and pains.

With the social organism, as with the individual, the ebb and flow of life oscillates between these extremes. These are the conditions which have sprung from man combatting with the forces of nature. This proves how the human race may overcome and assert its power to reign as the gigantic huge machine of the social organism wherein beats the pulse of life limited in its field of operation by the conditions within itself which cause pleasure and pain.

These forces being the aggregate of individual action fused together into a gigantic organism, it comes to pass that man, as a socially constituted individual, does social acts instinctively, so to speak, as a species of automatic action, without considering exactly whether they will bring him pleasure or pain. " He feels his own weal in the common weal, and it is his pleasure to exercise the function of which he is capable—in fact, it may come to be his egotistical impulse to act altruistically—his self-impulse to act unselfishly." In such forces a gleam of pleasure is infused into the social organism as the equivalent of moral feeling, and in that far helped to raise its capacity by inducing further impulses of a similar form.

Co-operation to a common end is the foundation of all

society. The desire aimed at is to act together, to feel together, and to think together. Social feeling thus fused together generates a moral sense, which develops its own form of force, just as any other intellectual combination does, and is to social medium its life—life, observe, which has been infused into it at the expense of the individual. For what the social medium gained in pleasure through the act of self-denial, is so much vital force parted with by the individual, viewed as a solitary unit. The social medium consolidates, and rises higher and higher potentially when man acts justly to his fellows. The order of evolution is such, that out of the opposing forces of the egotistical feeling, has sprung the social feeling, and from it, its highest function, that of exercising its moral element, by assuming it is well to part with what is prized, so that others may share in what is valued. Though such complications are not easily understood, it is nevertheless the conditions from which new feeling arises.

It is so. "'There is no loss of energy, no creation of energy, only a conversion thereof. What conscience gains, passion loses." The general truth is that the sum-total of energy is what it was at the beginning. When vital force first appeared on our planet, we had a transformation of energy from dead force into living force, inorganic matter into organic matter. A transformation which led to the consciousness of difference and agreement, say, in plants being gratified by absorbing the rays of the sun and depressed in its absence. The sum-total of energy is the same. Only the germs of a blind intelligence are created. The next step is that of imparting light to blind intelligence by enabling Intelligence to recognise the things that will gratify and the things that will depress. The transformation henceforth is from dead matter and energy into living matter and energy. Such energy can be defined, in the abstract, as absorbed when the oxygen is liberated on the green leaf of the plant, and reappears when the vegetable atom is split up by the carbon and oxygen reuniting.

Intellectual combinations of the greatest complexity are the highest forms of living matter known to us. For example, how vast the sum-total of the energy expended in intellectual work before the abstract that typifies one of our sciences is formed. And of this complicated nature is the very simplest abstraction, which only differs in degree from the most complex. All abstractions contain in their germ the sum-total of human energy spent in forming the conscious states that lead up to the abstraction. And intellectual combinations in functioning gives expression to their own forms of energy as Ideas, and represent vital force in motion. Of such is the conservation of the energy of consciousness reappearing in vital force, conditions which may in a way be applied to the human race, holding in its grasp all the energy spent in developing its intelligence, as the social organism I refer to.

We have no creation of nerve-energy, but only the law operating in the conservation of energy transformed into an external form of vital energy, in being participated in by consciousness and capable of reappearing as such in forming these conscious states—forms of energy which Humanity has created in vital union with it—the social medium for man's use and convenience, who is both the genius and the abiding form of that huge structure, which is immortal in Him. Yet the race is so constituted that Christian belief, the distinguishing mental quality, will operate at death so as to differentiate and separate the Christian believer

M

from the unbeliever in forming separate combinations of intelligent beings whose end and aim are totally different. We thus divide the human race into species, with the race as the genius, and belief the distinguishing quality. "Converted believers" represent the highest type of Christian belief, as sinners saved by grace, therefore in vital union with Christ their Lord while on earth. This being so, the Immortal social organism will not embrace the whole human race in the sense that it embraces that race on earth. For the belief to which Christianity gives birth so operates as to totally separate its section of the social organ from the race, when viewed solely as a human combination of earth-born intelligent beings; because, this section as individuals while on earth, were redeemed by the son of God, in being born again, thus transformed into the adopted children of God, the Eternal One. Thereby the human race is divided into species, with man as the genius and belief the distinguishing quality. These are the conditions which split up the social organism of Humanity—immortal in the immortality of every one of its units.

The immortality of the unbelieving section is secured by the operation of the law at work in self-preservation, animated by the energy of self-conservation, holding the individual unit—the Ego—intact, as active as ever on the death of the organism, which embraces the sum-total of energy, thus transformed into Ego, functioning conscious states, immortal as the energy of self-conservation, which will and must endure. Energy is transformed from dead matter into living forms in intellectual combination, having been participated in by Sentient Personality. The nature and combination of Intellect are to be found in its growth and development—its process of education. As such what moral feeling, and of what kind, is to be found in children without education and without a suitable intellectual and moral medium to develop it? "In the nervous substance that represents the results of ancestral action in moral relations, the child possesses the proper instrument which may be trained to action, but will not act without proper training. But immediately the proper stimulus brings the intellectual combination into action, there will be a certain pleasure from the moral exercise as there is from the exercise of other functions, and that pleasure is naturally felt as moral sentiment." The fact is, the instrument that will respond to its own stimulus is there, but the intellectual combinations which differentiate individual personality are to be found in the training and conditions that surround the child, through imitation and education, whether in a way conscious or unconscious. Always around are those strong social forces. Of these are Sympathy, which generates love — Custom, Opinion, Belief, and so on. For the social medium in which one is placed, operates to develop the special types of moral and social character.

These observations exclude the notion of an abstract moral feeling or conscience, but confirm the special phase of what is derived from the intellectual and social medium surrounding the individual, and from the moral ideal they cherish and preach. Morality may therefore contain a very weak or a very strong moral essence. It is with the particular feeling, not with the abstraction, that discussion must concern itself in order to be fruitful. Morality is properly based on an end outside self, which, in the highest form, aims at the good of the whole social medium as such, the difficulty lies in the application of the principle to the special case. To discern rightly is the trouble. Not to think and feel well, but to do well, is the end to be observed. The fact is, with the highest moral feelings we are brought in living contact with realities. Hence, we come in the end to a primitive basis of a concrete reflex action, if we are resolved to understand its exact meaning, action, or contents. As Maudsley says —" Pure internal feeling of pleasure and pain, of moral approbation and disapprobation, undoubtedly exists, but in order of existence they are rooted in action and developed out of experience, and must in the last resort receive their interpretation there. In the first instance, external considerations of good or ill determine suitable and useful acts, and perhaps the very kind of acts that the highest moral feeling would determine at a later and higher stage of development, the feeling which has been developed out of action exists independently of the external considerations that were effective in the first instance; and then the feeling by itself, which is purely internal, determinates action, its pains and pleasures therein being actually greater than those which spring from purely intellectual considerations of self-interest. But, if we would test the value of the feeling, we must always look to the social quality of the action, for there is not a vice nor crime of which human nature is capable that has not received the strongest approbation of conscience in one nation or another at one period or another of human history."

In these wise words we have the spring of moral action defined as rising from the pleasures and pains embodied in the concrete intellectual combinations that these emotions accompanied, forming the moral element which has been developed by our race as a phase of human education. The character of moral acts must in a measure, depend on the nature of the moral notions that surround the individual, and be judged accordingly; always bearing in mind that the germs of the highest morality must spring from the insight of the individual or society, in perceiving with clearness the effect the action meditated will produce on the general community in choosing the course that will develop the highest moral tone therein. For such action is helping forward the order of evolution of our social organism, the subject of this chapter, which would not be complete did I not introduce morality, its life-sustaining force. This is put in contrast with a process of degeneration going on. For the higher moral forms may be lost by the adverse process of degeneration. The activities of evolution and degeneration at work in the social medium are its phases of life or death. The developing process in the energy of self-conservation, the stay of the social medium, is to be found in the advancing moral attitude of that medium which leads man to act justly to his fellows, and to acknowledge and requite a favour received. A moral action awarded, so as to raise the general social tone, is successful where the one benefited is led to go and do likewise; but it is ill awarded when it leads to the opposite effect, and generates selfishness on the part of the receiver. To give indiscriminately is often an act of the most selfish kind. This is when it is stimulated by the lead of pleasure emanating from the moral element, and where the effect produced on the receiver is disregarded. Such gifts are most pernicious in their effect on some forms of the social organism. From the point of evolution moral action must be judged from the effect produced. Back we come to the concrete reflex act determined by action and counteraction, guided by intelligence. However, this is a condition only applicable to a race of high intelligence, such as is to be found in the civilized society that surrounds us. It has a marvellous capacity for intellectual growth.

This may be proved from the development of the various branches of the new sciences which have sprung up of late years, which leads man to bear and forbear with his kind, as well as to induce him to reason and reflect on the consequences his acts are likely to produce. But, alas, alongside of this intellectual phase of progress, which fits the community for producing the highest moral fruit, instead of such life-bearing fruit, we have to place in contrast the death-threatening phase of degeneration, in the immoral practices that have entered into many of our trades formerly referred to. When such are challenged, they are coolly brushed aside with "such is the practice in the trade," as if the accumulated practice justified the fraud. This is only one phase of immoral practice, and in a way it is countenanced by society. Thus, then, before passing on to another phase of social life, I would ask—Are we, therefore justified in calling this an age of progress in the social organism of humanity, beings knit together by the accumulated moral force of its ages?

It is true, a tremendous pressure from without in early times must have been used towards the individual, before the restraint of egotistic impulses could have been secured, so as to admit of the most primitive social feeling to be developed. The powers of nature and the wild animals around, would compel man to combine in order to survive. For it is plain those who did unite, so as to form the most compact organism, would best sustain the struggle, and so survive through the order of natural selection. Certain it is, that "to conquer by obedience and increase by conquest," give expression to all. The point to be decided in our present state of knowledge and advanced intellectual stage of race-development,

THE SOCIAL ORGANISM—IMMORTAL IN ITS DESTINY. 199

is, who is to be obeyed and who is to be conquered? This question I aim at answering before the volume is closed. It may be shortly stated thus. God is to be obeyed and the race is to be conquered through the influence of the law Christianity unfolds. But the onward course towards that end will be best served by following up in some short detail, the course that progress has assumed in bygone ages.

The power embodied in supernatural religion infused an element of gigantic power. That this element has almost always been abused by man is certain. Notwithstanding, it became the strongest power in compelling communities to combine and co-operate. The secret customs the social units adopt, which sprung from superstition, produce a certain order, often oppressive, and cruel in the extreme—the aim and effect being to compel obedience. This sprung from compulsory co-operation, and secured much for the race in compelling the social fusion that is absolutely necessary to ensure the advancement of the race, in the form we find it. What tyrant is equal to a savage ruler, enforcing the secret customs of his tribe, to which his subjects submit with abject obedience, offering no resistance? The custom of the tribe is a sufficient answer to give for all ceremonies or observations however cruel. It is well enough known that a strong Belief is what is required to stimulate to martyrdom for conscience sake. For an individual to be cast out of his special society by excommunication has always been regarded as a terrible punishment, both by him who endures it and by those that inflict it, so terrible, that to be put to death by his tribe seemed better than to be put out of it. The same agency is at work now in the social fears and pressure brought to bear upon classes of men, for the purpose of making them act together in trade unions and the like.

What is class interest but man united by a common bond of self-interest.

The creeds, superstitions, customs, ceremonies, laws, and so forth, by which social fusion in the transformations of egotism has been effected, was not the work of an individual, but the work of humanity, operating through the pressure of its environments, so as to determine its progress. Thus was the method framed in the order of evolution to give humanity some unity of action in the conflict with the terrible powers of nature with which it stood confronted. But such as these rites and customs were, they have done their work in the guidance of conduct, and faded away. The moral law, in its way, remains, though much that is useless has faded away. The truth is, that God meets humanity at many points, so as to direct its onward journey, and in doing so, adopts the form of intelligence which the phase of human development at the time could comprehend. Revelation was, therefore, unfolded in its own process of development, step by step, just as humanity was prepared to receive it, though imperfectly. For revelation is certainly a progressing force in an advanced form from what was the moral law, of an eye for an eye and a tooth for a tooth. Now, the moral, fused into Christian action, retains a great hold on civilized men in the guidance of conduct. Yet, notwithstanding the powerful influence of revelation, what we are justified in calling the natural depravity of man has retarded the progress of moral development, even in Christian nations, where God revealed Himself to man through the Christian records for centuries. I am quite justified in using the phrase "man's natural depravity," when viewed from the plan God decreed to rescue him by, in securing man's advancement into perfection as an independent individual, an end evidently designed to be accomplished in God's first revealing truth to the individual, which was eventually to be accepted by the race as God's message to them. In this way first raising the individual, then the race, above the purely natural forces operating in evolution as we know it. And viewed thus, it takes to do with God's place in nature.

The Lord, by special revelation, dealt with man as the representative of the phase of intelligence on the earth that He has given birth to in the God-appointed way and providence of God. However, in this special form of revelation, we find that the manifestation of the egotistic propensity in man was so strong as to cause many of the horrors, crimes, blood-shed, sins, and sufferings that might have been avoided, if the moral development induced by, and contained in, revelation had not been restrained through man's selfishness. In consequence of this impediment, the best possible progress in human development has been greatly impeded.

Nothing more fully proves what I have said of the effect man's selfishness has had in hindering the moral development of the race as a whole, than the present low standard of moral action among the Christian community when viewed from the high ideal Christianity teaches. Much, very much, of the waste of life and agony that has marked the features of the blood-stained course to which the race has been subject, might have been prevented, if men holding the truths of revealed religion had been less selfish, and permitted the moral element embodied in revelation to work its own course, by infusing its influence into the social medium, and to penetrate humanity by becoming the most powerful agent in social evolution. For revelation is, and was from the first, intended to be a progressive power in human evolution, had man's egotistic propensity permitted it to prove this. Just instance one percept of the teaching of our Lord, couched in these words—"As ye judge ye shall be judged," when understood as applying to man as an immortal being, liable to suffer the consequence of the course he pursues in his immortal habitation, how powerful these words would become, so understood, a child may see.

Observe how the intelligence of humanity is changing the face of the earth through the knowledge which scientific investigation has imparted. And yet how worthless is all, if morality, the life of the social medium, decrease. For it is with the social medium evolution takes to do in its onward course. And a progressive social medium is simply impossible if the morality of humanity decrease, for as is so often said, morality is the life-pulse beating in the social medium which ensures the progress of humanity. But in the individual egoistic tendency, there is a broad and easy way leading to degeneration and death, opposed to the straight narrow way that leads to evolution and fuller life.

The principles of good and evil have been recognised by all people in all ages. Indeed, some form of expression or another, meant to explain progress and degeneration, is necessary, and these contrasted ideas are doubtless the intuitions of the opposing laws, perceived as evolution and degeneration. The pulse of pleasure and pain beating between these two extremes, is the moral form of pleasure, we shall say, parted with by the individual and transferred into the social medium, generating gratitude, that marks the limit of the power of the human instrument which determines the advance of social evolution, or which, if withheld, marks the points of its degeneration; and this is true of nations also, where the moral element is holding the egoistic tendency of man's will in check, the social medium will be making progress, by knitting humanity closer together in the bond of sympathy—where the accumulating moral element in civilized humanity is a weaker power. The social organism of that medium will degenerate in civilized man and advanced nations becoming estranged from each other. The limit that must determine the moral course taken between man and man, and nation and nation, is to be found in the principle applied to special cases, regulated by a recognised principle of justice, as contrasted by oppression. Man, as an individual unit of his social medium, has a right to the form of justice recognised by that medium, in deciding in a general way the sacrifice the individual is to make for the good of the organism. The conditions which the term justice, so understood, well mark the ebb and flow between which the moral element of that medium may oscillate, guided by public opinion, which will determinate what is best for the progress of its social medium. Thus, then, what is called a just and safe course is to determine the limit of individual concession to humanity. That is, the sense of justice in man is to determinate in a general way the measure of self-gratification to be given up by the individual for the benefit of the social organism of which he forms part, so as to strengthen the tie of brotherhood, and not weaken it by inducing selfishness. This is often the effect of distributing charity indiscriminately, and the same effect may happen in many other ways.

A just and equal course indicated by public opinion is to be obeyed by the individual as the voice of the social organism to its unit. The limit must be conformed to, if the individual is to place himself in harmony with his environment.

That the founder of Christianity does not recognize the

limit of individual action restrained thus, is true, because his action is to deal with the utter depravity of man. Depravity was developed from man's selfishness, and stimulated by his egoistic tendency, even when it was recognized that God had revealed Himself, so as to enter into a covenant of works with man, the condition of which had utterly failed; therefore our Lord created a new source of obedience, in that which springs from love. He secured for the Redeemed a perfect state of eternal bliss on the condition of accepting the forgiveness He offers. By this means the social organism is split up into two sections, namely, the adopted children of God, and the children of nature, the product of our planet, to whom God has from time to time revealed Himself in a way conformable to their capacity and phase of intelligence.

From the point of revealed religion, the first covenant, the covenant of works, was expressed in the intellectual conception of—"Do this and Live." It may be said to take to do with the conditions I include in justice by a race who recognized a God revealing Himself to man as the Intelligence at the heart of everything, and the great centre of this form of revelation is the Moral Law. But the Moral Law, which did not rest in a sound belief in the immortality of a material soul, created of the individual states of consciousness generated on earth, and liable to suffer the consequences of a bad life in its immortal state, was not enough to secure the advancement of the social medium. Though a full conviction of these facts, fully taught in Christian revelation, and as fully confirmed by the science of human psychology, will in the future develop a moral element of sufficient strength in the social organism of humanity, capable of securing the higher and yet higher development of the race on earth while its history lasts.

Of the early revelation which ended in the Fall—whatever that may mean—one thing is certain, that the egoistic tendency of our race caused it. Further, the degeneration of man followed, causing much sin and suffering to the highest types of humanity. It was to rescue the race from the degenerating effect of the fall, that Redemption by Substitution was ordered. The moral influence flowing from this source is well known—as Christian life and work—and will be referred to further on. It is sufficient to say at present that our Lord's aim was, first to redeem a section of the social organism, by transforming them into the adopted sons of God. Secondly, to develop a moral element of sufficient strength in the other section of the social organism that would secure to that organism a form of everlasting development of the human type.

It is complained of by many holding the theory of evolution, that the Christian idea of God is built up of the negatives of all possible human conceptions—Infinity, Invisibility, Immortality, Incomprehensibility, &c.—Inconceivable, Incorporal, &c., and summing up all such negatives as making one called God. I would ask what better definition could we give, using human language, in trying to convey some sort of an intellectual conception to define the Being the Christian worships as God—the Creator and Ruler of the Universe? However inadequate these terms may be, they make the attempt at defining an inscrutable power that has been said to be past finding out. Doubtless, we Christians have the best term of all applied to God, viz., the Father of Jesus Christ. For in Christ, the risen Lord, we have a permanent objective existence, as the Son of the Intelligence everywhere at work, who came as the God-appointed means to save our race from perishing; a race steeped in selfishness, therefore constantly retarding the evolutionary instinct of humanity by inducing degeneration.

It is selfishness manifested in man's egoistic tendency to follow the lead of pleasure so as to secure a personal or national end, but indifferent to the good of the race as a whole, that has, hitherto, at every stage of human history become too strong an instrument to admit of a moral element of sufficient strength to be formed in the universal social medium, which would secure the permanent evolution of the race as a human instrument of progress on earth. But the time is close at hand when a moral element of sufficient strength to admit of this will be developed, in our race immortal in its units, in the form of force that its intellect confers on them.

To individuals on earth, death comes simply as an incident in their history in its onward journey. Death drafts the individual into a new sphere, where the instinct of the unsaved to follow the lead of pleasure will be as strong as ever, though the conditions surrounding the individual will so far be totally different, that the power of each will be limited by the course of action each pursued on earth.

To this all unbelievers must submit. This is taught in the words—"With what judgment ye judge ye shall be judged," &c. These and similar words of our Lord may be taken as the voice of the co-ordinating instrument of humanity, in Evolution Illuminating the Bible, addressed to the individual units which form the unsaved immortal section of the social organism. For these words give expression to conditions which, when enforced, will assuredly secure the pulse of evolution in this section of the social organism, by inducing it to act so as to neutralize the possibility of degeneration. Such conditions will induce self-interested man to act justly to his fellows—knowing the penalty he must incur if he acts otherwise.

Thus, then, the voice of the evolutional instinct of humanity is explained, in Evolntion Illuminating the Bible, as applied in the words of our Lord—" And why beholdest thou the mote that is in thy brother's eye, but considerest not the beam that is in thine own eye "—Matt. vii. 2—words spoken to the promiscuous multitudes to whom He addressed the Sermon on the Mount. A multitude which typified in its promiscuous character the social organism of humanity, was thus warned by our Lord of the consequences to which they were liable at death.

These conditions, however, ought to have been explained by the converted, as the condition taking effect after death, whereby the Immortal unsaved section of humanity were to be purified and redeemed, so as to secure the permanent advancement of the unsaved section of the social medium when applied as such to an immortal human instrument of progress, ever capable of advancing by the power that its human intellect has conferred upon it, though a form of advancement, including effort, into which pain enters. These conditions are applicable to all the human race, with the exception of the number elected, who—as sinners saved by grace, in virtue of the redemption purchased — were united to Christ in conversion, and are therefore the adopted children of God, and joint heirs with Christ. They are a portion originally forming part of the social organism, but disintegrated therefrom at conversion, in being inspired by the sentiment, issuing from the intellectual combinations thereby developed, which animates the church of the firstborn in inducing the obedience that love, animated by gratitude to God in Christ inspires. Thus, therefore, they are excluded from the section of the race that the warning voice of our Lord applies to. What chiefly concerns the warned section of the social medium is that these words of warning spoken by our Lord are conditions He can and will enforce.

Not only so, but they are words spoken by One who has secured the conditions whereby He can impart the needed strength to enable the individual to fulfil the terms of contract to which He has exposed Himself, however painful they may be. Painful they must be, when we note that the condition demanded by the evolutional instinct of humanity to secure the morality necessary is explained in its operation by our Lord, in Matt. xxiv. 26, ending with the emphatic words—"Thou shalt by no means come out hence till you have paid the uttermost farthing."

For such may be regarded as the voice that humanity has addressed to her children, uttered and explained by our Lord, as the retribution that will effect its end in the race eventually being purified even while on earth. Thus, then, the developing Intelligence of the race gives timely warning. Though it is impossible for these children of humanity, as individuals, to fulfil these conditions unaided, yet they can do so by strength divine.

Our Lord is in a condition to supply the needed strength which will enable each individual to overcome, however hard the struggle may be, and thus rejoice at last. The strength to do so will be found in the promise so freely given by our Lord—" He that overcomes will inherit all things," in the Revelation. For, when the individual is assured he will inherit all things if he overcomes, he is animated by a motive of sufficient strength to ensure a successful issue when our Lord has further promised that "to him that is athirst, he will give the fountain of the water of life freely." Adding, "I will be his God, and he will be my son."—Rev. xxi. 6-7. In the strength of such promises as these, it is easy to comprehend that those inspired by these words have the strength imparted to them, which will assuredly enable all to overcome, triumphing in the strength that their God, the Lord Jesus Christ, imparts. For, at bottom, have we not the old maxim of being willing to suffer a present pain because it insures a future pleasure?

However, as an abstraction, we must view Christ's promise "to give to him that is athirst the fountain of the water of life freely," read in the light of present knowledge to be that of Christ's felt presence imparting a sentiment of pleasure—say as an earnest or foretaste of the purchased possession. For this is the rational explanation conveyed in the "fountain of the water of life freely," as a well-known experience, common to all Christians in vital union with Christ, which indicates that a union is effected between the Redeemer, and the one, it may be, hardly pressed, yet struggling on in the strength the Saviour's presence begets —strength made apparent as the activity representing the Holy Spirit—the active agent that fills the space between is an influence of this nature, the spirit being a medium of activity always present and active uniting the Believer with his Saviour, Redeemer, and God. Assuredly, to thirst, is to desire the fellowship our Lord's presence imparts; and to convey this phase of vital activity by so affecting the Ether—that fills universal space—by impressing this influence on the space between in making that apparent, is the functioning power conferred on the Holy Spirit.

In an activity of this form, we have in the uniting
N

medium, the Holy Spirit, the promised Intelligence, who was to take of the things of Christ and show them to His people—John xvi. 7-15. Of the things referred to, assuredly is the power the Holy Spirit confers on Christians to perceive, wherein truth already revealed can be employed to include a new proportion into which a new phase of revelation enters, proceeding from a newly formed Intellectual structure in the brain of the one so inspired, and omitting its own phase of heaven-born joy. The joy of the Holy Spirit of truth ever active, unites all—the converted Christian the subject, Christ the object, and the spirit of truth the medium. You will observe we have in a group such as this, a section of the social medium differentiated and disintegrated therefrom.

It is, however, principally with the social organism in its immortal state that I wish to take to do and apply these words of our Lord, which give strength in showing how the worst of men may be strengthened to enable them to overcome the consequences of their wicked life, and to which many unconverted individuals have exposed themselves during their earthly life. For, from what is revealed, all may clearly perceive that God in Christ has decreed to redeem the whole human race from acting unjustly. Remember what is said of the destruction of the wicked in the Old and New Scriptures, refers to the destruction of wickedness — the sentiment that leads to oppression, tyranny, peace-breaking, lying, and will disappear in the race as individuals purify themselves in overcoming such anti-social tendencies through the strength that God, the Lord Jesus Christ, imparts. That this is so, may be perceived by all willing to reason fairly on what is revealed, read in the light of present knowledge, illuminated by the processes at work in the

Redemptive Purchase explained by St. John, as Christ being "the propitiation for the sins of the whole world." This clearly implies that the human race, as the social organism of humanity, will in course of time be Redeemed. The portion converted on earth so redeemed, and separated from the race, living in Christ, are animated by the love that desires God's glory as its chief end. They, for Christ's sake, have suffered and have been reproached on earth, when He was despised.

The remaining section of the social organism Christ will ultimately redeem in so far that He will cause wickedness to disappear—to cease. Finally, the human social organism formed of unbelievers in its immortality will ever find its evolutionary instinct beating in the sentiment that hope inspires, striving to gain yet a higher place in the universe of space, as a human instrument—an instrument which, led on by Christ, its God of Humanity, may be developing the intelligence of the visible universe. Anyhow, the immortal unconverted social organism is referred to in Rev. xxi. 23-24 (R.V.) as the nations walking in the light of the City, lightened by the glory of God, illuminated by Christ the Lamb, into which the kings of the earth do bring their honour and glory. A race having such a glorious destiny before it, may well exalt itself in the power its intellect gives, when illuminated by the Spirit of Truth, though human in its origin and immortal destiny. But not thus saved are the Converted, who though human in their origin, are "Divine" in their destiny, as the adopted children of God.

When Evolution admits of Revelation being explained thus, assuredly it illuminates the book of books—the Bible.

CHAPTER X.

THE BIBLE ILLUMINATING EVOLUTION, IS ILLUMINATED THEREBY.

THE impulses of Evolution, viewed from the highest point of its expression manifested in the great organic growth of Humanity, provide the medium of progressive aspiration in man's Imaginative Faculty. It may enable him to anticipate very exalted and far-reaching conditions looming in the distance yet to be realized. For such conceptions typify the unconscious form of cause and consequence, which a special phase of intelligence indicates. It is often the medium of this very exalted imaginative capacity inherent in progressive humanity, that God uses to reveal His purposes to man, by employing imagination for that end, in enabling man to perceive God's purposes afar off. It is from the aspirations man is capable of in his relations to the great organism of humanity, of which he forms part, that the higher ideal of understanding, feeling, and conduct, that earth has ever known spring. Even when his ideal is human, and is made by nature through man, though it is never realized, because, as practice improves the ideal uses in proportion, the ideal not being realized, the higher conception forming it has to adopt itself in the best way it can to surrounding social conditions. As has been said, by Lamarck, that "it is the want or need that creates the organ by minute increments of growth." For "what have we in the ideal but a sense of want felt by the higher mental organism, a yearning or striving to satisfy itself, and an impulse to develop in consequence:" shortly, the ceaseless activity of life grasping after higher attainments. The inspiration that manifests itself in consciousness as a want or need, grasped in the ideal, never realized on earth, is a condition made use of by God to impart revealed truth, by enabling man to anticipate conditions to be realized by the race either in time or eternity. For example, when humanity, in its far-reaching intelligence, formed an ideal conception of a future state in aspiring to immortality, it aspired to the condition that the providence of God had decreed to fulfil. In fact, immortality is inherent in the vital force that human intelligence embodies, as energy vitalized in having been participated in by consciousness. For it comes to pass that, conscious states and their energy are correlatives, and therefore immortal. The aspiration for immortality being realized in this way, was God's way of dealing with man made in His image.

When man, a unit of humanity, had so advanced as to be capable of forming some rude conception of the immortality of the soul, God would in a way intelligent to man, confirm by revelation the truth of the inference, that the soul was indeed immortal. The ideal conforming to the conception of immortality that Abraham's race had formed, is indicated in scripture language by the graphic words of " He was gathered to his fathers." And a more expressive rendering could not be given to convey the ideal conception embodied in immortality than that the friends now dead had gone to the abode of their fathers. " Very probably the conception of immortality proceeded from, and was developed through, ancestry worship." Let that be as it may, " Life's impulse to develop itself, felt in consciousness, as a want or need, which consequently gives the spring onwards towards intellectual development, is most probably the impulse displayed spontaneously by organic matter developing itself without consciousness." If so, the organic want, as such, certainly must precede the conscious conception of a special want, even in its most rudimentary form. Doubtless, the conscious need was developed as the sequence that accompanied the perceiving of the cause of pleasure and pain, and the desire to react accordingly. " Instinct displayed in even the lowest form of animal life, seems to point to its spring of action being derived from the ideal conception underlying the conscious notion of a want or need which would arise from life itself in quest of what would strengthen it." The inference to be drawn seems to be that organic matter, once formed, develops itself, animated by a conscious or unconscious impulse of a want or need. In other words, this might be expressed as the organism attracting what increases or strengthens it. For the ideal conception underlying all is certainly so, and shows how near akin the highest far-reaching intellectual conceptions are in the spring of their action, to the actions of the very lowest forms of organic life. In connection with this point, so as more fully to enable the reader to comprehend the spring of organic matter in its effort to increase itself, and to develop new resources in its onward and upward course, I will quote wise and comprehensive words of a well-known author writing on the analysis of the Will.

He asks, " Does not instinct, if we consider it well, signify a desire or want of something which is not actually apprehended, a dumb craving for the unknown? The analysis of the will, when we make it, brings us to desire, enlightened and guided by reason, that is, to the want of a known and approved object; but if we carry the analysis deeper down from complex desire to the most simple desire, and thence to appetite, we come at last to the question—Why a desire or appetite for something before that which is desired is known? Consciousness does not make the desire; it is that which lies beneath consciousness in the desire that stirs the consciousness, the unconscious appetite that makes the conscious desire. We must plant ourselves at the last on the fundamental property of life to maintain and increase itself, and we then find ourselves resting on the eternal nixus of evolution, so that by this way of proceeding we perceive again that our highest mental aspirations to the ideal are truly the highest evolutional manifestations as they take place in human consciousness. It is curious to note by the way here how man's true fundamental instincts, the self-conservative and the propagative, may be discovered at the foundations respectively of the two great doctrines of materialism and idealism; the former, coarse and common, so to speak, having immediate respect to the present, and the latter, more refined and glowing with the glamour of love, having a large respect to the future." These words may be said to give expression to all that is involved in the ideal conception underlying enlightened will as well as instinct. Intelligent Will in exercise is the desire fulfilled in being guided by enlightenment and reason, so as to secure the want felt, approved of, and desired. Desire, ever being understood as having for its lead a pleasure to be secured or a pain repelled. Therefore the desire—the motive always at the bottom—is of this nature, which, shortly, is the activity of life to maintain and increase itself.

A remote pleasure is wisely said to have a glimmer of love in it illuminating the desire in the distance, as love gives expression to the highest emotions within the experience of human intelligence, and, as such, may be said to be the inherent emotional instinct of humanity.

In the case of an individual in quest of personal gratification, guided by intelligent will to secure it, who has no regard for the suffering that carrying out the desired end may entail on another, or for the effect produced on the social organism is leading toward degeneration—intelligent will appears in its most degraded form. Then it conforms to the scripture language of "the heart of man is desperately wicked, who can know it." For does not our social organism lead toward degeneration, by so many striving to secure a personal pleasure, and are quite indifferent to how many may suffer thereby. The ideal conception embodying this is graphicly defined when revelation calls man utterly depraved. Such examples clearly illustrate the order in which " Evolution Illuminates the Bible," thus strengthening the inference that at bottom men hate each other.

Such being so, no final remedy could be secured for individual man's deliverance, short of providing the means of infusing a new sentiment into the individual. And this is done through the medium of the redemptive purchase, which not only ensures man of an eternity of supreme bliss, but imparts to him on earth the foretaste, as the experimental knowledge of the state of bliss in the glow of eternal love, marking the union of sentiment that unites Christ with the redeemed soul. The earnest of the emotion accompanying the ideal conception is realized in the human organism thus animated by divine love, which, while even the memory of it lasts, will induce the subject thereof to forego present enjoyment for the joy in prospect, the earnest of which has been vouchsafed to him. Further, while the emotion is constant, it creates in the human organism a sentiment so strong as to induce indifference to the pleasure that the world can give, the chief end being to glorify Christ in serving him here, in prospect of the happy eternity to be spent in His presence.

The end or spring of human action is the same—the desire of personal happiness, of which the earnest is given in the sentiment that Divine Love imparts. All that is now required is to wait, and serve, and suffer, so as to fulfil the condition enjoined in the "non-resistance creed." But, alas ! alas ! how little of such fruit is manifested by the very highest and most devoted class of Christians. Though all the clouds that intervene are lined by the brilliant light of eternal love, ready to burst upon the soul with overwhelming force at the moment of dissolution, by demonstrating the fact that all such die as conquerors; there may be a transit more marked, typifying in the words of Scripture, "Ye shall not all die, but ye shall all be changed," in the organism becoming so expanded through the action of the sentiment of love as to assume a process of evaporation, which confers on it power which we might well call infinite. This might be effected by the body partaking of the form of life now animating the nervous system, the truly vital part that feels, thinks, and moves, ever following the lead of pleasure. The lead in this case would be to transfer the organism from earth into the Redeemer's presence. Some such condition is evidently referred to by St. Paul, 1 Cor. xv. 51-52. To Christians thus changed, the want of a known and approved object would be attained in being transferred thus. This would be a transformation effected by the nervous system so acting on the substance as to cause the body to take its form of vitality, animated by love, the highest sentiment humanity is capable of participating in. We may fairly assume the effect would be to increase the capacity of the organism, so that the gravitating force of the earth would possess no power over it. In that case, the desire animating the organism would produce the desired effect in transporting the Christians into the presence of the risen Lord. If this process is the real fulfilment of the text, then assuredly Evolution Illuminates the Bible.

The sentiment animating the organism so as to secure this is certainly the rational explanation as to how such words of scripture are to be fulfilled; note, words which provide the structural unit, and their accompanying sentiment, the equivalent of volition. If we analyze the conditions in the concrete, we have in volition, enlightened and guided by reason, the desire of a known and approved object attained. By fully comprehending what I have said, we will find the highest mental aspiration of the ideal to be the highest evolutional manifestation as it takes place in human consciousness. For, apart, from the truth conveyed in modern science, it would have been impossible for me, or any one, to have given this rendering in forming these conceptions.

We have idealism in the desire to attain a known and approved object; Materialism in the desire attained through the transformation of the bodily organism. Viewed thus, "what explanation can we give of matter? Why, refuse to adopt the term material to conditions which will explain all." And yet how little does the bodily organism I have anticipated and pointed out as capable of securing the condition desired, resemble any form of matter with which we are acquainted. Such a body of force would seem to have all the properties of the force we know (as electricity, capable of penetrating everywhere, guided by the Intelligence of enlightened reason) and is animated by love divine having attained the highest degree of happiness humanity is capable of, and peacefully resting in that state.

Whatever you call the Ego, it is the Immortal form of human Intelligence, ceaseless in its activity, as it springs from the human form on earth, the life action of which is to maintain and develop itself by grasping what sustains, and repelling what weakens. The energy of life so rendered, I maintain, appeared at first as inorganic matter, transformed into what we call organic matter, capable of being affected pleasantly and painfully. These forces have further developed into forms of intelligence, grouped as organic matter, capable of perceiving the source of its pleasures and pains, and reacting accordingly. This action leads up to the marvellous power inherent in the human intellect from which spring the human soul or Ego. As such, I don't see it matters much whether we call it material or not. No quality of matter we know can have such properties, and yet it has come from transformed matter through a process of Intellectual Development; when we understand by intelligence the unfolding of the best properties of matter under conditions where a process of Degeneration, to a lower condition was possible. However, we know that the further Development of the Redeemed in the Kingdom ruled by love in glory, will be affected by a continuous flow of intelligence where no such opposing force has to be overcome, in the form of a resisting force.

There can be no reasonable doubt but "Humanity is based on the conditions that rest in Evolution, which substitutes a continuous creation for a creation by special shocks." Of the unfathomable impulse of Evolution, it has been said, "It cometh from afar, was before man was, works in his progress, prophesies in his instincts and aspirations, inspires his faith, is interpreted lamely in his creeds, and its end is not yet." One thing is certain, that no addition takes place in the matter or energy of the Universe. "New creations will be the production of the old, but not the old, having new properties and functions derived by the transformation of lower into higher forms of matter," the equivalent of more and more complex forms of intellectual combinations. As proof of this, it would have been utterly impossible for a Newton or a Shakespeare to appear among a tribe of savages, because the external medium required to secure their development would be absent. A suitable external medium must stimulate directly or indirectly the stored energies of the intellectual structure, so as to liberate the higher aspirations possible to men of genius. It is likewise in such conditions, applied to the highest functions of the most complex nervous organisation, manifested in the operation of mind "that we have to look for the purposive determinative energy that follows the deliberation called Will." Will is more or less exclusively dependent on internal influences. These influences are manifested through the law of inheritance operating in giving form to the strength and efficiency of mental combinations. Will is not solely a "mechanical process" summed up in the antecedent motives, for it possesses more than can be discerned in them; yet, motives secret and remote, open and far-reached, corporated in faculties and manifested in consciousness, always go before an act of Will, and are essential to it. Notwithstanding, there is a certain phase of truth in the "strong sentiment of Freedom of Will which assumes subjectively the form of self-determination."

Thus, then, when the Decrees of God come to be explained in the terms that condition and responsibility provides, the teaching of Modern Science and Evolution becomes a very formidable instrument to Illuminate the Bible. The enlightenment arising therefrom will not lessen man's responsibility, but, as an intelligent unit, increase it ten fold, in cause and consequence being placed before him in such a way as to stir in him new sentiments and desires, which will compel him to listen, take heed, and thank God for the stimulating power of the sentiment arising from the subjective indication "Free Will" gives, however elusive the freedom typified may be. For the Decrees of God must rest in the development which is inseperable from the higher and yet higher phases of intelligence capable of enabling man to perceive with greater clearness, cause and consequence, which, in their way, include a measure of freedom. Take for example the child of a drunkard, fully perceiving that through the law of inheritance he is doubly liable to fall a victim to this hurtful habit, and as a rational being does he not choose in self-interest to avoid the paths of temptation. For where the capacity of intellectual insight is clear and vivid, all is seen resting in cause and consequence.

It is in Sociology that we must investigate man's functions as a man among men united in a society which can discern and display his nature as a social, moral, and religious unit, that as such the aspirations are the impulses of evolution, "Supreme reason being the highest and latest evolved energy in nature, as Will-force is nature developing through man, so as to accomplish the progressive course of his life and its destiny." Man acted upon by his environment, socially and physically, reacts in turn. Man having been incorporated therein in the structure and constitution of his nervous system, exhibits the outcome of such an energy in a well informed Will, as the equivalent to a new step in Evolution, which is both productive and creative, in assuming the prophetic form leading onward into the unknown. Like instinct this form of Will-energy "seeks for what it has not, and knows not, but creates as the initial of the highest form of human development." Such instinctive development may be said "to bring man into complete harmony with nature in the creation he makes, being the realisation of the form of Nature's energy which man seeks." The case may be stated thus—man, the highest development in nature, creates the forms of matter which are adapted to his use. The most valuable form in our present condition is the creation of the imagination, which influences the notion of Duty and fortifies the "ought," in the desire to do right, by man striving to realize the ideal of his highest duties. To be inspired so in the path of moral law in social evolution, is certainly the aim and inspiration of the highest Will in functioning. If animated by the highest moral sentiment, man will not go the wrong way, to degeneration, but take the right way, so as to produce higher forms of human development. This course is the instinctive beat of the heart, which the understanding confirms as the right course for man to follow. Man being the best product in Nature, the highest aspiration in man will be the highest moral development, and will mark the point of the evolution of Will, which will secure his further development if hot tainted with degeneration. The objective course of action which "forms the base and sanction of morality in furthering the welfare and progress of the social organism, is the course which the highest type of men strive to promote." This being so, let us view the subject from the order in which the Bible Illuminates Evolution, and is Illuminated thereby. Then we find morality has the double advantage of the approval of the life that now is, as well as of the life that is to come. Viewed thus, the morality which Christianity enjoins is the means that God has employed to increase the vitality of the social organism. Christian morality has therefore the double sanction of God and man imparted to it. Take note, it is through the teaching of the pulse of evolution that the Christian has been enlightened so as to perceive this double sanction, for social evolution clearly reveals the fact that moral action is its life. The base of moral action rests in the individual foregoing personal gratification, so as to confer a gratification, on the social organism, which can only be sustained by the strength of such action. The case thus reduced to proof is a real addition to knowledge, which should greatly stimulate moral action, both in Christian and non-Christian man. Thus does Evolution Illuminate the Bible. The obligation to follow a line of conduct sanctioned as good, by two such great authorities as God and Humanity, and to avoid a line of conduct prohibited as bad, in being antisocial, is surely a course of action which Christian and non-Christian may join hands to help forward, where the highest aim of the one class will be to advance the glory of God in Christ, the highest aim of the other class to help onward the highest development of humanity.

If anything can insure the co-operation of an alliance between the two sections into which Christianity has divided the human race, assuredly the conditions referred to will do so, so that the harmony and peace which these conditions lead up to may flow in upon poor suffering Humanity, and lead it onward to immortality, animated by the higher and higher moral life.

The unchristian, and therefore unsaved section of Humanity, animated by the sentiment that seeks the advancement of man, as the servant of God, and the good of its social organism, will ever be inspired by an Ideal worthy of its destiny, and which will lead it on through eternity upward and onward towards the Infinite. The advancement of this section will rest in its power to overcome the resistance of opposing forces, animated by justice and truth—inspired by a higher and yet higher Ideal, as humanity advances onward through infinite space.

Whereas, whatever is included in the human term "Infinite," will be realized instinctively by the Christian section of the race through their union with Christ in God, the Christ of God to whom they owe all their glory, and in whose love they rest. They are led on by a glow of development, in harmony with their kind, the Redeemed of God, the Church of the first-born. How small the time-serving ends are that occupy so much our time on earth, when we contemplate the future in the light it may now be viewed in by the Christian section of a race so highly favoured of God, Illuminated by Evolution.

Notwithstanding the glorious destiny thus indicated for our race at one stage of its development, it was so depraved that the covenant of works, as a human instrument, utterly failed to secure the end aimed at. The failure made Redemption by substitution imperative, as the only remedy possible to secure the ultimate deliverance of the human race. One section is destined to be a progressive human instrument, ever liable to suffer, yet it will, on entering into the immortal state be led on by its God and Developing Intelligence, the Lord Jesus Christ, the only God it can ever know.

He was born into suffering humanity, and endured its ills through life. Though divine in His origin, yet He was made in this way human in His sympathy, therefore fitted to be the " God of humanity," capable of inspiring moral action, which will insure the eternal development of the unsaved section of that race onwards through space — a race with which in a way our Lord had a common origin, because born into it. Doubtless, it is the moral influence flowing through the redemptive purchase into the social organism, that will sustain and insure the advancement of the social organism of our immortal race as a progressive human instrument, stimulated by the assurance of success, which will "form a deep tranquil stream flowing beneath the tumultuous waves and angry movements of the surface, making aspiration prophecy, which, in the future as in the past, will make natural man in his progress ever wiser than his creed." This gives expression to one form of " the earnest expectation of the creation waiteth for the revealing of the Sons of God "—Rom. viii. 19, R.V.— the fulfilment of its predictions, which, when fulfilled, will find its further predictions, in a still higher phase of development, which, in its turn, springs from the one just attained. Conditions such as these, will invigorate and satisfy the aspirations of this social organism all through eternity. There, eventually, the peace of harmony will prevail, by the injustice of oppression having utterly disappeared from among men, this being the fulfilment of the Bible prophecy, which predicted the destruction of " the wicked." Whereas, the condition is that of annihilating wickedness, in this way, that the individual who acts wickedly will, in suffering the consequences, be regenerated through the influence of the onward movement, strengthened by the knowledge of what Christ—as God of this section has done and suffered for it, a social organism of which each individual forms a part, and cannot be therefrom annihilated or disintegrated. It is "wickedness" that will be annihilated and disappear from the Race. When this is accomplished, man will have overcome his anti-social habits, and the prophecy will be fulfilled in wickedness and oppression disappearing from the social organism of the race, led on by its God of Humanity, the Lord Jesus Christ, who is brother, Lord and Saviour of the Redeemed Section.

"On earth each mortal eager in his busy energy does his little piece of work, consciously or unconsciously aiding or hindering the development of the social organism of which he is a part." But in the immortal form of this organism, the individual will no longer be ignorant of the effect his conduct has produced in the past, and will produce in the future, on that huge social instrument. And he will thus become fully conscious that the effect of a selfish act will hinder social development, which includes his individual weal, and that the influence of a right act will help onward its development. He will fully realize that he is a responsible unit, "and that his well-being is inseparably bound up in the well-being of the whole, and that it is the organism as a whole, not a unit, but the organism in its integral form, that gives the distinctive direction to the sum of its many and varied units." The individual will then fully realise that it is the organism as a whole which creates the ideal to which the individual aspires. The intelligence of the social organism is the point which insures further development, both individually and collectively—individually in being the first to perceive or anticipate the higher ideal to which the social organism points.

The sum of the multitudinous conscious units is the moving whole, the action in the immortal state is the same as on earth, in so far that it is the united action of the social organism that creates the ideal to which man aspires. The difference in action will mainly rest in the fact that the immortal organism will come to be animated by unity of feeling, which will direct consciously its onward course of progress; having a conscious conception that progress rests in the unity of action which flows from the moral and religious sentiment that unites the organic whole, so as to provide a suitable solidifying medium for the race to rest in while developing the ideal conceptions destined to be realised, when enlightened by the form of moral and revealed truth that comes through the knowledge of "their God," the Christ of Christianity, the God of Humanity. Such is the work assigned to the great Immortal organic growth of Humanity hereafter, as the unsaved, because unconverted, section of the race who are not so united to Christ on earth. In an age when the process of unfolding the forces of nature, on which the sciences rest, is being accomplished ; which will, in part, represent the becomings of the future in typifying the ideal conceptions of this section of advancing humanity.

We may ask, What are the becomings? What is evolution? and from whence comes nature with its marvellous capacities for creating the ideal conceptions that lead towards social development. Bound up with the answer given to this question is the other question—whence come the forces that operate in evolving humanity? and whether does the human race tend? To both of these questions nature is dumb. It can give no reply. The scientific discoveries we value so much and justly, can give us no aid to help to an answer here. The furthest natural science can come, is to point to our dead bodies, and say or infer the end is there. The forces which gave birth to it live only in the social organism. As to the forces, their action is infused into it in forming and fashioning it. In language such as this, the case is stated fairly and rightly. For from Natural Science or Evolution no answer can be given, either of whence the forces of nature came, or whither they go. The voice which answers must come from God through Revelation alone—Revelation which authorises the Christian to point to the dead body, and say, Life does not cease here, but in the fullest and truest sense of all, individual life only begins its higher development.

The design working through evolution originated by nature's God, has produced humanity in producing man. The design works so marvellously in its integrity, that in the millions of the adaptive structures and instincts to be met with in nature, there is not one which has not been developed for the benefit of the species that produced it. This fact we Christians are justified in calling the integrity of design. That species only adopt beneficial qualities is a fact so marked, that even Darwin attached so much importance to this phase, that he offered to surrender his whole theory if a single instance was produced to the contrary; and, assuredly, a stronger evidence of Design could not be wished for. Yet natural selection provides further proof. For it is so, that though Selection preserves suitable variations, when they arise, it does not cause them. Now, as variations arise in every generation, and natural selection preserves the most suitable, surely we are justified in regarding such selection as a natural cause, and a strong link in proof of the order of design in nature.

A question sometimes asked is, why natural selection, &c., did not so operate as to cause all monkeys to become men? But the point is, apart from the action of a God of nature working through design, that the improvement did take place in one line of descent; and not in having taken place in one, it should have taken place in every other. However, viewed from the operation working through design, in the one case of variations, the germ of humanity was laid in the product of our race, endowed with such wonderful imaginative capacities, that enables man to anticipate far-reaching conclusions looming in the distance as conditions yet to be realised by our immortal race.

Linked with the faculty of imagination, is the line of action God makes use of in revealing His purposes to man. Further, Christian man, guided by the light that natural science gives — illuminated by what God has Revealed of His purposes towards man in the word of life — man may thereby anticipate the line of action through which these purposes are yet to be accomplished. The order of Design, clearly unfolded in the action of evolution producing natural man, is indicated in Gen. ii. 7, where we are informed that man was formed " of the dust of the ground." He had immortality breathed into his nostrils as the breath of life in the sentiment Hope inspired, by man having anticipated the possibility that his life would be prolonged on the death of his body. This anticipation gave birth to the aspiration designed by God to secure the condition desired, namely, immortality through the influence that hope produced in man hoping and trusting that his life would be prolonged indefinitely — a hope fulfilled in this, that the activity of the Ego does not cease on the death of the body, but in the human form continues active as ever. The breath of God, so understood, did breathe immortality into man's nostrils. This unfolds the process whereby the first man of the earth earthy was "made a living soul." 1 Cor. xv. 45-47. ThisInspiration, through the influence of the law of inheritance, came to insure the immortality of our race—for the forces hope inspired left a structural form in the brain, which increased in volume and strength by every succeeding generation so animated. Forces so developed on the death even of an infant would so act as to hold that infant's soul intact.

Could language more clearly illustrate the working of evolution in its process of unfolding, than the words of Genesis ii..—"Man made of the dust of the earth" does, written so many thousand years ago, and preserved by design for our enlightenment. Evolution, thus far, has fulfilled the work assigned it in pointing out how nature, as designed by God, operates in evolving itself so as to produce the immortal human species. For the form and intelligence which conform to the human race are produced—are evolved—and contain in themselves potentially a type of all the forms of life that preceded them. Further, the future development is the development of the natural section of the social organism, viewed as of the earth earthy. However, we cannot tell how long the organic human form existed on our planet before man became a living soul. For the ideal conception indicated in "Living soul," seen in the light of present knowledge, must be understood as applying to the condition whereby the individual unit viewed as the vitality of the conscious states of the human body would continue its activity, and hold together in the human form on the death of the bodily organism. This being so, we may infer that a very long period did exist in view of the slow process of evolution before the living forces animated by self-conservation had acquired the power of sustaining itself as a living form, separated from its bodily organism, which is the condition which conforms to the conception of soul or Ego, referred to in Gen. ii. 7.

Doubtless, the notion of Immortality, conforming to a very exalted ideal conception, which was to be realised, must have come through the working of the ideal conception inherent in humanity, which creates for man his onward course, in creating the exalted ideas which he strives to imitate, as the impulses which lead to a still higher development. In following the line of development indicated by revelation, it is well to note that, before man became capable of forming the ideal conception which included immortality, the work assigned to him was to be "fruitful, and multiply and replenish the earth, and subdue it"—Gen. i. 28. This proves that man had indeed attained to a considerably high state of mental development, before he could be capable of performing the work assigned to him, in overcoming natural impediments. Man's progress, then, as now, would naturally be that of his social organism as a whole. Viewing what is Revealed, from the order of Evolution, we may infer that the first conception formed of Immortality was, that man would continue to live on the earth just as he was.

The Adam in the garden clearly points to the conception formed of a continuous life on earth. If this is the rendering, the Adam of the garden would have been the first of the race to form such a conception. Fulfilling in this way God's design or decree, Adam would have the approval of God by, we shall say, God bestowing on him the mental condition which would ensure the end desired. And, I ask, would not this end be secured by mind—through mental states —so acting on the bodily organism as to supply the waste of the system from within, thus preserving it in a healthy condition. The mental state destined to secure this would be strengthened through the influence of the forces Revelation imparted. This being so, from what we know of life and its laws, the means used to secure the end seem very simple, say, by a continuous uninterrupted effort of mind so directed toward the maintenance of the organism, as to draw from the blood the material required to supply the Waste of the System from within ; the forces present in the blood would supply the material in matter and energy required, assuming that the unvarying mental state, necessary to direct the building up process was present.

Remember, that the mental state of doubt or uncertainty present in our day, which demands proof for every thing, would be absent in the simple-minded Adam of these days. He would unhesitatingly accept the revelation. And we shall say he continued to live on by the assurance it gave him, and it thus produced the effect desired. Conditions, if successful in our state of knowledge, would be so, guided by intelligence realising the nature of the process that the energy of mind was capable of accomplishing, in supplying the waste of the body from the material in the blood.

The conditions involved in the Fall of Man would end in Adam and Eve. The mental state I have anticipated, with its life-sustaining power, generating the mental state that anticipated death as the consequence their act of disobedience led to. It was followed by the most deplorable state of sin and death—sin because God entered into a covenant with man, which man sinned in breaking. For St. Paul distinctly explains that where there is no law, there is no transgression, Rom. iv. 15.

If the condition of the first Adam was such as I indicate, we may infer that the fruit flowing into the social organism from Adam's example, and progressive intelligence, would have so influenced the development thereof as to enable a female to be developed capable of becoming Adam's help-meet. Anyhow, at this stage of human development, the intelligence which Adam, during his long life had acquired, would prove a powerful influence in aiding the further progress of the race. Viewing the matter from this point, the advantage lost to Adam would in a way be conferred on his contemporary race. This race provided Adam's sons with wives. They were called the daughters of men. Though Adam's notion of immortality ended in his fall and death, the race would gain in the very fact that the conception had been formed which would lead man to anticipate some sort of life after death. A conception of this form would be helpful in furthering the onward flow of development in the race; it would be seized upon by the advancing social organism as a condition to be desired.

The conception must have sprung from the imaginative capacity of some genius of the race, anticipating the possibility of the immortality of the soul in a life after death, God would in some way intelligible to the individual, confirm by revelation the truth of the immortality he had anticipated. This conception in the order of evolution the social organism would immediately embrace as beneficial to it. This was the order designed by God, that evolution was destined to take, in helping forward the development of the race on earth, as well as inducing the condition which would ensure individual immortality as the equivalent of the conscious states which go to make up each unit, on the death of the body, consciousness being capable of absorbing energy from the surrounding medium to give expression to these conscious states. Energy and conscious states, so understood, are co-existent as the correlatives in which individual immortality rests. The design of God works through the order of evolution in this way, to breathe into man the breath of life, which makes man a "living soul." Or we might say, God working in evolution, created in man the desire which, at a further phase of development was realised, in man on the death of the organism finding itself a living soul, active as in the body. For the conditions I have anticipated, do create a body of energy, in giving expression to conscious states, its equivalent.

Further, we may safely infer, viewed from the order of evolution, and illuminated by Revelation, that in the conditions anticipated being realized, we have the first immortal man produced—though doubtless an immortality of some sort was conferred on Adam and Eve—which may have been in representing the contemporary social organism of which they both formed part; a race which in them would thus be represented as having existed, though not possessed of individual immortality. Let that be as it may, once a life after death was conceived, and the fact confirmed by Revelation, we can imagine what a power the belief of such a future would have on the advancement of the social organism as it gathered strength in developing itself. Till now, the immortality of the soul is held by almost the whole of the human race. With the exception of the most advanced men of science, who cannot conceive how the forces forming the individual intelligent unit, man, are to hold together on the death of the body, so as to form the "living soul," to which revelation points.

In questioning the truth of revelation, this class overlooks the fact "that connects feeling with all forms of life, and that the highest form of mental life, therefore the highest aggregate of feeling, is to be found in the forces which build up the human brain. Forces united by the sentiment of "self-conservation," operating to hold such energy together as the form of moving force, which does not cease its movement on the death of the body, but continues its activity by absorbing energy to give expression to conscious states in liberating it. This is the process that ensures Immortality, the equivalent of the sentiment of self-conservation. But how could we have an individual life after death, except it came in reproducing the mental states that the body has generated on earth in forming such ideas of the energy that surrounds the Ego. This is done by a somewhat similar process to that taking place in producing memory during life.

One thing is certain, that " the influence of the belief in immortality on human events has been of unspeakable moment. Further, that the primary conception of some sort of Immortality did spring into consciousness from the upward striving of impulses which are immanent in man, is evident as part and crown of organic nature." Ever since, a belief in Immortality so generated, became confirmed by God through Revelation, it " has throbbed in man's heart in the inspiration of Hope, of aspiration of Faith in things unseen. Imagination, as its manner is, constructs modes or forms of satisfaction of the instinct in conformity with the co-existing state of mental development." And such conceptions form the birthplace from whence springs truth designed of God to be realised. When such conceptions formed of old, were destined to be realised, God would in some way, through the power of a special revelation, intelligible to the man who formed the conception, confirm the truth of it. To have a conception confirmed so of God, would conform to a prophetic revelation, and entitle the man who formed the conception to be called a prophet sent by God. For so he was in anticipating conditions that God destined to fulfil. This is the explanation of the intellectual conceptions from which prophecy flows.

This instinctive far-reaching forecast of human destiny —which springs from the forces of evolution working in and through man, inspiring his imagination, enables him to grasp the facts, to which a phase of intelligence gives birth, by generalising and inferring therefrom—is a mental condition that forms a strong store of strength, to invigorate man's imagination, and spur him on to yet higher and yet higher flights.

The productive or creative function of mind in this way receives a very strong impulse from each new conception stamped as God's truth, through the phenomena that the process of Revelation chooses to make use of. For such new truths, confirmed by Revelation, will form the foundation, in its Intellectual groupings of a new productive or creative function of mind, leading to higher Imaginative flights in the same direction. When all rest on truth Revealed, the imagination will justly strive to grasp in anticipation the more advanced intellectual conception within the possible reach of the social organism, in its eternal habitation, formed of man in his natural state. For these conceptions will justly inspire the imagination, to strike out new paths in combining and arranging the probable conditions of the further development which the natural phenomena—with which man is at present conversant—seem to point to.

When employed to anticipate the surroundings of the race, in other and higher conditions, whereby the actual of human experience and reason thus transformed into new forms of thought may come to have the approval of the race on earth, because the conditions are seen by intelligent men to rest in the facts that in like manner satisfy the eternal form of revealed truth, human experience, and reason. By the conclusions arrived at, conforming with the evidences that satisfy the human Intellect, the working of God, as the God of truth, is clearly seen to be carrying out His purpose of design in the advancing sections of the race as a human instrument everlasting in its destiny.

However, the distinctions must be kept in view, that one section of the race, is a divine instrument, led on by the Redeemer, God, as the church of the first-born. The other, just referred to, is purely a human instrument, led on by the God of Humanity as the Son of God. Thus, then, the flight that the imagination takes in striving to realise the future of both sections, is quite different. The imagination in the first takes to do with the redeemed—in how what is revealed of their future is to be accomplished; in the last, with the future of the section that is purely human in its end and origin.

It is so, that by accepting in faith what the Christian records reveal of Christ, of His life, death, and resurrection, we give substance to faith in providing for these conceptions a habitation and a name in the human Brain. Further, in the flight that Imagination takes in forming new ideas, which do, indeed, anticipate the condition decreed of God yet to be fulfilled by our race, we are doing the work assigned by God for the imaginative faculty of man to accomplish. This, in few words, is enabling our race to anticipate what God has decreed to accomplish in bringing to naught the old conditions or conceptions, by the new discovery which is of far greater utility to the Race, in God choosing things which are not—until they were anticipated—to bring to naught things which are.—1st Cor. i. 28. We have prophecy in the most exalted form, when the imaginative faculty first conceives a higher form of revelation arising out of truth already revealed, which has yet to be fulfilled, and we may anticipate how this higher form can be accomplished by seeing how may be applied the Laws of Nature for this end. The Intellect can accomplish this through a process of generalization and inference—which, in the ab. stract, constructs things unknown, and also shows how they are to be accompanied by giving all a local habitation and a name in the ideal form. Human imagination animated thus, is the highest function of mind, and represents the becomings through which our race shall ever advance. Such flights of imagination do their part to carry on the evolution of the great social organism.

Remember, imagination cannot work except it be fed suitably and be well informed in truth revealed. Such an imaginative faculty rests in truth revealed, and it only concerns itself with the truths of nature when they can be used to illustrate Revealed Truth. To be in intimate sympathy with nature, Social and Physical, will enable one to gather what is behind and around, by combining it with revealed truth, so as to render revelation more and more intelligent, and lay in this way "a sound and solid basis for the forward reacting work of imaginative creation." The only difference between forming the theoretical conceptions of an advanced scientific truth, and that of forming a higher conception of what truth already revealed leads to, rests in the fact that the first is dealing with the things of earth seen to surround us, the other with what pertains to higher forms of Truth Revealed, but yet to be demonstrated as accomplished facts.

For may not imagination properly constructed on the basis of the unfathomable moral or religious consciousness, perceive higher truths yet to be realized than has been already revealed ? It was, doubtless, by a prophet perceiving the future, that would flow from conditions already revealed, that God made use of in confirming to the individual by revelation, the truth of the anticipated conception, that gave to the prophecies of old the stamp of God's approval. It is through the power of imagination, brought to bear on the Laws of Nature, that theoretical science grows and prospers. The same intellectual processes will be seen working in revelation, constructing theoretical conceptions, which, when in accordance with God's design He will stamp by His approval through a form of revelation.

That the "progressive becoming of knowledge anticipates understanding, foretelling the immediate *to be* before it definitely *is;* in the common use of it in scientific inquiry, for example, the theory which it constructs precedes the demonstration by which, after being tested and approved by the understanding, it is made knowledge ; and so it does actually go beyond the range of understanding, stretching forth into the future, but only from the base of understanding to come back to the test of understanding if it is of sterling value. What sort of a theory is that which is not based upon a competent appreciation of well-observed facts and their relations. And what sort of imagination that which is not based upon good, well-trained, and well-informed understanding, and can in turn appeal to the test of it." Now, it comes to pass that truth revealed rests on exactly the same base. For truth revealed to us in the

Bible will, in the immortal state, be found to have rested on the base of the understanding then realized by actual experience, when the base of understanding will have come back to the test of understanding. For Revelation mostly takes to do with the conditions entered at death, which immediately succeeds our life on earth, by the instinct of consciousness perceiving the body rigid in death unfitted for further use, and as its manner of action is, it maintains conscious states by absorbing energy to do so. For through a continuous flow of energy absorbed and liberated, as the correlative of conscious states, the life of the Soul or Ego is maintained as an Immortal Unit of our race, an Ego regulated and maintained by its own laws. Such is the law of Natural Science that secures the anticipated Immortality of the Soul, anticipated in the prophecies of thousands of years ago, not only fulfilled at death, but the conditions on which the fulfilment rests, through the aid of modern science, perceived, explained, and applied.

It is through the understanding, resting on the revelation given to man, that the highest conceptions of truth related to this immortal state comes. Such theoretical conceptions rest in conditions to be fulfilled after death. The facts anticipated will be accomplished, and resting on truth revealed, not one iota of them can fail, whether we accept or reject such, because, resting in the form of causation; whereas the theoretical conceptions of science have to be demonstrated as such here and now.

However, in both cases before the constructive power of the imagination can be of any value, we must make clear to ourselves "what we can affirm positively, what we can deny positively, what we must be content to leave unaffirmed and undenied." This, then, we Converted Christians can affirm with positive certainty, that the Old Testament Scriptures do contain a revelation in the prophecy of a promised Deliverer; that in the New Testament records we have the prophecy fulfilled in the incidents recorded of the Birth, Life, Death, Resurrection, and Ascension of the promised Deliverer, in the person of our Lord, who from the time of His ascension onwards, has been united in harmony of sentiment with every converted believer on earth, conversion being the link in causation, whereby all such find a home at death in His kingdom ruled by love, in the material human soul of such, while in the body, vibrating in unison of sentiment with the redeemed, in a kingdom anew created by our Lord's Life, Death, and Resurrection. This length the Converted Christian can assuredly go in his affirmation. Not only so, but from the teaching derived from unfulfilled prophecy, "this class" can go further and affirm with positive certainty, that the Revelations of St. John indicate the ultimate deliverance of the race, in "the new gospel," therein taught and addressed to the Race as the immortal body collective—the unsaved section of the social organism, the race Human—in the graphic words of our Lord, "He that overcometh shall inherit all things." Words so positively insisted on, as in one form or another to be repeated eight times in the Revelations. Now, the enlightened Christian can positively affirm, that in the history of our immortal race, this prophecy will be realized, in the effect produced by this gospel which will ultimately secure the deliverance and well-being of the human race, by enabling the unsaved to advance as an immortal human instrument on through eternity.

Thus, then, in these matters named, I make clear what the Converted Christian Church has a right positively to affirm. Resting here, I repeat in the words of an eminent author, the following — spoken regarding his class—" We are sure, and can affirm that a fundamental impulse of evolution is felt in the higher functions of mind ; we are sure, and can affirm that the impulse comes from afar, and is more than personal in any proper sense of the word ; we are entirely in doubt what it is essentially, whence it comes, and whither it tends, and are sure, that any positive and definite answer that we make to such question, must be fables of the imagination." The position taken up thus, by those who reject Revealed truth, is proper and safe. For they can go no further. They can give no answer to the question, from whence comes or whither goes the " fundamental impulse of evolution felt in the higher functions of mind," leading the race onward. For the answer must come through the truths that the Christian Records reveal, read in the light that natural science and evolution affords.

Taking for example, the first few verses of St. John's gospel, read in the light of present knowledge, and we have the birth-place of our Lord and Redeemer, as the only begotten Son of God in nature, and its Laws emanating from God. This operation revealed truth indicates in these words, " In the beginning was the Word, and the Word was with God, and the Word was God."—John i. 1. Words so rendered, must be understood to indicate an emanance from God, capable of producing the forms of intelligence, Nature and its Laws, viewed as nature, science, into which evolution enters, has produced in giving birth to intelligence. Further, that word a term, when viewed in the Concrete, must first include the intellectual conceptions or Ideas, "to be" developed through space by Nature and her Laws. Secondly, the effect this process or cause is to produce in the form of an Abstract, the crowning fruit of each system. Indeed, an abstract in the form of an intellectual unit that embraces the intelligence and accompanying sentiment of each system in space, therefore, an intelligence in personal sympathy with each separate system ; and, collectively, in harmony with all, is the only-begotten Son of God, and originator of all ideas, called " the Word of God." All Nature in this way, since the ascension of our Lord is specially related to Him. Therefore, as is revealed, He shall at the end return to God, and deliver up the intelligences developed in the universe of space by nature, and her Laws to God the Father, after having " put down all rule, all authority, and power"—1 Cor. xv. 20-28—which does not recognise God's place in nature. This will be accomplished when Nature and her Laws will have done their appointed work in producing the immortal intelligences of the universe, so modified by our Lord as to be in harmony with God the Father, when brought back from whence Nature sprung, by the only-begotten Son of God—to God, the triune, even the eternal originator of all.

In rendering what is revealed intelligent from my stand point, the case may be put thus. The various forms of Intellectual Systems Nature and its Laws have produced, in developing the various worlds (judging from the analysis that demonstrates myriads of planets in a similar condition to ours, we are justified in assuming as I do, that they do exist in the Universe of Space), have in form of intelligence and sympathy, the only-begotten Son of God, so related to the race that each world in space has given birth to, as to be capable of leading the race of each onward to a higher and yet higher phase of its own form of intellectual development. This office performed by our Lord as the originator of the fundamental impulses of evolution felt in the highest functions of mind represents "the Word," the actual essential which emanated from God, and returns thereto in the person of His only-begotten Son. In this way, He leads forward the Universe of Space in the special phase of intelligence each world has developed.

What concerns our race is to strive to understand God's mode of action as seen in nature and its laws, and His character as revealed by His Son, our Lord, who was in the world, and the world "was made by him, and the world knew him not."—John i. 10. Though as such His influence was "the fundamental impulse of evolution felt in the highest functions of mind," destined to produce humanity, in producing the form of intelligence human nature embodies, a form of intelligence capable of interpreting the action of such a God as the Christian records reveal in His dealings with a race developed by His laws. They are so highly gifted in the power that their Imaginative faculty confers, as to anticipate the becomings that natural science points to as the equivalent of new discoveries, as well as the conditions revealed truth indicates concerning the future of the race.

Evidently it is in the power the imaginative faculty confers on our race, in the capacity to anticipate from what is revealed, the future yet to be realized as a prophetic forecast of coming events that provides the explanation of what our Lord meant when He says—" I am the root and the offspring of David, the bright and the morning star."—Rev. xxii. 16. As the root, He was the origin of all that had been revealed to our race; and in very deed the offspring of David. For David was so highly gifted in sentiment, and developed in the form of intelligence that revealed truth imparts, as to be capable of anticipating the coming events of our Lord's birth and destiny. He conceived of Him as an Intelligence of a divine order, whose whole desire and whose activity centred in doing God's Will on earth. The Ideal conception thus formed, was the " foreordained " Germ brought together in the elements of its Ideal Sentiment, from which the person of our Lord sprung. In our Lord " the Word " was made flesh, and dwelt among us, " as the glory of the only-begotten Son of the Father, full of grace and truth "—John i. 14—who accomplished all required of Him.

In taking the following view of the matter, we have a whole series of causation. First, in the Ideal conception formed by David as the forces brought together in the Intellectual combination accompanied by its sentiment, which, in functioning, develop the only-begotten of the Father, our Lord, inspired to accomplish the work decreed. Secondly, you will observe the intellectual combination that David's reasoning gave birth to in springing from *revealed truth*, which gives a supernatural origin to our Lord, being the intellectual combination destined to form the Holy Thing—born of the Virgin Mary—the Son of God· This fact was evidently accomplished in following the lead causation took, as the result that faith produced in Mary having implicit confidence in the fulfilment of the promise conveyed by the Angel, that she would "conceive in the womb, and bring forth a Son, and call his name Jesus." This intimation by a supernatural agency generated the forces in the brain which developed the conception in the Virgin, and was miraculous, in so far as our race has no experience of the power or possibility of such a law. Yet, the possibility is that such was the process ordered by God to produce the Intelligence called the Root and the offspring of David, the bright and the morning star —Rev. xxii. 16—in causing the elements to unite, which formed the intellectual conception, that David was inspired to combine, and in this way developed the person of our Lord in the human form, ever active in doing what he felt to be the will of God. And so very intelligent at twelve years old was He, as to be found in the temple hearing the Doctors and asking them questions, so desirous as this was our Lord to find out what the will of God as revealed to our race was, that He might be ready to obey.

Evidently this phase of His character was checked for the time by His mother's rebuke, "Son, why hast thou thus dealt with us; behold thy father and I have sought thee sorrowing." Our Lord, we may infer, answered in the heat of enthusiasm created in hearing and understanding so much that concerned Him of what He required to know—"Wist ye not that I must be about my Father's business."—Luke ii. 49. Yet so impressed was our Lord by the rebuke, and the truth it implied of an act of disobedience to His recognised parents, that He accompanied them home and became subject to them, thereby remaining nearly thirty years in obscurity, till His mother induced Him to work His first so-called miracle. By commanding the atoms of water, earth, and air, to combine in producing the wine ready for the use of the wedding guests, He saved the host the pain that would arise from its being known that he had failed to provide enough to satisfy his invited guests.

It is evident that from this time henceforward, our Lord commanded the laws of nature in making them obedient to Him, by employing their power in ministering toward the good of His contemporary race while on earth, though He never used this power in any form to alleviate His own suffering. Possessing this power, which, when viewed from the stand-point of "Nature being one," we are justified in inferring that to command Nature as a servant obedient to its God, in carrying out His will, was natural to him. A similar power seems conferred on His converted ones, which, by its agency was to accomplish all that is included in our Saviour's promise in John xiv. 12-14, where He says, "If you ask anything in My name, I will do it."

Christ's intelligence while a man on earth did not surpass that of His contemporary race or class, with the exception of the intelligence He gathered from the Bible and applied to illustrate conditions of every-day life. Instance His parables. For assuredly the superiority of our Lord's teaching arose from His applying to present conditions the moral truths already revealed, to rebuke hypocrisy, falsehood, and fraud. For, in teeming nature, He only saw the product of His Father's hand, and as such the lilies of the field to be far superior in splendour than the glory of Solomon's court, a production perceived by Him to be the creation of man, which entailed in labour the penalty of much suffering on fellow-man. Our Lord's mind, so animated, was in a prepared state to grasp all; to see the activity of God His Father as much at work in the formation of a crystal, as in the production of man; yes, even man, who, enlightened by the intellectual capacity his Imaginative faculty confers, illuminated by perception, observation, conception, and inference, acting upon the whole of the evidence revealed truth and nature's doing indicate. By analysing and cross-examining the evidences in every way, a man of average ability can extricate from all an intelligent answer, which ought to satisfy the most sceptical human Intellect, that there is sufficient evidence to prove an intelligence at the heart of everything, regulating and governing all.

Taking into account our limited capacity, put in contrast with the vastness of space even known to us, we ought to accept with the humility befitting our case, the fact that the God we have to do with in the Christian Records is the governor of all; that our Redeemer, God, is the only-begotten of such a Father, full of grace and truth, who is the God of Humanity, leading the race onwards through eternity, as well as guiding onward all the intelligences developed or created in the uttermost confines of space.

Christendom can affirm with positive certainty that the climax of revealed truth centres in the Birth, Death, and Resurrection of our Lord, which gave to the only-begotten of the Father a permanent objective existence—in being made flesh—the essential conditions on which the term absolute truth must rest, because this term has in the person of our Lord, the permanent objective existence from which the actual conceptions of Christianity rise, therefore is justly called "absolute truth." However, it is only where these facts of Christianity are accepted, that the highest forms of the fundamental impulse of evolution can be felt in the most advanced functions of Mind. Because, henceforth, the essential of social evolution must concern itself with the Immortal part of man, which comes into existence on the birth of the individual, the fruit of the earthly social organism, and passes on through the gates of death an Immortal unit, capable of reasoning on the past, the present, and the future.

For such is the conception that conforms to man's actual future, and is no fable of the imagination unsupported by facts. Henceforth, any conception of "Nature's Doings," including evolution, that ignores the fact of man's Immortal destiny, will tend to develop forces antagonistic to evolution, and generate the forces of degeneration.

Evolution must now mean building up the eternal form of human intelligence into which Christian belief enters. Degeneration, pulling it down, ignores the fact of man's Immortality. Thus, does Evolution Illuminate the Bible. Degeneration is a positive deviation from the path of human progress. For during the earthly destiny of our race, human progress must come through man and be conditioned by the limitations of his nature; man is the channel of its flow to us, illuminated by the enlightenment that Christianity unfolds, resting on our Lord as its permanent objective existence and His vicarious sacrifice, destined to secure the ultimate deliverance of the race, whether viewed as a purely human instrument, comprising the unsaved section of the race, or as the sections saved by grace, and therefore the children of God, by adoption, the church of the first-born.

Revealed truth, resting on the foundation of proceeding from a permanent object—this permanent object since the Christian era is Christ—ought and must satisfy human understanding in having such a base. When we know that religion responds to an eternal need of human sentiment, a sentiment which Christianity satisfies, therefore it must come to be universally accepted as a form of truth proved and demonstrated, so as to satisfy the most sceptical mind. If further proof is required, it is to be found in Christianity inspiring the moral sentiment of humanity, and resting on the deep foundation of sacrifice of self, pity to the poor and suffering, faith in the triumph of the good. It appeals to both heart and understanding. " The heart is democratic, the intellect aristocratic "—the latter knowledge puffs up, but Love, the former, unites and builds up. Thus, then, Christianity must solve the social problem. For the Love begotten in union with Christ dominates the Intellect through the heart.

This is the very condition required to solve the social problem. Such a condition insures the deep fusing of human solidarity in whatever form you take it. For a Christian community in felt union with Christ, is to the social organism what the heart is to the bodily organism. When this influence ceases to beat, first in the individual conscience, then in the collective conscience of the community, moral force is lost, and the downward course of degeneration follows, and nothing will compensate the social organism for this loss. Even the scientific discoveries, justly called the glory of our age, will not compensate humanity for the loss of its moral force. This will happen if Christianity loses its power of solidifying the social force, if it is found wanting in the moral influence its originator enjoined. Christians should always remember that knowledge by itself is not necessarily good, it is certainly power, but power which may be used for ill, as much as for good. Further, "the effect of culture is to increase the individual's power, and to widen the gap between him and his less cultured fellows—to raise those that are high and degrade those who are low—to make the rich richer, and the poor poorer—to increase inequality without yielding anything to fill the gap between the classes" if Christianity loses its power. Increase of inequality means in the end revolution, and a new social fusion, except the people have fallen altogether out of the line of progress.

"The terrible suffering inseparable from social revolution is well known, and arises from widely separated classes and interests, which, in equalizing this condition, gives birth to a new social fusing. The blood that flows like water during these events, preserves human solidity at the cost of terrible personal suffering. Knowledge alone cannot supply the social base, without the consolidating cement that sympathy gives, in inducing moral action." Without this, the social organism cannot hold together. Now, it is just this relation that Christianity, in its most exalted form, begets by the vicarious sacrifice inspiring unity of sentiment into the community that realise they are saved by substitution. Thus, the Christian, in felt communion with Christ, realises the future in store for him in such a way as to make the attractions the world can offer a matter of indifference to him, in comparison with honouring and serving his beloved Redeemer by the life that a self-sacrificing love generates. However, those animated thus in the deeds of kindness they willingly confer, must in the future be guided by the desecration that seeks for proof that the effort they make to increase the comfort of others, develops equivalent sympathy by uniting in the bond of true kinship both receiver and giver. This would neutralise the degenerating effect that sometimes takes place in leading to indolence and selfishness, by drying up the sympathy of the giver, in perceiving that the receiver takes what is offered simply as a thing he requires, and which the giver has at his disposal to bestow. The friction so generated must in the future be avoided, if Christian benevolence is to do the work of solidifying the social organism, designed by its originator, in infusing the sympathy that tends to unite all classes, when Christian benevolence is viewed as a product of nature's God, in bringing human nature into harmony with its developing agent and originator, "the Christian's God and Redeemer," who to the non-Christian race is the "God of Humanity."

In partaking of our nature, He became flesh and dwelt among us, adorned in a natural body, capable of developing a reasonable soul, born in a stable, reared as one of the sons of toil, the equal of His class in intelligence, but not above them. The Human Intellect, the heritage of the race, was not to be usurped supernaturally by Him who was of divine origin, born into Humanity to develop its nature to partake of its material existence and its reasonable soul. As such, He returned the gift of human life the race bestowed in earning redemption by substitution and becoming its developing medium, conferred on the race through His life, death, and resurrection.

It was decreed of our race by the Godhead to give the second person of the Godhead a life all His own, though equal in power and glory with God the Eternal. He was thus qualified, as I have said, to return to that race the gift of the separate existence it bestowed in providing for all who accept Redemption by Substitution. This doctrine is lightly cast aside by many in our day as a fable of the imagination only, fit to impress the ignorant and the illiterate, such as the contemporary class into which our Lord was born, and lived amongst during His life—" a mass of oppressed toilers for a bare sustenance, worn down with labour." True and just for this reason the class prepared to accept the glorious future He came to offer as a gift free to all who " felt their need." Now, our Lord is qualified to lead on the Intellect of the race, that gave Him a reasonable soul, as its developing Intelligence through eternity. After His Resurrection, on His Ascension, He took His place in the Universe of Space as Co-originator and the Developing Instinct thereof. Henceforth He was to be known as the only-begotten of the Father, having an individuality in its way all His own, which unites Him in sympathy and intelligence with every race in the Universe of Space; because the material existence from whence the influence coming from afar proceeded " as the fundamental instinct of evolution felt in the highest functions of mind." Such now is He who accomplished " Redemption by Substitution "—a doctrine when held in the brain forming an intellectual combination when accepted by the individual as true, which is capable of developing that all-powerful and all-consuming love, as the earnest of the eternal union that unites the sinner with his Redeemer, the Redeemer born in condition far more humble than we know by a stable.

His followers, who diffused the truths He taught, were illiterate and ignorant, gathered from the lower grades of workers. But, behold the result secured in a century or two through the power possessed by these humble agents, through our Lord's influence, in their moral worth by adopting the non-resistence creed of these early days. Aided by the power which, as the servants of our Lord, the Christians possessed in commanding the laws of nature to obey their mandate, by producing in the organism the natural state of health before pervaded by disease. We find an example in Acts iii. 1-12, in the cure arising from Peter's words, in the name of Jesus Christ, "rise up and walk."

However, it is when we compare the moral power that vital Christianity infuses into the social organism, with the effect produced by the knowledge that puffeth up, that the full value of true Christianity can be comprehended as the leading factor in social evolution. Whereas, the gap that the knowledge that puffeth up leaves, has to be filled up at the terrible sacrifice social revolution involves. Let those who are enthusiastic enough to believe in the regeneration of society by the direct action of science, ponder on this, and provide some proof that scientific knowledge will generate the increase of moral force, in providing the instrument, to build up the social organism on which the development of the race principally depends.

The culture of the ancients, in some respects, was equal, if not superior, to ours. They failed to develop out of it the higher social evolution that would have knit the social organism together, namely, the sympathy that works for the good of the whole by uniting all classes. "And what happened? With all the intellectual acquisitions of Rome coming on the top of those of Greece, society went steadily towards destruction, and all that philosophy could do was to proclaim and lament it. Then was born of low parentage, in a mean way, in a distant corner of the empire, a person who passed in entire obscurity thirty years of His life, which ended at thirty-three years. For the three remaining years that He appeared in public, He was scouted as a miserable imposter, rejected by the priests and rulers of His own nation, hardly thought worthy a few words of contemptuous mention by the historians of the day, followed only by a few of the lowest persons of the lowest classes of society. At the end of His brief public career, He died an ignominious death on the cross, betrayed by one of His own disciples, denied by another, abandoned by all. And yet in Him was the birth of the greatest social force which, so far as we know, has ever arisen to modify social evolution. To have predicted it beforehand—nay, even so much as to have formed the dimmest anticipation of its coming and nature—would have been as impossible to all the intellectual insight of the time as it would have been impossible to predict, before experience, the organic molecules which carbon, hydrogen, nitrogen, and oxygen are capable of forming. The momentous fact may well abate the pretensions of philosophy to forecast the future of humanity; suffice it to know, that if it is to progress, it will, as heretofore, draw from a source within itself deeper than knowledge, the inspiration to direct and urge it on the path of destiny."—("Body and Mind," by Maudsley.)

That human evolution will progress is certain. It is also certain that the source, whence the race will draw inspiration to urge it on in the path of Destiny, will come from the originator of Christianity, so lowly born, spurned and rejected by His own nation, for whose earthly benefit, as proffered king, He came to secure for it a permanent kingdom while our planet lasted, by infusing the moral forces into the Jewish race which would enable it to provide a moral code that all the kingdoms of the earth would adopt. Thereby might have been developed the sympathy that binds the social organism together and insures its permanent progress. To a destiny so glorious as this the nation's response was "Crucify Him. Crucify Him." He died by the hands of His people, their proffered King. Their clamour for His blood forced the reluctant hands of the Roman ruler, who would willingly have spared Him, who knew that for envy the priests had delivered Him up.

This same Jesus will henceforth be enthroned as the only-begotten of the Father by our race, so highly favoured in its onward destiny as to have provided for the Governor of the Universe a grossly material form and reasonable soul. The destiny such a race must have before it, may well satisfy it for all the toil, suffering, and pain its countless millions must have endured, and will endure, not one of which has ceased to be, and to have before each and all a bright, a holy, and a prosperous future, in the Gospel of "He that overcometh shall inherit all things." In the Universe of Space there is field and place for all.

Who could have thought our race had such a destiny before it, when our progenitors began to assume a more human form than apes, though doubtless sprung from a considerably more intelligent class than the existing anthropoid apes; yet, progenitors considerably below the intellectual level of existent savages, who, even now, as shown by Romanes "Mental Evolution of Man," give evidence in the "click" of the speech of the Hottentots of the survival of a primordially inarticulate system of sign-speech, thus giving direct evidence of the survival of the primordially inarticulate system of sign-making among the lowest races.

From this the mental faculty in man can be traced step by step onward. Though it is not till articulation is attained, that higher mental progress is possible. Romanes shows this power to have likely arisen when our progenitors were more human than ape-like. In the foresighted intelligence the doctrine of evolution confers, Romanes finds no break or gulf to bridge in the continuity of the development between the brute intelligence and human reason, but a perfectly clear intermittent progress in organic and mental forms of existence. For when we have proof of the development of man from brute organ in bodily organisation, we need not hesitate to hold that it subsists in all mental powers. We in this way perceive how the Bible is Illuminated by the doctrine of social Evolution, in enabling man to anticipate where what is called human depravity came from, namely, through man's progenitors, the brute creation. Adam so generated, is held responsible by God as a covenant-breaker.

In giving an explanation as to how the higher mental powers in man came to be developed, Romanes turns to Language, and in the existence of speech he sees the means by which these general concepts and judgments are formed and retained, which distinguish so specially the man from the animal, as the great source of mental growth and attainment. As it is only the concepts or general ideas that require to be named in order to be thought, it comes to pass that in animals we find a kind of language or expression of generic ideas.

Now, to the converted Christian church, the doctrine of social evolution (so clearly proved by Romanes in "Mental Evolution of Man,") is a cause of great rejoicing, because it enables those Christians to form a clear, natural, and rational conception, as well as give the explanation of the material nature of the human soul, defined by Christ as the immortal part of man, "born of the flesh — flesh," put by Him in contrast with the spiritual influence that comes in the new birth, defined by our Lord as "born of the spirit and spirit," in having a spiritual nature infused in the heaven-born sentiment, referred to in John iii. 6.

Our immortal race, viewed as a product of nature, has provided for "the only-begotten of the Father" an Individual Life, in this far, making Him one of the race into which He was born and lived for 33 years. The race He divided through His work of Redemption into two classes of intelligences, animated by sentiments of a totally different nature, yet a race henceforth led on in both natures by Him. And what may yet be in store for such a race must be quite beyond the imaginative power of human intelligence—though possessing such marvellous powers—to conceive. Far in advance of anything yet attained, must the potential future inherent in the race be, led on by a Divine Intelligence related in this way to it.

Notwithstanding original research doing so much to enlighten the Christianity of our day in the Darwinian Doctrine, which enables us to give a rational explanation of what our Lord taught in John iii. 6, the advantage gained is not of unmixed good, as the sceptical tendency of the age proves, since it has infused into society what is evidently a deteriorating form of moral worth. Though having a clear conception of what social evolution involves is an indispensable factor in the progress of the social organism, yet we cannot tamper with the moral structure of the brain, and expect that it, like other structures, will not deteriorate and decay.

" Modern progress has certainly brought various modes of material well-being, and with these many desires of a selfish nature, demanding eager gratification. This is corrupting." For it must be allowed that all has tended to egoistic developments which are anti-social in their activities, leading towards degeneration. As at present permeating society, these forces are weakening the controlling forces of revealed religion, which formerly kept somewhat in check the egoistic tendency. As has been said—" It would not be easy to prove that it is an advantage to accumulate riches if man decay, to wear fine clothes and lose moral force. Are the men of to-day really better cultured than their forefathers, that is, better able to lead the race onwards in the more heroic action of self-sacrificing impulses. For a self-sacrificing act is a nobler thing and more civilizing than sending a message round the globe."

Viewed thus, what is the gain we have made in the progress of scientific knowledge, material comfort, &c.

Does it ensure a real advance in true social development? Is our advanced knowledge worth the energy in blood and nerve it costs, with the possible prospect of a revolution ahead to enable the gap which divides the classes, and breaks off the flow of sympathy, to be filled up? This question, with positive certainty, might be answered in the negative, if it were proved to be impossible for the truths Revealed Religion unfolds to be infused into the intellectual combinations, which scientific investigation reveals, of matter, of nature, of men, and of the laws that govern all. For the effect produced, as it really appears around us, threatens to disorganise in degenerating the social organism. But the remedy is at hand, in the fact that truth revealed, in the Bible Illuminated by Evolution, will so penetrate the most advanced intellectual conceptions, that the scientific enlightenment of the age develops regarding Nature and its doings by its Laws, which includes man's birth and development, so as to ensure moral energy of a higher form than could at present be anticipated to be infused into the social organism. By enabling man to see, to know, and to understand the fact, that they carry the discoveries they make, in a growth of conscious states, as the personal heritage each confers on the race into their immortal habitation—discoveries which represent nature as viewed by man on earth carried by man into a habitation comprising men of the same race, governed by the same laws as themselves, and as such can be understood and applied, it may be to further development; though as yet the purifying influence that revealed truth inspires has not penetrated, so as to purify, to the full power it possesses, the Ego that outlives the system on earth that developed it, is true The cause of this rests in the laws that govern the social organism not being rendered intelligent, by applying the immortal truths that Christianity reveals to unfold the responsibility and immortality conferred on the race. When this is effected, it will then be made plain, demonstrated, and proved, how man's eternal state is affected by his life on earth when his soul was created—for his actions on earth will determine his immortal destiny. The knowledge of this, in the light of present developments, will infuse a new purifying power into the social organism. The time is at hand when all will be clearly comprehended, and produce the purifying effect that our Lord will see and rejoice in. For, in His divine origin, He is not one of our Race though born into it?

The discoveries of Zoological Scientific investigation clearly proves that life is sensation; and, again, I repeat, to live is to feel—to feel is to live; that a living organism is an organism capable of feeling. This being accepted, leads to the fact being realized with clearness that as long as the human organism is capable of feeling, it is a living organism tenanted by the human soul, the immortal force to which it gave birth in functioning conscious states. Thus, then, when we recognise feeling as life, we find the highest aggregate of feeling manifested in human intelligence, which possesses the marvellous capacity for perceiving and classifying such a variety of all sorts of differences and agreements. It therefore comes to pass, that through the teaching of science, illuminated by the Bible in the truth revealed in Christianity, we know that man — these aggregate units of humanity so wonderfully endowed with vital force, that gives the power of perceiving all shades of feeling, ever following the lead of pleasure, whether seen as a present or remote gratification— passes on through the gate of death from earth into immortality, capable of apprehending how, under new conditions, the power of discrimination and inference which the earthly aggregate of intelligence, regulated by its own laws, bestows on individual man as an immortal unit held responsible for his life on earth. Remember, it is through the power which revealed truth possesses of infusing into the advanced phase of present knowledge, the facts which the immortality of the race involves including its responsibility and its capacities which hold natural man responsible for the consequence of his life on earth : a phase of knowledge that will act as the purifying influence of the future. This responsibility is henceforth seen to be of a nature which man, the offspring of humanity, can in nowise evade.

It is in union being effected between modern science and Christianity, by the Bible Illuminating Evolution, that the purifying power will centre, to infuse into the social organism the old truth of immortality seen through the new light that the scientific discoveries of our age reveal, into which the soul created by conscious states enters. The purifying power of science thus applied will be felt, so as to regenerate and build up the shattered social organism that is showing grievous signs of moral degeneration in selfish and egoistic tendencies. This will be the work of the future; it must be taken up by the joint alliance referred to. For this alliance will have the power in the influence both systems of truth possess of rescuing poor suffering humanity, in lifting it up through the power then fully comprehended that the gospel of atoning love imparts, to a higher and higher moral level, so that oppression will cease on earth, and justice and love take its place. In justice regulating the understanding, and love stirring the enthusiasm of the heart, it is very certain that an advanced state of civilization such as this is yet in store for the race. The reality of the promised millenium will be the fruit realized. It is not an ideal too exalted to be realized; but the conditions decreed to be accomplished by infusing into the earth-born social organism the power in active operation induced by the Redeemer's vicarious sacrifice, ending with His death, which led to His resurrection, and gives to humanity a permanent object who has partaken of its nature to worship, situated in some point of space, to whom humanity is responsible. To Him converted man can point as the source of his all-enduring power in life, and his sure portion in death. He wears the human form, and knows its weaknesses and temptations. He is, therefore, fit to illuminate modern thought, through the power and insight which Christian truth unfolds of the future of the race. This forms the cement whereby the social organism will derive a new developing impulse, so strengthening and purifying as to nullify degeneration.

The doctrine of personal immortality is the strong point of Christian power. It may animate the weakest with power divine, knowing that he, however weak, has an immortal individuality, a life ever flowing on through eternity, capable of what may be called infinite development.

In view of the two phases of truth that eventually must be amalgamated, though at present standing so far apart, we can easily anticipate the difficulty that surrounds one holding the doctrine of evolution, accepting the individual immortality that Christianity takes to do with. Having ignored revealed religion, this class sees only the living forces of intelligent life spring up and develop themselves in and through the bodily organism, as part of it, and as they reason, inseparable from it. They follow the destruction of the body undergoing corruption in the grave as organ after organ in due course, according to the tenacity of its structure, mixes indistinguishably with the surrounding soil, and see in this the subjective illusion of individual immortality (as they say) corrected by objective observation. Reasoning thus, they assert "when the functions of sense cease at death, and the mental organization that they have built up undergoes dissolution with the rest of the bodily parts, these become again a part of the whole, out of which it comes into temporary being, entering into and resuming their right in these cosmical operations whose range is outside the sense limit world of human experience." They thus assume that individual immortality must be annihilated as the result of what has taken place. Whereas, the very fact they affirm—that these forces when they resume their right in the cosmical operation as being outside the range of the sense-built world of human experience—might prove even to them how unreasonable are these assertions; when they have to do with a new quality of matter, come into existence as the life-energy of human consciousness the result of the feeling and the felt. Yea, more, the most highly endowed form of vital energy known to them, as the life-inspiring forces of human emotion, enthusiasm, and Intellect. To these the human organism and its environment gave birth, in producing these most highly endowed forms of energy, the energy of self-conservation, the equivalent of Sentient Personality. And this is the newly formed substance, to wit, which they assume, as part of the forces of nature cannot hold together its individual unit of conscious life on the death of its organism. In reasoning thus, it is the tenacity of human personality once created to maintain its individual life that this class ignore. They may reason quite right when they say the forces take the place they had before in the cosmical arrangement, if it is so. But as I have already explained, the conscious states that comprise the Ego in the human form as their correlative absorbs energy from the cosmus to maintain its life, a process which is the equivalent of Intelligence inherent in humanity. However, it may be so that the actual energy which goes to form conscious states builds itself as Sentient Personality, and liberated thus in the human form at death is the Ego. Remember I hold Lockyer's view of energy—viewing it as a quality of matter, dispersed by the sun as desiccated elements, and reduced by its heat to the condition we call Energy, so clearly demonstrated by Lockyer in "The Chemistry of the Sun."

The class referred to, by taking no account of the endurance inherent in the human vitality of self-conservation, which embodies individual immortality, ignore what to our race is of the greatest importance of all, when viewed in the light derived from the doctrine of evolution, namely, the enduring "sentiment" of self-conservation, the base of the subjective form of individual personality and the correlative of human immortality, emotion, and intellect; that is to say, the sentiment of self-conservation, in the ceaseless activities of its disembodied units is capable of feeling, of thinking, and of acting, by absorbing from its medium the energy required, which it returns in functioning. For in the human organism the truly living force, animated by the emotion of self-conservation, has attained the climax at which it can maintain its individuality as a living thing, independent of the organism at death, because its functioning power of sense and emotion does not cease on the death of the body, it only ceases to act through the body that has created it. For, individual personality was the truly living part of the body ever since its birth, being the part that feels, and therefore lives, comprising the aggregate Emotion that ensures the individual immortality of our race—a race so highly endowed with this vitality of potential energy, which starts into activity whenever an appeal is made to it by the Ego — appeals in the disembodied state provided for in the energy associated with the universal ether everywhere present.

It is marvellous how the class holding the doctrine of evolution, called materialists, can ignore the tenacity of this highly endowed form of the vitality of self-conservation, so as to deny or ignore Individual Immortality. Knowing and acknowledging, as they do, that to live is to feel, and that the tenacious emotion of self-conservation, springing into activity with every appeal made on it, thus forming a serial strain of sensations which continue to increase in building themselves up into Sentient Personality as long as the bodily organism is capable of imparting feeling. To know all this, so as to have made it intelligible to us who did not know, and yet not to have followed up the inferences by anticipating the fact that all such intelligence is held in the sentiment of self-conservation peculiar to the human Ego, capable of developing consciousness in forms of human energy on the death of the organism. These conditions comprise and retain the intelligence of the human race in the serial conscious states forming its immortal units onward since Adam. For from the stand point of the individual the world was not before he was, and the world of which he individually forms part will never cease to be represented while he lives. Such is the immortal unit created by the conditions which the subject and object gives birth to, and comprising in these individual units the immortality of the race, possessing the capacity of generating—that is absorbing—energy as I indicate.

Once more, I repeat, it is the bodily organism being capable of feeling that constitutes it a living organism. This has conferred on the human body the power of originating the ceaseless vital activity, of its own form of force, in creating its phase of emotion. For it is feeling, and not the material part of the body, that constitutes the vitality that consciousness created—Consciousness, not dependent at death on the bodily organism for its support, to enable it to continue its ceaseless activity, which rests in the vitality inherent in itself, namely, the power to feel.

To overlook facts like these, which point to the conditions that clearly illustrate individual immortality, is the great mistake that modern Christianity and modern science have made, since it has led to the scepticism of our day. In overlooking these facts, science and Christianity have become antagonistic forces, instead of conferring light and guidance in support of the truth that each system enfolds. When this is done truths will find their human explanation in terms that embrace and unite both systems.

Observe, it is Ego, the immortal vitality of Emotion and Intellect in its ceaseless activity, that feels, and which constitutes personal Immortality, that the permanent form of human intelligence rests on. Further, that this human Ego in the units of our race possess such an organism as absorbs energy, imparts vitality to it and returns it to its medium in functioning, is true. That the form is human, is also certain, but of its dimensions we can have no conception; whether the immortal forms of the unbelieving section remain attached to our planet or not, we cannot tell. What we do know is that the disembodied spirit of the Christian, in obedience to the emotion of love to its Redeemer, immediately transfers itself into the presence of its Lord. That the energies of Christians animated by this emotion are fixed in the unity of a definite aim, and are not dissipated in restless and incoherent vagaries, is true, as the expression of the natural law that regulates the Emotions when guided by Intellect, that leads to serve Christ in Love. Whereas, energy wasted in restless incoherent vagaries may be a common condition with the Ego of the unconverted, and especially true of such as ignore the doctrine of the atonement, which is of transcendent magnitude, and includes the belief in God. Those who ignore either must be in a totally different condition from those who accept both. For the Ruler of the Universe must be seen through the vicarious sacrifice He has provided, to be understood by our race.

The Belief in God was certainly the belief held by the Jews, to whom the Lord came, by whom He was reject ed, and through whose hatred He died an ignominious death. He suffered the just for the unjust, that God the Eternal might fulfil this purpose in developing the race to the fullness of its capacities, by ultimately ignoring the possibility of degeneration.

It is so that the rite of sacrifice, by which guilt was expiated or blessings gained, was one of the most remarkable and constant observations of different religious sects. This was decreed to illustrate and explain the necessity for the supreme sacrifice of the only Son of God, as the climax of the vicarious atonement. Certainly there cannot be a more rare, more pure, more costly sacrifice than that of the only-begotten Son of God. In this supreme vicarious sacrifice for the human race, the instinctive imaginative impulses of evolution have in that direction come to an end. It has reached the matchless height in the climax of the conception of sacrifice, and can never go one step farther. The permanent condition which secures the eternal development of the race is a result of the vicarious sacrifice that the Son of God has secured. In reasoning this from the stand-point of the Doctrine of Evolution, it enables us to comprehend the agency at work, in God's operations, running through all. We must consider and apprehend with clearness the fact that vicarious sacrifice is implied in the constitution of society, the very structure of which is "based upon the principle that we suffer for one another's sin, bear one another's burdens, expiate one another's errors, profit by one another's gains, gain by one another's pains." It thus comes to pass that vicarious sacrifice is an eminent law of the constitution and development of the social organism, manifesting its elementary factor in each being benefited by the gains and pains of the other. The idle, reckless, and improvident live on the fruit of the labours of the industrious, prudent, and provident. The greatest benefactors of mankind are often the martyrs of humanity. "Everywhere the same story meets us, that vicarious atonement and vicarious recompense are essential principles of social union." For vicarious sacrifice so understood stirs social development and represents the providence of God in His decrees to the race. Further, it was from a dim instinct of the operation of vicarious sacrifice in the social organism that inspired the leaders of the early social movements to adopt these rites of sacrifice which have been a marked feature in so many religions, which led up to the appreciation of the work accomplished, and yet to be accomplished by that divinely endowed being, our Lord, who was decreed to lead the race onwards through eternity.

When viewing all from the working of social evolution, led on by the decrees of God, in His providence infusing revealed truth into the social organism, which imparted to it a new and living power leading it on step by step to anticipate the individual immortality of its units. Such a phase of intellectual development is justly called a divine essence, " a thing of itself," enfolding a special form of revealed truth applicable to the conditions of the race to which it was given, which is never lost, however intermingled its form of intelligence may get in its association with human intelligence.

A phase of Intelligence which included all in the Jewish race came to be embodied in the term " Lord of Hosts," leading them onward through their pilgrimage. It reappeared in Christianity in an actual form as a man who embraced potentially " the thing in itself ;" that is, all that revealed truth ever imparted to our race was embodied in the person of our Lord Jesus Christ, who came to atone for sin by means of vicarious sacrifice, and to lead the race on through eternity.

Revelation, " the thing in itself," operating in and through social development, so moulds human intelligence, as to lead man to anticipate conditions conforming to the Decrees of God, as a phase of development whereby nature is ever being made better by those who lead the race onwards reasoning on truth already revealed—inspired to grasp a truth which embodies a higher ideal, an ideal which a section of the race would strive to attain as the condition revelation leads up to. In this way the prophet developed for the race a higher ideal conception than those previously held.

Take special notice, that all rest in, and spring from, revealed truth. With this clearly realised, it will be seen how revelation acting through human intelligence, operates in the social organism by enabling man to anticipate conditions which will determine social development in the right direction. Animated thus, the Old Testament prophets were inspired to predict our Lord's sufferings and death. Isaiah specially had the key that unlocked prophetic revelation, in reasoning on what he felt and knew of the race. Isaiah thus so clearly foretold the conditions of what would be accomplished by our Lord in His life and death, as to induce some of those who do not believe in a revelation to suggest that Isaiah must have been describing a case which he had witnessed himself. Whereas, the case was, that as a genius of the race, Isaiah, animated by inspiration, anticipated the conditions decreed to be accomplished by our Lord, so clearly indicated in Isaiah liii. and lv.

On reasoning on the past, the present, and the future of his race, the prophet anticipated all this, and much yet to be understood in the 54th chapter that intervenes, and led on to Christianity being universally accepted by the race, so as to nullify oppression. Then it will be said with the sincerity that springs from conviction, that nature developed the means whereby nature was made better, in the only-begotten of the Father seen to be working in and through nature, in revelation to our race, as the influence determining all true and lasting development.

In so far as the unsaved portion of the race is concerned, the case would be correctly stated thus. That "the organism of humanity having reached a certain stage of development, gave birth to a supremely endowed organ, by the functions of which its future development was determined in the right direction," by infusing the moral which insured true social progress. "The supreme atonement was the personification and glorification of the social principle of vicarious sacrifice." The ideal conception conveyed in these words viewed from the broadest point of the social development our race has attained—a race greatly strengthened by the belief in and worship of a personal God—included the whole series of Intellectual, Emotional, and Moral Development, whereby the influence, in the antecedent condition of our Lord's history, viewed as the races developing intelligence, was leading it onwards and upwards as a purely human instrument in a general way, being to our race the supremely endowed organ whose function was such.

But to the Jewish race, to whom our Lord ultimately came, the influence of the organ referred to was much more, in so enlightening their phase of intelligence, as to enable the prophet to predict conditions to be realised thousands and thousands of years after, nay, even at the end of the world. One climax in the intervening series predicted is close at hand, when the religion the rejected King of the Jews gave birth to, namely Christianity, will be universally accepted as the permanent religion of the race, led onwards by the rejected King, the child of Mary, but the Son of God. He, in the concrete, embodies all forms of revelation, whether unfolded to Jew or Gentile.

In the ideal conception of a personal God everywhere present, a final ideal conception of God had been reached, beyond which it was impossible for human thought to go. It included the recognition of one God, the maker of heaven and earth, who orders and governs all things by laws which, viewed by human reason, are the manifestation of His will. Now, the very end that revelation had in view was to lead man to form this conception of God as the last—the most exalted—of the series that all forms of revelation lead up to, and the highest which the human intellect can grasp. The mental operations of the human intellect is to generalise and to infer. Therefore it led to anticipate one God ruling everywhere. This being realized is the very end attained by a revelation given, which God in His fore-knowledge had decreed.

As it has been said, the unifying impulses at work in the human mind procured the base on which the mental operation rested. It is man's nature to make for himself some sort of mental synthesis of the world around him in order to live in it. For man must bind phenomena into a unity of some form, as it is binding phenomena into unity that gives continuity, and enables one to act methodically in his relations in life. Development would be impossible either morally or intellectually apart from the unity of synthesis. God, the Creator from whom matter emanated, has so ordered it that unifying impulses are indeed instinct in living matter both in its conscious and unconscious relations, therefore organic life is a form of synthesis, and the human mind is no exception. The body in every part is a synthesis, for each organ is so, and each element in each organ is a synthesis. Organic life is kept up by the increase synthesis indicates. In like manner is mind, which reflects nature in being its counterpart or its correlative, which is necessarily a form of the synthesis of unifying impulses.

However, synthesis in an untutored mind is more the child of feeling and character than that of intellect. For to mind, emotion and passion are the forms of the primary unifying impulses; it is even so, that unifying impulses go to build up the sciences. This has led to the growing conception formed by anticipating the unity of all science. The magnitude of such a conception has even kindled in the philosopher's bosom an outburst of emotion; and well may the unifying emotion of success thus proclaim the approval of such an exalted "subjective creation" of the purely human unifying impulses of man, a result attained by man using his senses to the best of his ability. The senses are justly called man's five gateways of knowledge, whereby man has unfolded the unifying operation at work by God, the great Originator of nature, apparent in the laws of nature. The base of all is the unifying impulse, the essential principle of life, and of individuality. For the body, with its brain and nervous system, creating the immortal Ego, is a synthesis, each organ a putting together, and each element a putting together. Organic life itself is constituted and kept up by the increase of its form of synthesis.

However, apart from the fact that mind—the human Ego—is immortal in its units, as a product of human nature, even the exalted forms of subjective creation, which spring from the scientific investigation of human intellect, directed toward matter and its laws, they might, for all we know, be void of foundation in objective reality. They are just the result attained from the unifying process that arose from nature affecting the human organism through its five senses. But, as the units in the Ego are immortal, and continue to use these five senses, their conception of matter may change. Yet matter in some form must and will be the surrounding medium that continues to affect these senses and to be known as such by the human intellect that it created in creating consciousness or conscious states on earth. Viewing the creation and growth of the Intellect as a unifying process, how magnificent is the result attained in the con-

R

ception formed of God—as the self-subsistence—who gives unity to the universe. It is true that by the limitation of man's faculties, it is impossible for him to think, and interpret the universe, save in terms of himself. This being so, he unavoidably limits God, the so-called unknown power, when he tries to form a conception of Him, because man's limit is the limit of humanity, finite in its range. Though in reasoning on what is revelation, man does feel the energy outside knowledge working in him, giving impulses and aspirations that he can recognise to be through his Redeemer God.

Viewing the subject from the point of Evolution Illuminating the Bible, and the Bible itself thereby illuminates Evolution, it is clearly perceptible that once the conception was formed of God giving unity to the Universe, this idea opened up the way for the progressive power of the Intellect forming the conception of God, giving His only Son to redeem the race—a conception realised in the person of our Lord. He alone since His humanity brings the Divine within the compass of human intelligence, in giving to the Divine being a magnificent human personality, a character, and a name, of whom we can say man is made in His image. For our Redeemer God is animated by human nature, bears the human form, and imparts to the race the conception of a God of Love, who has procured its redemption through the vicarious sacrifice of His only-begotten Son. This only-begotten Son, the divine personality which personifies revelation, who is also its origin and source, is therefore truly Divine. Even now the permanent object who supplies the subject the Ego with an objective existence capable of developing forms of human intelligence that the Ego can comprehend, having in this conception of our Lord, what constitutes the permanent object, the equivalent of a permanent subject, in form supplying the condition on which conscious states depend, as the equivalent of sustaining and developing the Ego. The Ego was created of change of states. It demands for its further development a subject and an object, that is an Ego and a non-Ego. In our Lord the race has thus a permanent non-Ego or objective existence — recognisable as the source or flow of life, including also Divine Intelligence.

The divine flow of intellectual aspiration imparted by our Lord to the race will through eternity provide that race, as well as the Universe, with the objective source that intelligence depends on to sustain it, which takes the form of the non-Ego, in supplying the impulses from without. Thus, our Lord and His surroundings supply the condition on which human Intelligence rests and develops, by providing for it a permanent objective source of perception. It flows from one who can comprehend humanity, for He has taken its form and nature, the exact image of the creature man. In so far our Lord is a human intelligence, being conditioned by our nature, and capable of comprehending and imparting intelligent conceptions to it. This being so, the cosmogony, the Universe, in that part of it which expresses itself through human nature, the product of that part of nature which is, and is being humanized in man's development, has in man, in union with our Lord, a new and purely human development, having a genuine human solid base, where the true, the good, and the beautiful will unite, and in uniting will find in the God of Humanity a higher and yet higher phase of development on through Eternity. Thus, then, the Divine, though outside human intelligence, will express itself through Human intelligence imparted by our Lord, who is specially the developing intelligence of our race, and in a general way of the Universe.

Let it be understood as an axiom of my creed, that it was the divine nature of our Lord originally operating from time to time that produced the intellectual conceptions imparted by Revelation to our race. The Divine Being comprehended by the Jewish race in the Ideal conception of "The Lord of Hosts," was represented by Him, and at a later stage, took a human form in the processes and sensations that led to the conceptions and birth of our Lord by the Virgin Mary, and on through His life, death, and resurrection, in providing the vicarious sacrifice that ensures man's redemption, by imparting a new sentiment, that induces man to serve God in love. Our Lord, viewed in the concrete, was the origin of all. All that was ever revealed to our race was a "thing in itself," capable of being rendered intelligible in human language, yet not limited by human nature, because Divine in its origin.

Further, mind created and developed by the organism and its environments, is likewise a "thing in itself," capable of existing independent of the human body.

CHAPTER XI.

HUMAN DEPRAVITY FINDS ITS ANTIDOTE IN CHRISTIANITY.

THE conception of human depravity as advanced by some students of sociology, is confirmed by scriptural evidence, and finds in Christianity its Antidote. Therefore human depravity is a matter of much importance, when viewed from the standpoint of social development. The question that arises is, can anything approaching to a scientific explanation of the case be attempted. Viewed as a social unit, man's depravity arises from his nature, which leads him to seek his own advancement, in striving to secure a personal end, when indifferent to the pain this course would cause others. This understood as man's nature is the force seen to be operating in the laws of social degeneration.

Society has attained to a comparatively high moral development, by strengthening the tie of sympathy which secures social well-being by adding luxuries to comforts. This condition which usually leads to ease, in one class exacting more than the other is willing (or, it may be, justified) to give. Then the intellectual combination of which the moral element is formed falls into disuse, because an organ not kept in constant use functioning, so as to preserve the tie of sympathy unbroken in welding all classes together. For degeneration begins here. It leads to envy, jealousy, and hatred, in setting class against class. Whereas, true social development rests in the sympathy that binds all classes closely together—and generates individual contentment in the universal well-being of all. And assuredly we have the germ of degeneration in the moral element not being kept in constant use functioning. " Disuse of function leads everywhere to decay of organ; by decay of organ going on through generations, that which was complete and capable becomes rudimentary and incapable." The same law holds good in the moral structure whether you view that structure as seen collectively in the social organism, or in man individually. In the process of the backward course, the moral structure may reach an extreme state of degeneration.

Degeneration, take note, is used exclusively to denote a change from a higher to a lower moral state. It is of interest to note that national degeneration begins in what is strictly demoralising—notably in the loss of "patriotism, which inspires self-abnegation and the sacrifice of individual interest to the good of the community, which consolidates a nation. In like manner, in the individual, it is the function of will in the highest moral sphere—the region of moral feeling which, representing the highest reach of evolution, is the consummate inflorescence of human culture—that will be the first to exhibit signs of impairment; the latest and highest product of social evolution, that which is latest organised, is least stable, will be the first to undergo dissolution."—Maudsley. It thus comes to pass, that individual degeneration commences in the region of moral feeling, which represents the highest reach of evolution—the highest point of human culture. As moral feeling is the latest and highest product of social evolution, and as such is the organ less stable, it will therefore be the first to exhibit signs of impairment, so as to undergo a process of dissolution if allowed to fall into disuse. When this is so, poor suffering humanity is being deprived of its only support—the sympathy that moral feeling develops. That the facts of observation agree with this is very certain, and we may find in the healing virtue vital Christianity provides, an antidote for Human depravity.

With man there are two terms between which all sorts of variations may be ranged—namely, the lowest term of moral degeneration and the highest term of evolution. This concerns us all, for towards one or other of these points each individual is tending. "Some persons are high on the upward, others low on the downward path. Many are just entering upon the one or the other; but there is no one who is not himself going in the one or other direction, and making the way which he takes easier for others to follow in." For example is one of the most powerful stimulating factors either to induce social development or lead to social degeneration. When we view man as the organic unit, and the social organism formed of such units—depending on sympathy for the unity of its harmony—this brings home to the mind the necessity of taking a scientific view of moral defects, and of a scientific inquiry into their nature. Man may show no defect of ordinary intelligence, even when the moral degeneration is extreme. This serves to show how the fine layer of moral feeling, and the supreme reason imbedded in it, so to speak, may be deranged, or clean stripped off from the mind. This is the sure indication of social degeneracy, though the ordinary intelligence is not seriously touched.

As social evolution really rests on the advance made individually in the moral development of its units, the sad result observation seems to point to is, that moral degeneration of one generation will generate, in the succeeding generation, probable mental derangement, madness, or crime; and in a third generation moral imbecility or idiocy. Such Ideal conceptions serve to mark the main line in the course of degeneration. Though, as a matter of course, such may be modified greatly in many ways, as well as completely checked by the effect produced through the sentiment vital Christianity infuses, in the "New Birth," taking full possession and providing a new mental structure of high moral worth in the intellectual combinations that the Christian doctrine of rescue by substitution unfolds. Christianity, however, is in a way outside the subject matter in hand. As at the present phase of social development, its students take too little or no account of the power revealed truth actually possesses. This being so, the broad lesson that remains has been stated thus—"That the acquired infirmity of one generation will, unless counteracted by breed or surroundings, brought to bear meanwhile, become the natural deficiency of a succeeding generation."

Note, in this series we have the processes indicated in the moral law explained and confirmed by scientific investigation in the iniquity of the fathers being visited upon the children unto the third and fourth generation. "In the fathers having eaten sour grapes, the children's teeth are set on edge."

The sins of the fathers are, indeed, visited on the children, leading to social results in cause and consequence, so operating as to enable a rational explanation to be forthcoming of the decrees of God. When viewed from the standpoint of inherited tendencies, " that there are laws of hereditary action working definitely in direct transmission of qualities, or indirectly through combination and physical constitution of every individual, that a good result ensues in one case, a bad result in another." These are conditions clearly stated resting in established facts. Fully to understand the consequences involved in the laws operating, it must be clearly understood and ever borne in mind, that man is following the action that his natural life leads to, when acting selfishly, because his nature leads him to pursue a personal pleasure and repel a personal pain. It was his case being so that called for the necessity of Divine interposition, if the race which is immortal was to be rescued and purified in one portion as a human instrument, being led on through eternity by its God of Humanity. The other portion, redeemed through substitution by the only-begotten of the Father, are led on as adopted children of God. This is evidently the future in store for our race.

It is certain as the result of the vital activities of our nature, that we, as the creatures of defective parents, are fairly degenerated before being generated in the sentiment of our individual being, "self-conservation," which demands that its life will be continued under happy conditions. This could only be secured by nullifying the struggle that leads to all forms of social disorder, and ends in degeneration. For, had the infant in arms a giant's strength in its outburst of transcendent passion, in going into a rage, when it is to be washed, it would be as destructive and dangerous as any mad man—it is the helplessness of its body that renders it innocent. The activities that exist are not for the most part innocent, the real germ at work is seen in the fact that children are "naturally boastful, scornful, passionate, envious, selfish, idle, prone to steal, apt at dissimulation, and ready liars; easily moved to immoderate joy, or thrown into excessive grief by trifles; not willing themselves to suffer, but eager and pleased to inflict suffering. It is a description that would suit well for savages in a low state of civilisation, though no one would be vehemently eager to ascribe purity and innocence to them." The truth is, if you take away from the child the potentiality of moral development, you leave the natural passions and instinct free play. "Not the fundamental instincts of animal nature only, but the secondary or acquired egoistic passions" into which the complex social state, with its different interests, have got infused through the development primary instincts have undergone. "To lie, to counterfeit, to deceive, to envy, to hate, to steal, to devise cunning means of gratifying sense or instinct, are human enough qualities; everybody may, I suppose, be said truly to be a potential liar, a potential thief, a potential adulterer, even a potential murderer; since whatever sinner any man has been, every man needs to pray that he may not be." It is in these words that Dr. Maudsley points to the utter depravity of human nature.

This utter depravity is set forth by revealed truth as succeeding the disobedience of the fall. This is an obscure event that might be made a little more intelligent, by inferring—what is likely true—that in the universe of space there are myriads of intelligent beings, animated by a form of vitality similar to that of our race, whose natural developments and surroundings are also similar. But to them a revelation has not been made. Yet they are placed in contrast with our race, to whom God had manifested himself, in entering into a covenant of works with man, in terms of "do this and live"—conditions which those of our race concerned violated and fell, and consequently led the way to the degeneration of a race which, but for this disobedience and fall, might have progressed by a process of continuous development all through eternity. Now, it is by placing our race, with such a history, in contrast with other races of intelligent beings similarly surrounded and animated, and, it may be, with some of whom God entered into a similar covenant, which they kept, thus proving what was possible for human nature put in contrast with our race who fell.

The section of the Christian race, though now redeemed through divine intervention, yet, alas ! manifesting a form of human nature so depraved as that referred to by Dr. Maudsley as applicable to a Christian nation where Christian influence has been at work for many centuries, over a thousand years. Yet many depraved thus believe in the birth, death, and resurrection of our Lord, as the only-begotten of the Father sent to redeem the race. How sad this condition would appear placed in contrast with a race similarly endowed, who had secured its own religious and moral perfection. Yet, doubtless, all such contrasts, if they exist, are decreed of God henceforth to lead to higher and higher individual development.

What most concerns us is that, after nearly 2000 years of Christian influence on our planet, an influence sufficiently strong to have neutralised among its adherents human depravity by inducing a new mental structure so animated by love to the Redeemer, and sympathy for the unsaved race, as to produce a community whose lives were in harmony with Gospel teaching. But, alas! the real social condition, fair and impersonal authors such as Maudsley found surrounding is truly a most depraved type. How different the conditions might have been, is proved by the Law of Zoology illuminating the law at work in inherited tendencies which long ere now might have clean swept away from the brain the structures that induce a selfish impure life, by developing structures which would induce such a life as the converted believer enters at death, unselfish and pure, arising from the sentiment he carries with him, so strengthened by Love to the Redeemer, as to bind in sympathy and harmony all the redeemed—yes, redeemed by conditions that demanded the blood of the only-begotten Son of God. For so depraved is our race, that the class of men I refer to find it, by observation, so utterly depraved as to corroborate the truth the Bible reveals of the depravity of human nature, and it therefore provides an antidote. Facts thus confirmed by the modern student of natural philosophy can no longer admit the possibility of any reasonable man honestly doubting the truth revealed, pointing out the necessity that rested on the Creator of the race of providing a rescue. This truth is a self-evident axiom.

We, therefore turn to truth unfolded in the Christian records to find such a rescue fully provided, in the vicarious sacrifice of the only-begotten of the Father. He, through the merits of His son, infuses at conversion a new sentiment into the individual, thus born again, which changes his nature by inducing him to find his pleasures in glorifying Christ, his Deliverer; in helping poor suffering humanity by deeds of kindness. It is the old old story, told in nature and unfolded in grace, which proves the healing virtue of vicarious suffering, and it finds its climax in the effect produced in the work accomplished by our Lord—a self-sacrificing form of work henceforth to be repeated by His people, so that the race may be gathered in. Now, there can be no reasonable doubt of human depravity, nor of the necessity for a deliverer. And when Christianity anticipated the conditions that the student of sociology proclaims of human depravity, and provides the remedy—" the antidote"—the sceptical tendency of the age is compelled to pause and listen. And if such evidence is rejected, it is in the face of appalling consequences.

Viewing the complex social development that surrounds us, it is well to take special note that the downward process of endowing commences with enfeebled moral feeling. It could not be otherwise, when the altruistic impulse is formed out of social fusion, and transmutation of the egoistic impulses. Moral action is far from an instinct in any, even in the very best. But moral energy in an instinct form would have been established in Christendom long ere now, if the sentiment that springs of "faith working by Love," had been cultivated so as to have its structure transmitted by the law of inheritance, in the form that gives stability and strength when kept in constant exercise. This course would have given the intellectual combination thereof the stability of instinct. Whereas, even among the best of Christians in taking a moral course which causes them pain there is almost always the consciousness of a desire to take the opposite course, which has to be resisted before the moral action contemplated is performed. Thus far human depravity has not found its antidote in Christianity, inspired by sentiments that seek Christ's glory as its final end.

The fact, even now is, apart from a few high-typed Christians, that if the evil imagination of the natural heart was laid bare, there would be good evidence for saying that men naturally hate each other. When the secrets of all hearts are laid open, there will be a sad display of evil thoughts having passed through the mind of the best of men. Thoughts, indeed, that they would shrink with horror from letting the tongue put into words and would willingly have resisted if they could.

But, alas, depraved human nature is such, and as such

has been graphically defined by our Lord in the words of "out of the heart of man proceed evil thoughts, adulteries, fornications, murders, thefts, covetousness, an evil eye, blasphemy, pride, foolishness. All these evil things come from within and defile the man."—Mark vii. 22 23. Yet, notwithstanding this, if "faith working by love," had been cultivated, the case would have been quite different among Christians long ere the 19th century dawned.

For there is no reasonable doubt, viewed in the light of present knowledge, but that the capacity of the purely organic constructive energy of the brain, which each of us possesses for good or ill, is a definite measurable proportion decreed of God, whereby we individually can add to the sum-total of the social development of our day or retard it in inducing degeneration. The possible good in us is the energy of development, the possible bad the energy of degeneration. For, as has been said, "not" to exercise and to grow in exercise of one's better nature, is to exercise and to grow to the exercise of one's worse nature. There is no standing still. However, what is of real interest to us individually now, is how near we have approached to the limit of the possible good in us; not how much one does more than another, but how near each has approached to the limit of his or her capacity for good. Bearing in mind that individual human life is the moving force ever in motion which does not cease at death, but gains in activity when the bodily organism is then thrust aside as a worthless garment. Thus, then, where death finds us, judgment must find us. Because the Soul or Ego is the product of the life on earth, the energy generated as consciousness, which we have to give an account of, and can neither add to or substract from the sum-total thereof. As this life—this form of vital energy—was developed by the bodily organism and its environments, which will never occupy the same position again, it must therefore be that where death finds us, the judgment, which demands an account of the deeds done in the body, will find us.

It is through the muscular or nervous system that the external world is built up in us, and is represented in the organic Ego, as it has been moulded by the fit muscular action of habitual internal states. This being so, we can never again be placed in this external condition, so judgment must meet us at the point where the actual Ego parts with the organic Ego, which is part of the bodily organism—nothing can be more certain than this. If evidence is wanted in proof of the materialistic process at work building up the organic Ego, the following paragraph of Dr. Maudsley's will suffice. His words are, " It is through the eye mainly that we take in or apprehend the world, so it is through the eye that the world, as we have apprehended it, looks out; or, speaking more correctly, as it is through the muscular system that the external world is built up in us, so the world, as it has been built up, is expressed in the whole bodily features, as they have been moulded by the fit muscular actions of habitual internal states. He is a poor medical psychologist who cannot see idiocy in the walk as well as in the talk of his patient; and he will be a very expert psychologist in time to come who shall read a full knowledge of the whole character of any individual in his gait, carriage, conformation, features, and look. With that reflection I take leave of the idiot."

That judgment is in store for the individual and race is certain, but viewed from the standpoint of surroundings and influence of inherited instinct, individual responsibility is in so far considerably lessened. It is a fact of observation, that mental degeneration in one generation is sometimes an innate deficiency or absence of moral sense in the succeeding generation; add to this the fact that moral feeling is the first function of mind to be affected at the commencement of mental degeneration in the individual. These are observed facts which in one way lessen individual responsibility, and in another increase it.

However, what does increase general responsibility is the observed fact that as man begins to degenerate alike as individual, as family, as society, as nation, as humanity, the moral feeling takes the lead in the downward course. To know this certainly does increase the responsibility of all, in indicating the value of moral feeling more and more in its operation on the race, apart from the after consequences to the individual.

It is a point of much importance to those who believe in revealed religion to know that the moral taught therein is proved by the student of sociology to be essential for securing race development. Facts such as these assuredly secure for revealed religion a scientific base, similar in its nature to the base on which natural science rests. Pointing out to the natural man how he can secure a desirable immortal place among nature's sons, by obeying the covenant of works—"Do this and live:"—or, act well your part—and rejoicing, live in helping forward the development of thy race. In the precept taught by revealed truth thus rendered, surely we are justified in claiming for it the scientific base that its own phase of truth unfolds—which is demonstrated by the natural form of the moral law. Further evidence is supplied in the fact that the moral nature of an habitual drunkard is wholly depraved, put in contrast with 1 Cor. vi.

10, as one of the class that cannot inherit the kingdom of heaven, because his moral nature (as well as the other named) is utterly depraved—anti-social. In this form how could he inherit eternal life, that is, get possession thereof by right. For the term inherent implies having a right to the condition. Whereas, a good man as a social unit assuredly does earn this immortal right as one of the sons of nature, though the drunkard, with his class named therein, covetous, revilers, extortioners, can have no right. —1 Cor. vi. 10. In proof of the habitual drunkard's moral depravity, I quote Maudsley again, who says, " Nowhere is to be found a more miserable specimen of degeneration, of moral feeling, and of impotence of will, than is presented by the person who has become the abject slave of either (alcohol or opium) pernicious indulgence. His finest moral sensibilities are extinguished and his least fine blunted. Steadily sensitive to his own selfish wants, and persistent to gratify them, he is insensible of the feeling and claims of his family, whose dearest interests he sacrifices without real compensation, and indifferent to the obligations and responsibilities of his social position; he will often profess you very fine sentiments, and perhaps indulge in the pleasant debauchery of a visionary imagination, inspired by intensely egoistic feeling and stimulated by the drug, but uncontrolled by realities, the disciplinary and disagreeable hold of which the drug has deaded or destroyed; for the most part he is untruthful and untrustworthy, and in the worst end there is not a meanness of pretence or of conduct he will not descend to, not a lie he will not tell, not a degredation he will not undergo, scarce a fraud he will not perpetrate, in order to gratify his absorbing craving." It is the condition that leads to such depravity that revealed religion denounces in saying that no drunkard can enter the kingdom of heaven (that is, earn the right to enter). And if the case was different, few would care to enter the kingdom. And does not the moral degeneration indicated throw clear light in providing cause and consequence, which proves why revelation prohibits those morally depraved from inheriting eternal life (or geting it by right), because the life they have lived has so depraved their moral nature as to unfit them. However, it is with much pity we should view the case of one who has inherited the original taint, so that once the craving for drink is stirred in him it is kindled into an uncontrollable desire, likely to lead to his certain ruin. How sad to think of a parent leaving this vile heritage to his child. However, this corroborates revelation in providing another link in the chain of evidence in proving, so as to demonstrate the fact, that the parents' sins are visited on their children.

"Habitual criminals are a class of beings whose lives are sufficient proof of the absence or great bluntness of moral sense. It is the common experience, and the common testimony of those who have much to do with these anti-social varieties of the human kind, that a certain proportion of them are of distinctly weak intellect. . . . Their fate is, indeed, a hard one — congenital outcasts from the social organisation by the pre-ordination of the society that has produced them. It is, nevertheless, demanded of them that they should conform to the laws of a body of which they are not part, but from which they are a part." Sad it is to see a class thus situated; yet it is sadder far to know that two or three generations of habitual drunkards leave to their children the inheritance of an enfeebled intellect and impaired moral sense, thus adding to the criminal class. Sad, yet true this is. For we know that defective moral sense leads to moral degeneration, which means undoing the structure that mental evolution has built up, and that the moral life Christianity enjoins means building up the mental edifice which conforms to mental evolution. Such is the self-improvement Christian life leads to, by furthering mental evolution, in building up a structure that ensures individual and race development. For Christian life and work cuts at the root of egoism, intemperance, vanity, envy, &c. Now, we all know that envy certainly corrodes the mental structure, and eats out the good character, as does suspicion and other such tendencies. Whereas, Christian life and work provides the antidote in doing the work of evolution, and retarding race degeneration. Thus, then, to the student of sociology such conditions as the building up process of the social organism enjoined by Christianity, and put in contrast with the anti-social course man in his natural state is prone to follow, greatly add to the guilt of a man of intelligence, if he refuses to accept or seriously consider the claim put forward by Christianity to be of divine origin. For the tendency that weakens this claim, in generating unbelief, and many evils, leads to social disruption and all the ills that follow, being an anti-social force.

An early stage in the down grade is seen to be in corrupt men uniting together in order to gain their end at the cost, and often in the ruin of the ignorant and unwary, whom they delude and defraud. Yet the immoral course adopted does not overwhelm the guilty authors in infamy. So base a condition as this does the complex social organism breed in itself as the elements on which such corrupt anti-social creeds flourish in it. The worst feature of all is that the wrong-doer so often goes wholly unpunished. But the time is close at hand when the delusion entertained that evil deeds can go unpunished will cease. For evolution illuminated by Christianity will unfold the material nature of the mental organ in such a way as will leave no doubt that it is impossible for man to conceal any thought or action of his life, or to escape the consequences thereof, in so far as he is responsible. All this follows as the natural sequence, in his soul having been formed of his mental states on earth. His character in his soul-formation will represent him after death to all, exactly as he is. The evolution on earth that accompanies these accepted facts will be to purify the corrupt mental organ by the influence produced in the Christian doctrine taking to do with man as an immortal unit, capable of continuous progressive development, yet responsible for his actions on earth, the consequences of which do not end with his earthly life. For the Christianity of the future will be moulded by the operation of the materialistic views which will explain all mental terms in forms of matter.

Materialism, as the equivalent of the objective world, thus confirming the materialism held by our Lord, and so prominently taught in all His parables, but especially so in "Lazarus and the rich man" who begs a drop of water to cool his burning throat and tongue.—Luke xvi. 19-31.

With man and his destiny, when all mental states are explained in terms and forms of the energy of matter in intellectual combination as the result of human life and its laws, the short thread of earthly life will be realised as the beginning of a never-ending progressing life, where man's eternal prospects are affected by the course he took on earth.

When all this is clearly seen by the light in which the materialistic views of matter and mind will be rendered intelligent in time and eternity, man will begin in earnest to contract new forms of thought, which will generate higher moral feeling and its equivalent action, in response to his self-regarding interest, as viewed from the immortal standpoint. That such is the true sequence in the history of natural man is certain.

It is also true that the same fact will quicken Christian activity hundreds of fold. Then the Church of the firstborn will clearly perceive the end to which their birthright in Christ leads, as regenerated units, immortally united to God in love by His Son as their spiritual and material Lord, Mediator, and Redeemer. He is a Mediator in virtue of being a sharer in the natures of both the parties between whom He mediated. Our Lord was both human and divine. Thus, then, the Redeemer shares our nature and God's nature, and therefore human depravity finds its antidote in Christianity. He infuses the divine nature into us, first in being united to us in the new birth, followed by the efficacy of absorbing the truth unfolded in the promises which have a divine origin. These combined actions are the process through which Christians become partakers of God's nature, and in eternity will act accordingly, and which may remove Christians far from their human kind, both in organic form and intelligence. For whatever God is, members of the Church of the first-born may become. Their characters being such, their nature, and therefore their Will-energy in volition, will give expression to the Divine in them, working, it may be, after the earthly model, whereby the co-ordination of their mental functions necessary to effect this has been attained. But to understand this, we must perceive with clearness what Will-energy means, is it the "conscious expression of the co-ordination of mental functions working to an end; that co-ordination imperfect, will is imperfect; exact and complete, will reaches its highest quality and energy, its highest functional expression, in the particular person."—Dr. Maudsley. And in possession of such exact and complete wills are the particular persons of the church of the first-born in heaven, animated by the divine nature carrying out the decrees of their Lord, Mediator, the Redeemer, God. But on earth, while the character is being formed, Christian experience is disruption of co-ordination in disruption of Will-energy—thus does Evolution Illuminate the Bible. And of this form of disruption was the struggle so graphically defined by St. Paul as his experience in Rom .vii. 15-25, as he strove to give conscious expression to the co-ordinating mental function working towards a desired end, by getting the divine nature in him into the harmony that seeks only the glory of God, and in this way takes the place of human nature whose action is to serve self. He thus creates anew co-ordinating mental structure to give conscious expression in functioning of his individual Will-energy in harmony with the spiritual teaching enjoined by his Redeemer God. Assuredly in this co-ordinating process human nature finds its antidote in Christ.

What I have said of the divine nature working after a human model, will be made plain in the rendering of Will-energy understood and applied to sift cause and consequence, so as to provide a clear conception of the nature of the mental struggle to which Christians are subject in their effort to adopt the non-resistance creed, enjoined by the covenant of grace. This process, when placed in contrast with corrupt human nature, as every student of biology will see, requires a new mental structure of a totally different mould to give expression to the new form of Will-energy the non-resistance creed requires. It thus comes to pass, that during a period of Christian life, the inhabited co-ordinating mental centres are sadly impaired, and greatly hinder carrying out the precepts indicated in Christian life and work. St. Paul's case, a typical one, was this. The energy of will-force was constantly meeting with a resisting force, which neutralised the mental function working toward the end he desired. So much was this realised as to draw the bitter cry from him of "O wretched man that I am, who shall deliver me from the body of this death," to be followed by the indwelling reaction habitual to one in close fellowship with his Redeemer God, therefore able to perceive the strength imparted in all times of need by the glorious anticipation of insured success in "I thank God through Jesus Christ our Lord,—I can do all things. So then with the mind I myself serve the Law of God; but with the flesh the law of sin. For in truth, there is therefore no condemnation to those who are in Jesus Christ."—Rom. vii. 25; viii. 1.

> "Here conscience ends its strife,
> And faith delights to prove,
> The sweetness of the bread of life,
> The fulness of Thy Love."

The causation of such a mental state as the warfare of the new nature indicated, before the co-ordination was attained, is fully explained by the student of biology in the complex mental organ that has to give way so as to admit of a more effective one that ensures race development in moral action to take its place. For the action of "the flesh," the body of sin, St. Paul so bitterly lamented, meant the corrupt forces of human nature, giving expression to the egoistic tendency, as viewed from the Christian standpoint, called our cardinal nature, which had built up the complex mental structure St. Paul was striving so hard to pull down, so as to have the new structure take its place which would function in the direction he wished, and thus give conscious expression to the co-ordination of mental function working towards the desired end.

Such a flood of light as this is opened up in St. Paul's experience, when read in the light illuminating Will-energy in the rendering, supplied by Dr. Maudsley, in giving the rational explanation of the mental combination to which volition is justly applied; so as to enable the converted Christian to place corrupt human nature in contrast with the self-sacrificing life Christ enjoins converted corrupt man to adopt, in building up the requirements of a new life-action, ensured when doing so, that "there is no condemnation to them that are in Christ Jesus."—Rom. viii. 1. By the mind resting here, much, of the mental struggle ceases, in the calm assurance arising from the converted believer serving Christ in Love. However, in the contest the struggle is explained, that must take place, extinguishing the old corrupt egoistic tendency, in the structure and sentiment enjoined by our Lord taking its place. It shortly is, the new Adam—formed of the forces generated by "being in Christ Jesus," therefore a partaker of the benefits arising from His vicarious sacrifice—taking the place of the old Adam acting under the covenant of works in "Do this and live." This command corrupt human nature failed to fulfil. The new Adam at death is free from the encumbrance of the bodily organism, and will act in harmony with the sentiment that animates the "inner man" in the human form that survives death. Will-force will then give expression to the actual character as the co-ordinated forces working towards the desired end, viz., that of glorifying God in Christ in obedience to the Law of Love unencumbered by corrupt human nature.

Just a word to show more fully how Will-energy, in its co-ordinating process, may have been the acting agent decreed to procure the birth of the promised child Isaac, in the effect produced on both parents in the promise conveyed by special revelation that they were to have a son, in the mental functioning power of Will-energy imparting the needed strength from within. For assuredly the forces to do so are present in the blood if they could be got to take the right direction. That in this case the forces were so directed seems proved in the fact of Abraham afterwards being the father of a large family. Thus, then, we shall say a miracle was effected in the birth of Isaac through the operation of conscious will guiding the co-ordinating mental function working to attain the special end promised by a personal God in whom infinite belief in His power to fulfil what He had promised was fully realized, and so operated on the bodily organism as to produce, in both parents, the fulfillment of the condition anticipated. As it is, modern science, unfolds cause and consequence in such a way as to show how the end could be secured, and we will do well to listen to what the diligent student of mental pathology says in the future, if we wish to understand Revelation.

It is by the diligent study of the facts of mental pathology that we obtain an intelligent conception of the process mental states spring from in forming the Ego, the immortal part. For pathology gives us an idea of the nature of the mental organism as a great organic growth, whether viewed in the particular person or in the race, giving expression to human intelligence as its co-ordinating function, which we could not otherwise have. Once having formed such a conception, we cannot fail to apprehend the "exquisitely fine and intricately complex organisation which is the physical basis of mind, every interest of the entire body, every organic energy, has direct or indirect representation; there is nothing in the outermost that is not, so to speak, represented in the innermost. Not one organ, but all organs; not one structure, but all structures; not one movement, but all movements; not one feeling, but all feelings: all vibrations of energy, of what sort soever, from all parts of the body, the nearest and the most remote; the meanest and most noble; conscious and infraconscious, stream into the unifying centre, and make their felt or unfelt contribution to the outcome of conscious functions. The brain is the central organ of the bodily synthesis, sympathy, and synergy; and the will at its best the supreme expression of that unity. Therefore it is that in will is contained character; not character of mind only, as commonly understood, but the character of every organ of the body, the consentient functions of which enter into the full expression of individuality.

This being so, it is made evident that disorganisation of the union of the supreme cerebral centres must be more or less a dissolution of the conscious self, the Ego, according to the depths of the damage to the physiological unity."
—Maudsley.

These words bring out with much clearness what is known of the physical basis of mind in the particular person, especially so when taken in connection with the ideas advanced and demonstrated by Dr. Luys in the mode of study he has adopted to illustrate the brain and its functions.

The work of the physical base of mind being to create the immortal Ego with which revelation takes to do, and which joins with Evolution in proclaiming human depravity, which finds in Christianity its antidote, so as to understand the stability of the immortal part, when viewed from the standpoint of the materialistic conception conveyed by Pathology; we have first to remember that it is from this complex organic physical base of mind that the immortal part is evolved; further, that during the period of its evolution—that is during the earthly life of the individual— it is inseparably united to the organism as a part of it, depending wholly on that organism for its growth, its continuity, and its development; so much so, that it can act no independent part whatsoever. When the supreme centre is disorganised, the Ego, as a natural consequence, suffers also, this being comprehended, understood, and accepted on proof. The question that suggests itself is—how are we to be insured, say, apart from the assurance conveyed in the Christian records, that the soul, the living force, will survive the dissolution of the organism that created it, and of which it forms its vital part? Now, it comes to pass that the assurance so much desired just rests in the fact of the ceaselessness of the human form of vital activity—the soul. Individual immortality is co-existent—is the correlative of the ceaseless vital activity of the human form—the form and intelligence that created the individual Ego. The Ego, once created, essentially retains the individuality it possessed all through, since created in its first sensation which invested it with the ceaseless movement of immortality. This ceaseless movement, that finds expression in sensation, alone constitutes vitality, and gives to the body animation, movement, and what we falsely call natural life, if we infer by that term that the vital force of the individual ceases on the death of the organism, without which, the organism could not, and would not have been. For to be a living organism, is to be capable of feeling, and to feel in this case is to create a human being in the ceaseless movement of vitality that the Ego possesses, which constitutes its immortality in not ceasing to be capable of feeling on the death of its organism. The Ego, in virtue of having been created of its first sensation all along, if disembodied at any moment, possesssed this quality and power. It simply continues its normal movement, absorbing energy in the form of the organism—of which it so long formed the vital part—on the death of that organism. It is thus the Ego continues its immortal life, and finds itself in the human form possessed of the power of generating the forms of energy to which its activities gave birth as the equivalent of earth-born feeling. This is the result of the ceaseless activity generated through the human organ in sensation. This form of vitality is capable of demonstrating by reproducing the whole series of the individual life-history, which ended with the last bodily sensation.

The disembodied Ego, so formed, continues to act its individual part in the laws governing its own form of energy, no longer subject to frail mortal flesh. Humanly speaking, it is the ceaseless activity of the elements of ideas forming into the intellectual combinations of intelligent conceptions that secure for the Ego its movement, its continuity, and life, and in a way is its immortality. For, in the Ego, animated by its own laws, all feeling, the equivalent of the vibrating energy of what sort soever, that had been generated in any part of the human organism, is reproducable, not as character of mind only, but as the character of every organ of the body united as a whole, and operating through the co-ordinating function to which the Ego is subject in giving expression to thought through the human form. If the Ego is not united to Christ in conversion, it is animated by self-conservation, and manifests all the phases of degeneration to which the Ego was subject while in its body, as well as all its moral impressions and actions.

Thus, then, we have the living force created by the organism, now separated from the organism, a living immortal unit of humanity, capable of giving expression to Ideal combinations, such as we may justly call, "reason made substance," for the forces of the Ego will express themselves as such in the forms of intellectual combinations of vitalised energy, as the ceaseless activities of life forming its individual units, which, in consciousness, survive all changes, yea, even the dissolution of our sun. Although the actual basis of all is in our sun, the series is thus the "fundamental condition of the progress from simple to compound combinations of matter, from dead to living matter, from low to high organisms, from simple sensations and movements to moral feeling and Will." For such is nature and its laws, which include immortal man. The originator of all is God, the Father of Jesus Christ, who ordered or fore-ordained that, for organic evolution, and for our earth, practically the sun is all and all. When its life and heat expire, all energies on earth which it animates will expire. However, there is one class of energies formed through organic evolution that does not cease, namely, the energy vitalised in giving expression to human consciousness as the intelligence that the organic base of mind creates in functioning in creating the human Ego, which, in absorbing energy, reproduces all in " reason made substance." The organic process of the operation, we may say, was rendered visible through the magnificent arrangement adopted by Dr. Luys photographing thin sections of the network of nerve cells and their tissues to illustrate the functioning power of the human brain, the organ of mind, built up as the central region of the system. Assuredly, we have in the labours of such men the organic base of mind demonstrated, that is, rendered visible, that creates the ceaseless activities of life in creating the Ego explained, and in its way made visible, as the process taking place in the human body during the period of its earthly life when the Soul or Ego is being created. The reason why the Ego retains the human form arises from the ceaseless activities to which it is subject, having sprung from the human organism, and therefore a phase of intelligence which can only express itself through a human form.

The whole case may be clearly stated thus : the disembodied Ego is an individual self-conscious unit incased in the force of its own ceaseless action of vitalising energy. It lives in the human form in virtue of the human organism having given birth to it in developing sensations which may be said to crystalize in forming their own intellectual combinations of vitalised energy. Energy they absorb and return in functioning to sustain consciousness. Such are the laws that individual immortality rests in.

Such, then, is the renewed mind in the disembodied spirit referred to by St. Paul as the " new man which after God is created in righteousness and true holiness."—Eph. iv. 22-24. There thought must express itself in outward signs such as speech and character, &c., in characteristic action. These efforts are effected by the Ego—disembodied spirit or soul—as self-consciousness absorbing energy from its surrounding medium and returning it in functioning, either by speech or it may be, in written characters of light, or any other form as the process one Ego communicates with his fellow. Each manifests its own form of thought and action by absorbing energy to do so. This process is somewhat similar to what takes place in the brain during natural life. However, then intelligence leaves its traces in the brain in deferentiating it; whereas such energy is used by the Ego in function, in the human form taking on the sign representing the intellectual combination then present in consciousness, such sensations having the power in themselves to absorb the energy required in functioning.

As a consequence of the condition that human life rests in, the sum-total of the energy at the disposal of the Ego must be equivalent to the energy used by the Ego, accompanied by consciousness, while being developed through the organism. The Energy is equal in power to the Ego's capacity in quality, and is determinated by the motive prompting the activity and the effect produced on the social organism. The actual amount of available energy possessed by the race, will be the sum-total of energy used up in functioning by that race into which consciousness entered, in transforming dead matter into the immortal living forms of human intelligence.

Individual immortality is formed of human sensations regulated by the laws of feeling that build themselves up of every thought that thrills its organism. They are produced thus when disembodied, and they possess the power of reproducing all in forms of energy. In these units of nature as disembodied spirits not united to Christ in belief, their immortality circulates in the sentiment of hope that vitality itself begets, in its effort to secure something which it has not in possession. Hope so rendered is the highest aspiration of the natural man. But the aspiration may be of a very exalted nature in the desire : and, alas ! very mean in the worthlessness of the object desired. For human depravity, finding its antidote in Christianity, may lead to such exalted ideas as at present to be quite beyond the power of our race to imagine.

For such is the immortal hope that leads onwards and upwards, ever hopeful of a higher and yet higher development. It gives expression to the law stimulated and sustained in the ceaseless flow of human intelligence. These individual units "Live, and hope to live;" and in obedience to their social instinct will group themselves into societies, called in scriptural language nations, formed of units animated by similar sentiments which act in harmony to renew the battle of life, striving to attain something they have not in possession, still liable to the death-threatening shock of pain in damping the vigour flowing from the sentiment of hope. Remember, this class has no guarantee that their life will be eternal, neither that human depravity will find an antidote in Christianity. Notwithstanding, man as the latest and highest outcome of the long travail of nature stimulated in the form I have formerly indicated by the sentiment of hope will never be bereft of the evolutional energy of enthusiam; will never be without aspirations without an ideal. For the living activities flowing from the anticipation of an eternal existence will secure all this and much more.

The inspiration of hope, which includes all in man, is nature propagating itself through him in stirring him with enthusiasm which strives to attain to the ideal conceived and animated by the activity of life. Nature lives in man or in humanity, and has attained so much, and hopes to live to attain much more. Thus inspired, man will ever be passing onward. Animated by the aspiration hope begets, he is inspired by all the glorious possibilities the future may unfold. Thus inspired, man realizeth, however brilliant the future of the nations may be, he, as a unit thereof, will share therein. For, alas, alas ! except united thus egoism which is man's natural sentiment, would generate degeneration that would end in annihilating the race, or in producing such an offspring as that referred to in the scriptures as the Devil and his Angels, whose fall was brought about on these very lines. A graphic description thereof is given in Isaiah xiv. 13-14, where Lucifer, son of the morning, said, " I will ascend into heaven, I will exalt my throne above the stars of God ; I will sit also upon the mount of the congregation in the sides of the north, I will ascend above the heights of the clouds ; I will be like the Most High."

Further, Lucifer's attack on our Lord was directly similar. In striving to induce our Lord to use His supernal power to secure a personal benefit—first, that of appeasing His hunger by commanding a stone to become bread. The other two were of a similar nature, in striving to induce our Lord to exalt Himself. For well Lucifer knew if our Saviour, as the Son of God, acted thus, it would have unfitted Him for His office as Mediator between God and man, He who—though of Divine origin—came to the world to suffer and to die, the just for the unjust, that He might reconcile us sinners to God.

However, our Lord proved Himself equal to all emergencies, for though God, He was also perfect man.

T

A joint alliance so formed enables our Lord to inspire His people with the new sentiment that union with Christ the Lord begets.

That Jealousy, Hatred, Envy, Malice, and all sorts of anti-social energies are not confined to earth, but are carried into the eternal state as part of the earthly heritage of the Ego, proves that human depravity must be a prominent feature in that state of disembodied spirits, and leaves no doubt of the necessity resting on the Creator to provide a rescue. Thus a most effective rescue for about two thousand years Christianity has possessed, in the God-inspiring sentiment of Divine Love, as the means to create anew the human soul. In the opportunity lost, church and suffering humanity have lost what neither can redeem.

This power to purify was lost individually in ignoring the necessity of conversion, which alone could fit for heaven, and collectively in the ease, luxury, and excessive egoism of its members, which left poor suffering humanity a prey to every vile passion, in its members striving to secure a personal pleasure heedless of the suffering thereby caused to others. Even so animated, man passed through the chambers of death into immortality. For this in its way Christianity has to be responsible—for the work might have been done—for myriads died animated by corrupt human nature, who might have been now glorifying the God of the whole earth as their Redeemer and Deliverer. If the Christian Ideal had been of the exalted nature that its origin typifies, a race, guided by motives, would have had in such an Ideal the highest of all motives to work while on earth to win humanity to purity, peace, and eternal glory through Christ, in giving up the pleasures of earth, insured of rest and peace in the Redeemer's Kingdom, which is ruled by Love.

Such is the responsibility of the effect produced by the Christian ideal ceasing to be of this exalted nature. In thus far Christendom stands condemned by its God and by the unsaved race also.

Evidently it is because of such a responsibility resting on Christendom, that at the final end, when He who sitteth on the throne has made all things new, and has so ordered it, that the tabernacle of God is to be with man—when he who overcometh shall inherit all things. Then Christ says, "I will be his God and he shall be my son." Apparently at this stage of human development, led on by the God of humanity, there is provision made for a possible intermingling between the two sections of the race, though so differently constituted, in the one section being purely human, the other Divine in adoption.—Rev. xxi. 1-8. Of the nature of the anticipated mingling, those who read must form their own conclusion. I feel it expedient to leave the matter so.

Remember, that the new gospel of "He that overcometh shall inherit all things," came first to the seven Churches mentioned in the Revelations, intended to typify Christendom on earth. It was a gospel intended to act on the Churches by inducing the purity that develops every Christian virtue, in every individual being animated by the love that casteth out fear. Though finally addressed to each individual of the unsaved section of the race, this is a condition only made possible in Christ having died for the sins of the whole world. His first act, after having finished His great work of redemption, was to visit the spirits in prison, and as a spirit preach to these spirits in prison. As our Lord is surrounded thus we need have no hesitation in affirming that here, and by Him for the first time, the gospel of "He that overcometh shall inherit all things" was preached.

So that humanity, so utterly depraved as the scriptures indicate man to be, conditions confirmed by the student of sociology, had through our Lord visiting their dark abode, the sentiment of hope imparted to them in the "He that overcometh shall inherit all things." For henceforth Human depravity finds its antidote in the strength Christ provides.

CHAPTER XII.

CHRISTIANITY—ITS END AND ORIGIN.

IN viewing human nature from the standpoint of evolution, we have developed in the Moral and Religious elements the intellectual combinations that form a base for Christian activities, in enabling a man to appreciate the benefit conferred on his nature by the sentiment Christianity imparts. This being so, the discriminating powers of the human intellect may be awakened to the importance of the facts which the Redemption Purchase unfolds in perceiving the distinction which must arise; and which divides the human race into two great sections, separated by the mental state of believing the glad tidings conveyed in the Redemption Purchase, and not believing them. The first class believes in our Lord, the permanent objective existence with whom the Ego is united and can hold communion; the other class is cut off by unbelief from any intercourse whatever with our Lord. The importance which this difference makes is clearly seen, when it is realized that mental life on earth depends on a conscious union formed between a subject and object, and that in Christ we have a permanent object, to whom the subject is in this way united. Further, remember, that the development of the Ego rests in the union formed between the subject man and his environments, the objective world. The Ego is the vital combination that builds itself up of the feeling and the felt so derived. Thus, then, the vital activity that unites subject and object in developing conscious states is the Ego in process of formation growing in complexity just as the conscious states grow in complexity. It is ceaseless in its movement, and on the death of the organism continues to live, in giving expression to the conscious states of which it is formed.

In the disembodied state, our Lord is to the believer his special environment. The unbeliever has no such environment, for by him Christ, the Lord was ignored, therefore his soul is deprived of the source of intelligence our Lord's presence would impart. For, as an unbeliever, he is bereft of the mental state, including all that the believer enjoys in felt communion with Christ. Thus, then, the discriminating power of the human Intellect is perfectly capable of comprehending the vital importance attached to what I have said, viewed in the abstract as a soul bereft of all that is included in the Redemption Purchase of Christ the risen Lord; and to appreciate the value of the development, which union with Christ at conversion would lead to, in the religious element becoming animated by a new sentiment expressing itself in Adoration, Love, and Gratitude to God the Father through His Son our Lord.

These conditions, like all knowledge, spring from the discriminating power of the Intellect enabling man to perceive and classify points of differences and points of agreement. This proposition is understood and admitted. With revealed religion this chapter chiefly takes to do. It is with what is revealed in the Bible that we are specially concerned, and how this environment affects the human Intellect. As the revelation given to the human race, whose vitality grasps a pleasure and repels a pain in its instinct of self-preservation—an instinct prone to generate selfishness, which leads to all forms of vice, because each unit comprising Sentient Personality is first and most of all concerned to secure what will confer a pleasure on self. From Scripture testimony, we have at the beginning two beings thus animated, approached by the Governor of the Universe entering into a covenant of works with them, in "Do this and Live"—conditions which the creatures addressed did not prove capable of fulfilling. In Bible language "the fall" ensued. This catastrophe brought with it the most appalling and deplorable results. What followed would seem to be that the highest forms of intelligence were bereft of the elevating influence that an exalted Ideal confers. The capacity to advance, thus induced, would, as a natural consequence, fail, and lead to race degeneration. Degeneration which, as its nature is, when coming from a complex organism, would produce the most degraded forms of intelligence, so as to lead to most deplorable results. Because of its complexity, the organ of mind would show traces of degeneration impossible for a less complex organism. This seems to be really the condition of the fall, which left man so degraded, and led to race degeneration. Anti-social conditions such as this would naturally follow as the result of the fall of a pair so gifted and honoured of God as Adam and Eve, having imparted to them a phase of Divine Intelligence which created exalted ideas. In striving to attain, they would develop in complexity their mental structure hundreds of times; so that when sin entered by disobedience, and communion with God ceased, Degeneration and all the evils springing from complexity of mental organisms would then make their appearance, culminating in Cain killing Abel. This would arise from Cain's complex mental organs enabling him to discern points of difference between his own mental state and that of his brother, where one possessed of a less developed mental organ would see no distinction at all. The distinction perceived where degeneration had set in would naturally lead to a depraved act. Cain manifested this in killing his brother Abel when inspired by hatred or jealousy. He was induced by the conceptions he was capable of forming. These conceptions were of a nature impossible for one of Adam's contemporary race to have formed. To a contemporary race the Bible evidently points to. He was a step in advance of them in degeneration, and this Cain's complex organ would enable him to take. Except for the Fall complexity would have led to a higher development — Cain would have striven to imitate Abel.

The fact is, that a race highly endowed by degeneration, would lead to a fall from possible development to a positive degeneration of a very depraved type, ending in undoing all that had been done. The course adopted by God is different in this far, that in Revelation God appeals to man's enlightened reason, as an intelligent being capable of perceiving and classifying conditions that differ from one another and conditions that agree with each other. In reasoning thus, human intelligence rests. God addresses men in language which the human intellect can comprehend and reason on. Man in this way is capable of forming conceptions of God, His nature, His character, and His laws, that are human. The power to perceive a more complex revelation would arise from the conceptions previously imparted to a less intelligent race held by a race of higher intelligence, in enabling that race to comprehend more complex phases of Revelation. In this way Revealed truth would advance in complexity as the intelligence of the race advanced. Each section of the race advancing, so, would be capable of comprehending higher and higher conceptions of revealed truth. If progressing, to these exalted ideals the race would strive to attain, and in striving, they would rise to a marvellous complexity of structure in functioning thus.

A race capable of this high development had become so corrupt in the degeneration which the fall led to as certainly would have led to its final ruin, had not God interposed, by providing a deliverer, who was to Christianity its origin and end; in Christianity being destined to infuse a new sentiment into man at conversion, which springs from a new vital source that ensures success in inducing a new mental development, whereby the lusts of the flesh—classified in Gal. v. 19-21—" Adultery, fornication, uncleanness, lasciviousness, idolatry, witchcraft, hatred, variance, emulations, wrath, strife, seditions, heresies," will give place to the fruits of the spirit, classified by Paul as " Love, joy, peace, longsuffering, gentleness, goodness, faith, meekness, temperance.', Through this process, the new man St. Paul alludes to, is formed ; and of such are the adopted children of God, comprising the church of the first-born, the redeemed from among men.

That the other section of the race embracing poor corrupt suffering human nature will ultimately be redeemed, in so far as to be rescued from its corrupt tendencies, including race degeneration, called the lusts of the flesh, is certain. They will be clothed in garments possible for this section of the race to attain, through the regenerating power hope inspires, enabling the seed of the first Adam to regain the condition of forming the exalted moral Ideal that the second Adam, the originator of Christianity, will confer, which the race lost at the fall. That is a purified human race, as a purely human instrument led by our Lord, *its God of Humanity*. The race of the first Adam thus inspired, will eventually regain its lost position, this being the end and origin Christianity had in view for it.

Regenerating the human race, and dividing it into two such sections as I indicate, are assuredly the Decrees of God working through human development into which the Divine entered, which led to the end accomplished by our Lord, the God-appointed Deliverer. The Decrees of God involve such magnificent results, and are not to be supposed to end with the Redemption of the human race, but through the merits our Lord has provided in His Redemption Purchase, to benefit eventually all created intelligence, which, we may justly infer, have been and may be developed or created in universal space, visible or invisible, by our Lord becoming to all, the visible and recognised source of development in many special ways, when what has been revealed comes to be eliminated by advancing science taking to do with Nature —the material medium — and its Laws. However, what specially concerns us at present is that poor suffering human nature will be rescued from suffering and degeneration. This is clearly revealed in many passages of scripture, notably when our Lord, the Redeemer, will have delivered up the race to the Father.— 1 Cor. xv. 24-27.

The terms used in the Bible to indicate the destruction of the wicked, are terms intended to convey the operation whereby evil tendencies will disappear, by the phase of intelligence and sentiment Christ imparts, annihilating wickedness in individual man being purified through power divine, which the crucified One imparts. First, through divine love flowing from the Saviour "as man's substitute."

Secondly, in the hope-inspiring sentiment begotten of the power our Lord imparts in "He that overcometh shall inherit all things." For man (a unit of consciousness) will not and cannot be annihilated through evil, and all anti-social sentiments will, and must be annihilated, as the end Christianity will effect.

Remember, the eternal distinction which divides the race into believers and unbelievers is to be found in those animated by the purifying sentiment induced by conversion. The unsaved are those who have not experienced this change as the medium of union effected between Christ and the human soul while in the body. The body in the scripture sense must rise again. Then such a distinction must be of such a nature as every one will see to be of vital importance. It seems apparent from scriptural evidence that the converted cease to form part of the human race in becoming the adopted children of God. They have the right to approach Him as sons crying Abba Father, just as Christ in His manhood may have addressed God.

The necessity for a divine deliverer always present in the life action of the race, was made apparent by the Fall. The cause of it seems to be a process employed by God to test the power of human capacity, to prove to Humanity, and it may be to other forms of intelligence similarly evolved, the utter impossibility of our life action, surrounded as that pair was to triumph over the self-regarding instinct, and introduce the sentiment into the race whereby man would find his chief pleasure in glorifying God the eternal one. It would thus be demonstrated that if humanity, as we know it, was to be redeemed, it must be through divine interposition, which embraces the end and origin of Christianity in the necessity being so.

When read in the light of the Christian dispensation, we see the Redeemer of the race, as man, in His divine nature revealing truth in the form of intelligence that man can comprehend, so as to enable the race to anticipate such an event as that decreed in God giving His only-begotten Son to redeem the race. For the divine nature of the Son of God in assimilating itself with our race—all through its history—imparts conceptions that the race could comprehend, of God's character in His dealing with it. Through this process one climax was reached when the race anticipated God revealing Himself to it as the universal ruler. This anticipation of God as universal ruler exhausted the evolutional instinct in that direction, as no more exalted conception of God was possible. The next step onwards to the end decreed, was to anticipate the depravity of the race to be of such a nature as to necessitate redemption by substitution, in God giving His only-begotten Son to redeem it. When these conceptions were formed and inspired by the influence of our Lord's divine nature, working through the race, the instinct of race evolution in another direction was exhausted. For what more priceless gift could God give than His only-begotten Son, to secure man's redemption. It is divine truth through revelation assimilating itself with human intelligence that enables the race to anticipate such coming events. Human intelligence, through such processes, became so flexible as to be capable of moulding divine truth into its own intellectual conception, which in the ideal form, of intellectual conceptions present in the Ego so transformed, reappears before God the Father and Son in the point of space our Redeemer's risen body now occupies, into which the human soul that is redeemed gravitates at death.

A transformation of Divine Intelligence, somehow

humanized, may have so operated as to develop the form of intelligence defined by the Jews as the "Lord of Hosts." An intelligence, divine in its origin, but human in its form, assimilated itself with the Jewish race, because they were the seed of Abraham, the friend of God, whose faith never wavered. They were a race intrusted with the oracles of God; and in the divine power they called the Lord of Hosts, they had a form of intelligence which reappeared as the Son of God in the Christ of Christianity, embodying the Divine nature from which flowed the organic growth that developed the miraculous conception, which assumed the human form in the person of our Lord; the second person of the Godhead, destined to redeem the world, by infusing a new sentiment which will modify man's self-regarding instinct so as to render harmless the vitality of self-conservation, which leads the race to ruin, decreed of the triune God, Father, Son, and Spirit. These decrees find their concrete in the person of our Lord, their complexity in God, in nature, and in the spirit of truth, which includes revealed truth, as well as the Laws of Nature represented in the sciences. This clearly is Christianity in its end and origin.

From first to last, it was our Lord's divine nature operating in humanity through revelation, which took effect in the miraculous conception, and leads to the vicarious sacrifice in the life, death, and resurrection of our Lord that redeems the race, in ultimately infusing purity and peace, led on by its God, the Lord Jesus Christ.

Our Lord is possessed of the attributes of God, and we can only comprehend them, in so far as they can be explained in human forms of intelligence. However, as our intelligence is capable of increasing while supplied with new conditions, which include points of difference and points of agreement with what is already known, human intelligence may be developed into a very high form of complexity, which may, viewed from a human standpoint, be called Infinite. That is something so vast, that human language at present has not terms that can define or even convey its meaning. Another advantage human intelligence has in the simplicity of its mode of operation, is that the unlearned, as well as the learned, are capable of understanding everything when instructed in the points that differ from and agree with each other. This simplicity greatly increases the range of vision opened to the lowest as well as the highest intellect, when enlightened by Divine Reason, far beyond any conception that the race can form at present of intellectual advancement. This advancement is of such a nature that the mysteries to be unfolded in what we may call infinite space would hardly satisfy the eternal aspirations of even the unsaved section of the race, led on by "its God of Humanity" in his Human and Divine Nature as its Developing Intelligence —an Intelligence which took on its first Human phase in the first revelation made to our race—a race that in revelation has, like all proper names, its signs, standing for the intellectual combinations, forming the concrete mental structure called into activity by the terms used. The structure or idea increases as the terms do. Thus, then, the first revelation created a human conception of the divine in originating conditions that are never to end. For this is involved in the end and origin of Christianity.

For in the first revelation the Divine—representing the triune God—assimilated itself with the human by adopting a human phase of intelligence which the capacity of the race conld comprehend ; because it ended in the Son taking the human form to give expression to the divine nature in the person and work of our Lord Jesus Christ, who henceforth is developing intelligence to both sections of the race, one section of which is purely human in its mode of operation, the other, the adopted children of God, essentially divine ; may or may not continue human.

In what I have said, I affirm I have given the rational explanation of the Origin and the end of Christianity—as far as its end can be anticipated—in tracing its origin to the first revelation given to our race. This operation continues on through its history up to the time of the miraculous conception, when in that event the accumulated divine intelligence, which had assimilated itself with the human race, took the human form and unfolded divine truth therefrom ; an intelligence in the forces accumulated in the miraculous conception that developed in producing a Divine being whose presence marked a new era in the history of humanity; and doubtless in the destiny and history of the Universe, visible and invisible

The end to be accomplished by our Lord I will now glance at—though repeating what has been said and will be said again—because I hold it to be the one thing essential for the race to know, believe, and comprehend. The highest end to be attained is that of infusing a new sentiment—a new life action—into the individual, divine in its nature and origin, to take the place of self-conservation, in inducing the individual to find his pleasure in the sufferings that a self-sacrificing life entails, that God may be glorified thereby. Influenced thus, the natural sentiment of self-conservation is nullified. Self-conservation in its most corrupt form, is a force so degraded that, on the death of the body, the Ego, might end in annihilation after being subject to untold misery—misery which, from the nature of things, would have been utterly impossible while in the body, or if annihilation was possible for even such a set of corrupt forces, on the death of their organism. To live on in the misery such corrupt tendencies would entail, would lead to conditions equal to the worst conceptions of Hell ever formed.

But through the efficiency of our Lord's life and death, a very different future awaits the race, though, in forwarding that future, the corrupt must suffer as a consequence of the purifying process involved. For the end to be attained by Christianity is that of rescuing and purifying the race in two ways. First, through the medium of conversion during natural life. Then the converted section becomes, so to speak, disintegrated from the race human, as the adopted children of God, to whom Christ is both Brother and Lord, a section animated during earthly life with the sentiment that approaches God in the adoring love of the Abba Father. Secondly, the remaining unconverted and unbelieving, therefore the unsaved section of the race, will find their deliverance in overcoming their evil tendency by paying the uttermost farthing. Thus, the wicked acts done in the flesh entail rending off the corruption and defilement of the flesh in obedience to self-interest. Then self-interest will induce, the equal division of labour to be recognised, and oppression will cease in the harmonious action everywhere present in the unsaved section of humanity.

It is well to give the Christian explanation for the term Faith, because faith includes the mental state that divides the race in transforming the convert into an adopted child of God. Faith so rendered arises from one feeling himself to be a sinner, and as such, accepting the forgiveness Christ offers, in having become the sinner's substitute. Just by letting the sinner grasp the offered forgiveness as we would accept a gift or pledge offered by a friend which, because of its value, in response generates the love and gratitude that finds pleasure in serving and suffering for the one loved. Though our Lord, the object loved, is not present to the eye of sense He makes His presence felt in the communion that the new sentiment generates. The token or sign of conversion is realised in many ways. Notable in the love for the brethren it begets, in each realising that all such are one in union with Christ their Lord, who was crucified for their sins, rose from the dead, and ascended to heaven, where dwells the permanent objective existence who created Christendom, and to whom the converted cling in Love. That is in the new sentiment that Christ Himself imparts, for such is conversion and its felt power. So as to comprehend how much is included in having in the person of our Lord a permanent object, we must have a pretty clear conception of the laws on which mental life depends—laws which require for their base a subject and an object, such as a living organism and its environments. We know that the human organism and its social medium are the conditions that produce mind in developing the human Ego formed of Ideal conceptions as mental combinations or images, to which the organism and environment give birth in generating thought, emotion, and reflection.

Thus, then, the social medium makes itself felt as thought, by generating life's current as consciousness in the individual human brain organism. This is the condition always at work in every mental state whatsoever. It forms the source of activity as the origin and growth of human mind, for without a social medium we can have no human conceptions or ideas. Nothing can be found in the human mind or Ego, except forms of thought that have sprung from its environment during the period of its development. There are always the objective existences at the bottom, as the condition on which mental life depends to sustain it. This being so, if Christianity is to maintain a permanent place, it must conform to these laws in possessing the evidence, that the person of our Lord Jesus Christ did exist about the time indicated, as the originator of Christianity (facts supported by secular evidence), which developed a religious system that rests in the evidences of His life, death, and resurrection, handed down by the church in an unbroken line of evidence from His day till now, a religion which has in these conditions enough to satisfy the claims advanced by Christianity of resting on a permanent objective existence. This condition is as well established as an historical fact of the same date.

Christianity contains in its history these strongly fortified facts, and appeals to the non-Christian world as the permanent religion of the race. But to its converted adherents it provides another and stronger evidence in the felt communion that demonstrates the fact that the converted are united to their Redeemer God in love.

Thus fortified in having the manhood of our Lord proved, Christianity will ever possess a permanent object as its environment, capable of satisfying the claim that the human Intellect makes for proof. For such proof is ever at hand in the subjective and objective conditions formed between Christ and a section of the race that provided for Him His human form. The conditions on which the progress of the mental development of the race depends, is that the race be provided with a permanent objective existence as its developing intelligence, which provides for it a permanent environment; and assuredly of this nature is our Lord, Redeemer, and God. This being clearly understood, the all-important point is for the indidividual in conversion to get united to this object—our Lord, the essential environment—during his earthly life. To secure this end, rests in the individual having a clear intellectual conception of the cardinal points of the Christian system, namely, that Christ, the Lord, is the sinner's substitute. This understood, all that is left for the sinner to do is to accept the forgiveness the Redeemer offers. For this is the free gospel, that when the sinner accepts forgiveness, he is converted, and has passed from death into life. Whether he feels assured or not, it is in accepting the thing offered, that union with Christ rests in. If one desires to be saved, and will make the mental effort to believe, clothed in the words, "Lord, I believe, help thou mine unbelief," which is a mental effort equivalent to,—Lord, I am striving for the mental state assurance gives, that my sins are forgiven by Thee. That mental effort and prayer, if habitually persisted in, will soon be crowned with success, through the individual becoming fully assured that his sins are forgiven, and that he stands before God "as a sinner saved by Grace," that is, saved by Favour. Feeling assured of this, will soon generate the Faith that worketh by Love—the sentiment that stimulates and regulates the inhabitants of heaven. Through a process of so simple a nature as this, does the gospel of peace take effect in the human soul. For our Lord, as the sinner's substitute, does exist in some point of space as the man Christ Jesus—our Lord, who does make His presence felt in the human soul or Ego, in such a way as to lead the converted section of the race to care very little for the joys of earth, because fully insured of the everlasting joy of heaven, an earnest which he has on earth as a foretaste thereof.

In view of the free Gospel, let the reader note that our Lord, in virtue of His vicarious sacrifice, in dying on the cross, has suffered the greatest penalty which could be demanded from the most corrupt depraved human being on earth by his fellow-man—that of ridding society of the corrupt wretch by putting him to death. Viewing redemption from this point, Christ suffered the worst penalty man can inflict on his fellow-man, for by taking the life of the worst, he cannot again trouble society. Christ, the Son of God, pure and sinless, in every part, having suffered thus for man, was in very deed his substitute. It is true, Christ suffered the death sentence meted out for Him by His own nation, who themselves were the Elect of God, yet so corrupt that the purity of the doctrine He taught in condemning their wicked practises so enraged them, that nothing short of the death by crucifixion of the sinless One would satisfy them, for they professed to see in Him the chief of sinners. This proves how depraved the very class had become to whom the oracles of God were entrusted. Their lives were so corrupt, that when reproved, nothing short of the reprover's life-blood would satisfy, so terribly vile as this had the seed of Abraham, God's elect, entrusted with His oracles, become. Thus fallen, they sold their birthright, and opened the way for the decrees of God to take effect, on which redemption rests, in securing for the vilest, deliverance by substitution. We have in the corrupt lives of some professingly converted Christians of our day a case somewhat similar. Of course, such, if converted, are of the class entrusted with God's inspired word, to whom God in Christ has revealed Himself through the in-dwelling power of the spirit as a God of love.

But the all-important point is that, in viewing the Jewish race as the elect of God, entrusted with His oracles, they had in this way become the mouthpiece of God in demanding retribution for our race, where life itself rests in vicarious sacrifice which entails the necessity for the innocent to die to sustain life in one animal living on another. Apart from the heathen world, the Jewish nation itself, as individuals, could not be saved as the elect of God, in the same sense as now. It was in this way brought about that the Jews, though unconsciously, were inspired by the oracles of God as God to carry out the decrees of God in meting out to the innocent one the very penalty they themselves had incurred, so demanded the life of the Son of God as the substitute decreed to die for the sins of the whole world.

The case may be put thus : a divine revelation applicable to a human medium was communicated to a race called and elected of God because the seed of Abraham, who had become so corrupted in their age and generation that when the Son of God, in the likeness of man came to take His place as their King, Deliverer, Leader, and Guide, they rejected Him, treated Him just as they themselves ought to have been treated of God, as outcasts, forsaken and deprived of life, because unfaithful to the trust committed to them —that of imparting to the heathen world a false impression of God's character. In this way, Abraham's seed, the elect of God, therefore divine, though a most corrupt organic growth, took God's place, and as a human organism gave the judgment that their own corrupt natures led the way to ; because they could not tolerate the idea of being reproved by one of his humble class, though living a pure and blameless life, they judged and condemned God's Son, so that the just did die for the unjust. It is when looking at divine truth, as we must do, acting in or through a human medium, that we can form a true conception of what is implied in God demanding a substitute before divine justice could be satisfied and the race redeemed.

It was the divine in Abraham's seed that was speaking through a medium of human intelligence representing a just God demanding a substitute to satisfy His justice, because His Laws had been violated—a conception of God which relates to our race and the condition of the life thereof. Being a race to whom God had revealed Himself, and in so doing, had in a sense imparted the divine to it, when the Jews judged, God acquiesced in the judgment they meted out to his Son. In virtue of His vicarious sacrifice, thus brought about, the justice of God (viewed as a human being) was satisfied—terms used to represent the divine, in these Jews demanding satisfaction, though themselves so corrupt—the condition God's plan of redemption involved.

Laws originated by God decreed to develop our race, makes the race in that sense the offspring of God, and a race whose very life rests in the form of vicarious sacrifice in one generation dying so that another may live, which on entering into its immortal habitation (unconverted), has its life there regulated by the law of retribution in the "ye shall not come out hence till you pay the uttermost farthing." As such, the unsaved section, as the offspring of God, will have the rejected King of the Jews as the God of Humanity, the only God they can ever know, leading them on through eternity. Whereas the section saved by substitution, in being the adopted children, can comprehend God's attributes in another and a higher sense than through a human medium, for to them our Saviour is Lord, Redeemer, and Brother, whereas to the unsaved section He is their God.—Rev. xxi. 7. Divided thus, the race is equipped for eternity, the one section human in end and origin, the other, Divine in adoption, freed from the power or consequence of a wicked life.

We may safely infer, the place our race is destined to take in the Universe of space, is that of a race pre-eminently intelligent, and pre-eminently depraved, which required to be rescued from the consequences that such a complex and highly developed organism entailed—animated by the life-action of self-conservation—through the operation of a divinely organized plan of redemption specially appointed for that end. Equipped thus, the race will appear in the Universe of space redeemed by the Son of God suffering in their stead. The necessity of such a deliverer will then be seen to rest in the vitality of the race, leading man to oppress his neighbour, so that he may gain a personal advantage. In such conditions we have the *end and origin of Christianity*, this chapter takes to do with, though I add a paragraph that concerns the Christian only.

Before ending this chapter, it is desirable to explain the meaning I attach to one Intellectually united to Christ in belief. One justly called an Intellectual Christian believes in the facts of Christianity, but has to be awakened to the importance of Conversion by realizing he is a sinner in need of salvation. Such an one is to approach God in the words of "Lord I believe, help thou my unbelief." This prayer is to be interpreted as, Lord I am making an effort to take hold of the glad tidings of the free Gospel by believing they are true to me; enable me to realize the truth these words imply, in such a way as to feel I am a sinner saved by grace—that is saved by favour—and accepted as Thy child for whom Christ died, therefore entitled to approach Thee, O God, in the spirit of the Abba Father, which gives expression to the changed relationship that has taken place between me, "the sinner," and God. It is true, one so animated is accepted, because Christ has said, "whosoever cometh unto me I shall in nowise cast out," and His words cannot fail; but until the individual has realized it is so, the mental state indicated by assurance is absent. And the mental state of one assured and one not assured is of a totally different nature. For one not assured is living on in the bondage of doubt. Whereas, one assured, feels himself in possession of the thing desired—one saved by grace, free from the penalty of sin. Fear is an element in the one case of this nature, that the thing prized may be lost; fear is absent in the other case, because he has the thing prized in his possession, consequently he is animated by the love that casteth out fear. It is evident to any one how different the mental states of both are—in both having realized the need of salvation, so as to be rescued from the penalty of sin—say, rescued from having to pay the uttermost farthing, in being accepted as an adopted child by God the Father of Jesus Christ.

I now address myself to the unassured, beseeching them to be ever making the effort to grasp the glad tidings, so as to feel the forgiveness Christ offers to be true to them, in having taken the sinner's place, and reconciled them to God as sinners saved by grace. For when this mental effort is continued, assurance will soon break through and take the place of doubt, and enable the individual to say, in the emotion of a joyful acclamation, "I know whom I have believed, and am persuaded he is able to keep that I have committed to him against that day."—2 Tim. i. 12.

When this is realized, the mental state of doubt has passed away in assurance taking its place, by the individual grasping the eternal truth that unites the sinful soul of man to God through the Redeemer, whose merits that soul pleads in approaching as a " sinner saved by grace." To live on in a state of doubt is an abnormal mental state no Christian should tolerate, because his assurance rests on the merits of another, who has already paid the penalty demanded, and doubt indicates a want of confidence that the case is so. This being so, assurance is a mark of confidence, and not that of presumption, as is so often assumed, by those who do not possess assurance themselves and seek to damp the joy of others who possess it. A Christian's success so much depends on his being assured, as it is the mental state that generates the Faith that worketh by Love, and renders him indifferent to earthly joy, in so prizing the future the free gospel he has accepted ensures. Assurance is being in possession of the thing desired, which generates the faith that worketh by love, in building up the new man who takes the place of the old man who finds his pleasure in serving the loved one who has rescued him. The emotion of love, whether human or divine, is always the same; the difference rests in its origin and the end to which it leads. The origin of Christian love is heaven-born, and springs from the personal Saviour, who though not seen is loved.

The sudden manifestation of Love that sometimes accompanies conversion, is the Saviour making His presence known in felt communion in the language of the emotion of love, which indicates the union effected between the Saviour in heaven and the sinner on earth. While the intensity of the emotion lasts, the subject is in the condition that he loves and must serve—he loves and must follow. The human soul, so animated by the spirit of God, viewed from the Christian stand-point, explains the doctrine of necessity in the overpowering sentiment of love which leads the individual to follow the lead of pleasure in serving the object loved, whatever it costs him. The object is Christ, His glory the end. It is only while the overwhelming emotion of love lasts, that the term, necessity to serve, in this sense can be applicable. However, for the Christian to act so as to strengthen the emotion of love, and to avoid whatever tends to weaken it, is of the greatest importance; the temptation to take the course that weakens it, ought to be avoided, however much that will cost. For when love quenched, the manifestation of the spirit of God is damped. Love damped produces apathy and indifference which will mar the Christian's usefulness, and render him indifferent to the emotions of divine love, from which truly acceptable Christian work only flows. To produce a continuous flow of work generated so is the end and origin of Christianity.

When deficient in love, the Christian becomes a poor shattered, shrinking, human soul, ashamed to meet the Lord who redeemed him, not having one trophy as the fruit of gratitude to cast at the feet of the Lord of Glory. That is the fruit conversion should generate. A more pitiable object could not be imagined among the Redeemed, many of whom have spent their lives on earth, serving Christ in love. And yet the object of this indifference has as good a right to be among the redeemed as any there; not even excepting the glorious army of martyrs, all radiant in joy and love, who cast their crowns at Jesus feet, to crown Him King of all, with their shout of Hallelujah rending the third heavens; for all are saved for what our Lord did, and not for the services done in glorifying Him for the good things the Christian got through conversion, which ought to stimulate them with the sentiment of Love.

God's way of dealing with sinners on earth while the Christian dispensation lasts, is forcibly put by our Lord in the graphic words " whosoever cometh unto me I will in nowise cast him out." Now, as all converted have come, Christ will in nowise cast any such out, for the God man is pledged so to act. He who died the "just for the unjust," has a free pardon to offer to all, and all that accept are saved, however ungrateful some may be in permitting the sentiment of love to decline, after accepting this priceless boon, that cost the life-blood of the Son of God. Alas, alas! how sad a spectacle to behold, a redeemed soul ashamed to meet its Redeemer and God. Then shame will proclaim its emotion on every feature : the averted eye, the bent form, may speak in accents louder than word could do of the self-reproach the dejected spirit feels. In redemption by substitution through conversion, which induces communion with God, all such had a strong enough motive to induce them to avoid the path of temptation that damps the ardour of love, and may lead to being ashamed in the presence of their Redeemer. To such, there was no law of necessity to force them astray, if they had maintained the devotion love generates in building the structure that flows therefrom ; it was the first false step that made all the others easy, which never should have been taken.

Finally, the origin of Christianity is to be found in vitality of self-conservation, the life-action of our race, which leads the immortal individual unit to seek his own glory. Its end is to redeem a race animated so, by a process that includes all that is contained in the term redemption by substitution, which makes Christianity the permanent religion of the race, in the permanent Christ, the God man, its Lord, Regenerator, and Redeemer.

CHAPTER XIII.

VITAL CHRISTIANITY, WHAT IS IT? LOVING AND WORKING.

THIS phase of Christianity, the fruit of the realization of belief, is the progress made in sanctification, viewed from the sentiment the following lines convey:—

> We love and must follow,
> We love and must serve.

Our Lord in calling St. Paul by special revelation, had a special work of the greatest importance for Paul to do. And it was this. To unfold the process at work that insures sanctification, which is "Faith working by Love," that is, Love and Work; for this is life divine begun as the fruit of faith on earth. The sentiment of vital Christianity is sustained in " Faith working by Love," animating in a more or less degree every one converted—that is, born again—and may be tested in this way. Ask a converted soul, let it be ever so worldly-minded, living on in the uncertainty of hope, would you, if such a thing was possible, sell your hope of salvation by Christ, to secure the success of your most prized earthly undertaking. The unhesitating response would be the emphatic no, never. For from the very nature of the case it must be so, as Christ is an object of love to every soul united to Him in conversion, and may be so in a way with not a few intellectual believers, that hold the truth of the Christian doctrine of salvation, just as they do any other well-established fact in nature, inspired to love by the beauty and purity of our Lord's character. But let that be as it may; to the convert Jesus is an object of Love, cold though that emotion may have become, even though at conversion the emotion may have expressed itself wlth great intensity, making the zeal of the young convert very marked.

However, what most concerns the converted soul is, how best to sustain in ardent zeal the emotion of Love's enthusiasm, and this can only be done by avoiding the path of temptation—which tends to damp Christian zeal—whatever that may be. For the path of temptation to be avoided must be of varied forms, closely relating itself with the temperaments different individuals are most liable to. The course to be taken to obviate this must be decided by the individual himself, in noting with constant care the effect produced on him. This calls for earnest prayer by one willing to be enlightened, who asks for guidance, and who as a Protestant is personally responsible for the course he takes. However, as a Protestant myself, I have not much sympathy with the popular phrase so often in the mouth of some Christians, namely, "A Christian should not go to such and such entertainments," &c. And yet this notion takes its rise from the intellectual combination underlying what I warn Christians to beware of, in following the path that would damp the enthusiasm that is inseparable from the strong emotion of love to the Saviour, by entering the path of temptation.

When the ardour of love is cooled, so as to lead the individual to question the fact of his own conversion and place him in a state of doubt, it is of vital importance for such a one to comprehend in its fulhess what is included in being in a state of Grace, which shortly is, taking the position of "a sinner saved by Grace," for whom Christ has suffered the penalty of his sin. That having taken the position this change of place indicates, is what secures forgiveness by substitution—and nothing else does so—this is the Gospel of peace that generates love.

And to be in doubts of having taken this step *may* be a fatal error which includes what is called in the Bible the loss of a soul. For a human being who believes in Christianity should have no doubt as to whether he is or is not in possession of the mental state this simple belief indicates. In simplicity it is on a level with being convinced that New Zealand or any of our colonies exist. It is not with the evidences of Christianity *it takes to do*. That point is understood to have been settled by the individual. It is as to whether he has accepted the offered forgiveness Christ makes or not; and a Christian of very low mental capacity should have no difficulty in answering this. Those who cannot ought to let bygones be bygones, and make sure of the future in accepting the Lord's offer of a free pardon now, and at once, thus solving the doubt, and henceforth rejoice that Jesus is theirs, so taking the position that conversion indicates. It is as sinners saved by Grace we begin and end our Christian life, and enter Glory—not our own, but bought with a price, in entering as the adopted of God. Let the converted, but not assured, dwell much on these simple facts, and the mental state of apathy, and its first-born child *doubt*, will soon be changed for the mental state of joyous assurance, in the emotion of Love to God, in Christ, filling the soul as the inspiration of "the Spirit bearing witness with our spirits that we are the children of God."—Rom. viii. 16. For all Christians must remember that at no stage in their career do they get beyond being a "sinner saved by grace." It is resting on the assurance that this great boon is true to one's self, that places the feet on the rock that cannot be moved. For immediately the individual begins to question the truth of this right as true to Him, his feet slips from the rock, and with that slip, the faith that worketh by love is damped and begins to decline; because the intellectual combinations to which the assurance of being saved is attached shows signs of weakness. It has not been kept in vigour by the vitality that faith working by love imparts, when kept in active exertion by the individual realizing that he is saved, and what is in store for him.

In realizing this, we have the old old story, of the converted Christian rejoicing in the assurance of the good thing in store for him. But when the intellectual combinations, including all that is thus implied ceases to be in the active vigour of *realized belief*, the joyous anticipation ceases too, and a state of apathy takes its place. Where such apathy continues, the rudimentary form of the intellectual combination in the brain, will only remain and express itself in the individual taking shelter in the generalized idea that Christ died for sinners, and as one, he hopes to be saved. Then he has fallen from the platform and sunlight of assurance, to the shadowy platform of doubt. Such an one will no longer appear before the Saviour glowing with the sentiment emanating from the intellectual combination of " I know in whom I have believed, and am persuaded that he is able to keep that which I have committed to him."—2 Thes. i. 12. Alas, how the mighty has fallen from his first love, in falling from the mental state of assurance to the shadowy or misty state of hope or doubt. The special cause of the change rests in worldly-mindedness. Thus worldly, the individual wilfully becomes indifferent to the words of Jesus—" Ye are not of the world, for I have called you out of the world," because the things of time are then more valued by the believer than those of eternity. For in ceasing to realize the glory that awaits one, the sentiment that raises the convert above the desire for worldly pleasure, profit, or reward, is absent, in the absence of the quickening power of the Faith that worketh by love, and raises the believer above the things of earth.

Our Lord's kingdom is established on the self-denying service that emanates from love. The work of a bond servant our Lord does not recognize. His servant must be free, prompted by love. How to maintain this form of activity is what chiefly concerns the converted Christian. To my judgment the first step towards securing this is to make a public confession of conversion as soon as the change has taken place; and form a close intimacy with those already converted and professing to be so, who are living in harmony with that profession. By acting in this way one converted shows he is not ashamed of Christ, and is prepared to take the responsibility attached to the profession, which includes that he is prepared to act so that Christ may not be ashamed of him living an inconsistent life, and in this way give a false impression to the world of the character of the Redeemer he serves and calls Lord.

In the convert being animated by the joy that springs from the new birth, the world is justified in expecting from him the fruit of the joy—the labour of love—that strives to glorify Christ his Lord on earth. For Christ has committed the keeping of His character to the care of His people, in appealing through them to the unchristian world. Thus, then, when the Christian acts unworthily, he wounds Christ in marring the Re-deemer's glory on earth. With this ever present in consciousness, and the importance of it fully realized, the work of sanctification will make progress in the convert by the new man taking the place of the old man, and Christ will be glorified in the old corrupt mental structure, built up of self-conservation. disappearing with its fruit. Then the world will have lost its power over the individual, and therefore over the true Christian church universal, formed of such individuals, in the continuous stream of good work done as the labour of love, flowing from the abiding evidence of Christ's presence realized by each individual.

When the Church—the collective body of Christ—realises the place in the universe of space that belief in Christ's merits confers on it collectively, it will rise above the world and seek to glorify Christ only.

This will be effected through the strength imparted by Christ, building up intellectual combinations of great stability by the individual resting in the full assurance that he can do all things by Christ strengthening him; trusting and believing, the converted Christian will be advancing and overcoming, in getting the needed strength to overcome every difficulty in Christ. Trusting to the promises, and going onwards in their strength, will and must secure success, because our Lord is Himself pledged to fulfil all His promises. Therefore He will never desert a soul that trusts in them. Both church and individual so trusting, will get possession of the substance of things hoped for the evidence of things not seen—Heb. xi. 1—(which is the correlative of the material forces of the energy thus immortalised in building the soul of such mental states).

The truth of promises are demonstrated to us subjectively in the strength of the moving current proceeding from the intellectual combination built up of trusting in this

v

simple way to the fulfilment of the promises our Lord has given. It is through a process of this nature that we come to realize the power that the promises impart, and can comprehend with clearness what Peter meant by saying we may become partakers of the divine nature, having escaped the corruption that is in the world through lust.—2 Peter i. 4. For when these forces come to be so strengthened that the world has no power over us, we will not lust after its pleasures. Thus, then, when animated by the divine nature our Saviour imparts, it is very certain we rise above the desire of worldly pleasure. Inspired by the nature divine love expresses itself in, we are in possession of the mental state our Lord refers to in the words, "The kingdom of heaven is within you." Whereas, regarding the other promises referred to, it is only the last and great day, when our Lord delivers up the kingdom to the Father, that will reveal the work effected through the strength imparted in the words of St. Paul, "I can do all things through Christ which strengtheneth me."—Ph. iv. 13. For if Paul could and can do all things, so can we. There was no virtue in Paul as Paul—his strength came in his union with Christ, and it will come to us if we work, and wait, and trust, and will enable us to rise above the world too.

For there can be no necessary limit to the power in Christ that these words imply. The limit must be associated in some way with unbelief on our part. Another intellectual combination transferred as such from the word of life into the believer's brain that imparts a fount of strength, is the assurance that all the promises of God in Christ are yea, and in Him Amen, to every converted believer: "For how many soever be the promises of God in Him is the yea, wherefore also through Him is the

Amen, unto the glory of God through us."—2 Cor. i. 20, (Rev. Ver.)

These words clearly established our right to take possession of all the promises. All doubt is clearly swept away, and the fact established, that all converted individuals, therefore the converted church collectively, is entitled individually and collectively, to take possession of every one of the promises of God, and make each and all their own. This being a settled matter, all may strengthen themselves in the strength of God, by taking full possession of one and all of His promises. Paul clearly saw the importance of leaving no doubt whatsoever on this point, as uncertainty here would lead to doubt, and mar the success that implicit confidence would insure. So that the course of reasoning he adopted removes every shadow of doubt, and leaves the converted believer fully confident that in Christ he is authorised to take possession of the life-inspiring promises as his inheritance in Christ. The intellectual combinations giving expression to the Ideal conception in the human brain that confers this priceless and unprecedented boon, rest in the fact that Christ is the seed—the Elect of God—and that every converted believer is united to our Lord as such, thus forming His body, in the Ideal Christ having an actual habitation as a centre of activity in the believer's brain. The believer, so animated, is the seed or elect of God, a condition which confers on such a similar right in so far with His Lord and Master, Jesus Christ. For in virtue of the union referred to, the converted believer is the seed or elect of God.

Why should we, the church of the first-born, shrink from handling in this way the tools the materialism of our age puts into our hands, so as to make the material doctrine our Lord so fully taught intelligent to our contemporary race. Viewed from the material standpoint, we have the mystery cleared away—hid from ages and generations—now " made manifest to the saints, to whom God makes known what is the riches of the glory of this mystery among the Gentiles, which is Christ in you"— the converted believer— " the hope of glory."—Col. i. 27. And with an activity of the nature I have indicated, manifesting the presence of the Redeemer God in the human brain, is not this promise literally fulfilled, " in God making known among the Gentiles the mystery of Christ in us"—converted believers—" the hope of glory."

In the Ideal Christ in the human brain, as the centre of activity, the energy radiating from there, finds its correlative or equivalent in the risen Lord, who reacts in harmony. For such a material form as this is the union that unites the converted believer with the point in space God in Christ inhabits. Christ, united thus, demonstrates to the Gentile world that election is the seed of God in the human brain as the Ideal Christ radiating in unison with its source, the Redeemer God, Christ its Lord. This mystery is rendered intelligent, and can be explained in human language by recognizing in the personifying Christ, the Elect of God, the object the believer grasps, and in doing so, takes subjective possession of Christ—the object—who thus becomes a part of the individual's soul, elected and redeemed, because the Ideal Christ has a place in that human soul. So simply as this is the mystery of election explained. It places the developed human mind in its ceaseless activity in vital union with a permanent object ever capable of supplying it with new ideas.

Union with our Lord comes in belief, so that in a

general way all true believers are elected. But the final distinction that separates the intellectual believer from the converted believer, is the vitality conversion confers on the individual as an individual being in the vital union of realised belief with Christ, therefore an elected individual. Whereas the intellectual believer is not in this vital way united, therefore he and his class, as intellectual believers, are only elected in a general way as the class or nation forming the general community of the visible Christian church on earth. The converted are in this community, but are not " of it," because they, as individuals, are in vital union with Christ, a connection doubtless marked by the radiant energy forming the medium between, that unites and gives expression to the type of energy conversion assumes, resting in realized belief, which includes Covenant blessings; and nothing short of being assured thus, will raise the individual above the world, and insure his affections being set on things above, as one whose life is hid with Christ in God, so that when Christ who is his life shall appear, he shall appear with him in glory—CoL iii. 4. Not only so, but as one now and here united, and that fact made visible in the presence of our Lord, by the energy gene rated in the human brain, through a process of combustion, which, in the strength of the emotion, wafts itself outward as the equivalent of the emotion so generated arising from this highly vitalized intellectual combination, which springs from the Ideal Christ, recognised as the sinner's substitute, onward through space to where the Redeemer dwells. Connected thus, Stephen beheld the glory of God—glory which *to him* typified " heaven opened, and the Son of Man standing on the right hand of God." — Acts vii. 56. In this conception Stephen saw our Lord as two separate and distinct individuals, in His two separate and distinct natures, as human—the Son of our race—as divine—God. For our Lord in thus far has two distinct personalities in His double natures. They are distinct and separate, as nothing short of this is sufficient to satisfy the claim His various offices set forth as viewed either from the human or divine standpoint, in the relationship our Lord occupies toward our race.

Our present point, dealing with sanctification, is that converted Christians, living in the full assurance (which belief in God's word justifies) that all promises including all covenant blessings are true to them, will alone secure the mental state that enables the believer to mortify the deeds done in the body, so as to rise above the desire of worldly advancements called in Christian language "the corruption of the world through lust." It is as individuals so completely selfish in their nature as our race is, that the Christian religion takes to do with us. It is only when the convert feels fully assured in realizing that he indeed and in truth is saved, and therefore he will get all the good things the Saviour has promised, that the converted individual is enabled to triumph over the world, the Devil, sin, and the flesh.

One thus equipped in feeling assured that he has "received Christ Jesus the Lord, so he walks in him, rooted and built up in him, established in the faith as he has been taught, abounding therein with thanksgiving."—Col. ii. 7. These words of Paul, when fully understood and realized, will inspire with the zeal that St. Paul himself experienced. The thing to be remembered is, that it is in resting implicitly on being justified by faith, that facilitates sanctification; thereby it is so that the world losing its power over one fully assured that Christ has in store for him something far better than the world has to offer, places one so equipped in the position of despising, viz., being indifferent to worldly advantages. Shortly, such an one is following the lead of pleasure, in loving, following, and serving Christ, going on the way rejoicing in the footsteps of the Master, animated thus by the sentiment that ensures sanctification as the equivalent of Christian devotedness. For so it is.

All rests in taking full possession of the promises and making them all one's own. First and last, resting in the assurance that I (the personal pronoun) am a sinner saved by grace—redeemed by Christ's vicarious sacrifice—therefore elected in Christ the seed and elect of God, resting thus in forgiveness and acceptance is the condition God Himself has provided. Therefore, humanly speaking, God is Himself responsible for the effect produced. For such is Loving and Working. But the sentiment of love that leads to all this must be the real language of the heart ; not the lip language of assumed love that takes it for granted that all this is true to the individual, because he is a Christian believing in Christ's merits as sufficient to save the chief of sinners. The individual must have felt that he himself is the sinner saved by Favour, therefore entitled to all. It is not the glad tidings of the gospel accepted as true in a general way that has the sanctifying effect; but the sentiment that arises from the gospel of glad tidings taken possession of by the individual. It is in realizing that all is true to him that inspires the sentiment that insures sanctification, and induces following the lead of pleasure in loving and serving Christ, the object loved.

But, remember, we are warned by the word of God of the danger we are exposed to in the world, and commanded to watch and pray that we enter not into temptation. If converted Christians cared nothing for the world or its opinions, they would have fewer temptations to fear and overcome. It is true, worldly-mindedness places many temptations in the Christian's path, which induces him to strive to attain what often proves hurtful to his growth in grace, and therefore will mar his eternal lustre. It is often that we so ardently cling to the world, because there is so much in it we have set our hearts on. Conditions, though inspired by the most secret devotion, are dividing our hearts between love to our Lord and the strong desire or love we have to accomplish the work we have wrought conscientiously in and set our hearts on to bring to a successful issue. The missionary to the heathen—say in the centre of Africa—who is in the first rank of the self-sacrificing community that has given up the world for Christ, even such is not always free from a divided heart of this nature. It is true there are few of the converted indifferent to the world's opinion or to worldly comfort. For true it is, we rush into temptation and get accustomed to conditions, as Christians we have no claim to; conditions such as belong to the unconverted part of the race, whose comfort and happiness mainly depend on what the world has to give. Put in contrast with this, is Christ united to the converted Christian in what ought to be the continuous flow of energy which Love generates as the equivalent of the moving current that unites both in giving expression to the highest phase of pleasure known to our race. United thus, Christ's inspiring words are, " Ye are not of the world, for I have chosen you out of the world," to be sanctified by the revelation given to the race in prophecy anticipating a deliverer sent by God to redeem the race—that anticipated deliverer you have found in Me Christ; and by Me you are sent to be sanctified through truth revealed by God.—John xvii.

By letting your lives manifest, prove, and proclaim your physical and spiritual union with Me, that to you I am King, Brother, and Lord.

But if the convert rush into temptation, and imbibe the spirit of the world, so as to find much of his enjoyment in what the world has to give, how can Christians be sanctified? For the lusts of the flesh must be conquered if the convert is to go on his way rejoicing worthy of the high calling to which he is called in being elected in Christ. Otherwise he may be acting so as to be ashamed before Him at His coming. To be full of the glory of God is to be following the lead of pleasure that love to Christ begets, and choosing the self-sacrificing course that our Lord Himself took and enjoined. For Faith, working by Love, gives expression to the power of the new life, that is, the new source of joy imparted by Christ manifesting Himself as an object of love in the human mind constraining the convert to follow and serve by willing obedience Christ—the object loved. For such is the flood of the life's inspiring vitality that agitates and emanates from the marvellously constituted web of nerve tissue that surrounds the muff-guarded cylinder of the human brain when inspired by love either human or divine. The object and abode of that object is the only condition in so far that marks in deferentiating the physical connection the glowing energy manifests in—we shall say— uniting the subject and its object of love.

Christian faith in the activity of harmony is reason intensified by the feeling which the intellectual combination forming the ideal Christ, the object of love, imparts in functioning that sentiment. For faith, working by love, is the intellectual combination in its ideal form, which the term reason intensified by feeling would explain as the operation taking place in the organ of mind, by one realizing that he is saved, and that therefore all the promises of Christ are true to him. The natural condition of the organ of mind inspired thus, would be expressed in "I know whom I have believed, and am persuaded he is able to keep what I have committed to him." I ask, would it not seem impossible for the Ego, the vital force of material mind, animated thus, to cease its activity on the death of the body, surrounded as it would be by energy or the universal ether which the vitality of the Ego naturally would absorb in order to sustain its movement. That vitality would cease its activity animated thus and surrounded so, is far more difficult to imagine than that consciousness actually does continue its activity in its natural way by the Ego absorbing the energy that surrounds it to do so.

A further point of strength to the Christian so inspired is that fear, the death-threatening sentiment, is absent, because God has not given him—the Christian—the "spirit of fear, but of power and of love, and of a sound mind"— 2 Thes. i. 7. "Being confident of this very thing, that he who has begun a good work" in the Christian "will perform it unto the day of Christ Jesus. For it is God that worketh in him both to will and to do of his good pleasure, according to the eternal purpose which he purposed in Christ Jesus."—Eph. iii. 11. Thus assured, the converted believer is no longer tossed to and fro, and carried about with every wind of doctrine, but is established in the faith, speaking the truth in love. Having the practical experience that the fruit of spiritual life, generated by love, is righteousness and truth.

Such knowledge and experience comes to the converted one as the evidence of the new sense union with

Christ, giving expression to—as a new life-sustaining action—a new source of activity more or less apparent in every converted Christian; activity which, issuing from the developing intellectual combinations of the new sense manifesting its growth in grace, may be called the evidence, token, or *title deed*, the subject has in his possession which assures his right to eternal life, as a sinner saved by grace, rejoicing that it is so, in striving to live worthy of so high a calling, by loving and working. For those thus inspired have proved the sincerity of their love, and have the witness in the title deeds I have indicated, as intellectual combinations developed In the brain by the energy the new life imparts in loving and serving. In this way is unveiled the mystery of the hidden life that springs from God in Christ, by explaining the conditions thereof in the language that human intelligence places at the Christian's disposal—language developed as the equivalent of the laborious labour modern research imposes on its votaries, in providing proof of the material nature of the Ego. Their incessant labour is ill requited by Christian contemporaries, who have in great measure ignored the phase of intelligence developed by modern research, in brushing it aside from the place it is designed by God to take, to illuminate truth revealed, so as to demonstrate the rational conditions on which the conceptions of the spiritual life conversion unfolds, rest, which at present are held in faith as a matter of belief.

It will be seen from what I have said how completely separated converted believers are from the race in the new life, arising from Faith working by Love. The activities that the new sense manifests are the equivalent of the sanctifying power displayed by the church of the first-born, formed of individuals converted during their life on earth, animated by the divine emotion of love which conversion generates. The convert has accepted the good things put at his disposal by the Christ of Christianity, henceforth to be recognised as the God of humanity. Sanctifying grace is the manifestation of the glad tidings accepted by the convert. The general result of this, as classified by St. Paul is what the converted believer received after believing, in being sealed with the holy spirit of promise.—Eph. i. 11-14. He is sealed in the sentiment inspired by the promise realized, inducing the self-consecrated life sanctification indicates. All springs from the glad tidings received, generating the emotion of love after believing. For it is the emotion of divine love thus explained that leads to sanctification, the fruit of the divine life imparted in belief. Sanctification, so understood, is necessarily the fruit of the emotion of love imparted by the sentiment which has a divine origin, inspiring the church of the first-born, who works under its influence. The manifestation of the works done by this church in the sanctification of its members animated by the emotion of love is the tribute of gratitude rendered to the object loved—a tribute of gratitude manifesting the new sense which springs from a new vital source, originated by our Lord's vicarious sacrifice, therefore of a totally different origin from the vital energy of self-conservation animating unconverted humanity. The new vital source is God as a God of Love, imparting His own nature, through the operation of Christianity, to the portion of the Christian church that has been converted, called the church of the first-born. A church led on all through eternity as sinners saved by grace, animated by the nature of God, into which gratitude has been infused and takes a prominent place, working through the influence of love divine on earth, and ever more in eternity.

It is needless to say much more on the subject of the distinction that divides two sections of the human race. For from the light of present knowledge no distinctions could be more marked. One section is animated by self-conservation, called in Scripture the unsaved; the other section, who are inspired by the emotion of love divine, are insured of a peaceful eternal life, and strive to glorify in serving the object of its love—Christ the Lord, who secures this priceless boon. The vital activity of the first is regulated by self-conservation, the latter is regulated by the emotion that induces to serve the object loved, namely, the God of humanity.

Such distinctions do not only divide the human race, but also the Christian church, that is, Christendom, eternally into two distinct nations or sections, guided by totally distinct sentiments. The one, the section of intellectual believers, guided by the natural instinct of self-preservation, illuminated by the Christian records, though not converted, therefore not disintegrated from the race human on earth by the sentiment conversion induces, called by our Lord a "Being born again." Whereas the other section of Christendom is "converted," disentegrated from the race in being born again—saved—animated by a new vital action, divine in its origin and nature, inducing service to its Divine Head, the Son of God, in the love that gratitude to a recognised, acknowledged, and "*accepted*" Deliverer begets. So differently constituted as this are the Intellectual and Converted sections of Christendom believers, in one section being animated by human nature—the other by the nature Adoption begets. Viewed from the highest point, the aim of the one is so to live as to be saved ; the aim of the other how best to serve this God of love who has already saved them. You will perceive the one class is striving to secure, that is striving to gain, what the other class already possesses. Both classes are Christian, holding as head Christ the Son of God, but the motives inducing service in both are totally different: the one is hoping to be saved in believing, and living a good, religious, and moral life ; the other is saved, and knows it is so, in having its nature changed by divine love infused, and as the nature of this love is, finds pleasure in serving the object loved.

The idea embraced in the term " holding the head," is the Intellectual combination which points to the permanent existence by whom infinite progress is developed—a term that embraces the full meaning of the words spoken by our Lord, " Without me ye can do nothing"—John xv. 5 ; also, " Whatsoever ye shall ask the Father in my name, He will give you."—John xvi. 23.

These general propositions apply to both sections of the church. This being so, it places each member of the intellectual section of the Christian church in a totally different position in the universe of space than that occupied by the unbelieving section of the race. For from the order of things, such must be true in the present dispensation at any rate, until Christ is accepted as the God of the race, who in the Old Testament Scriptures is referred to as " the God of the whole earth, shall he be called "—Isaiah liv. 5— applied to the Lord Jesus, who Christendom believes is the only-begotten Son of God, without whom we can do nothing.

CHAPTER XIV.

INTELLECTUAL CHRISTIANITY — WHAT IS IT? DO GOOD WORKS AND LIVE. INTO WHICH A FEW REMARKS ON BRAIN STRUCTURE ENTERS.

INTELLECTUAL believers, who form the unsaved section of the Christian Church, are unsaved because, as individuals, they have not been converted—that is, "born again," therefore they are not in the vital union Love generates toward the object, Christ, in the individual who feels he is already saved by the Redeemer, and rejoices as a sinner saved by Grace. The class referred to may be called saved as the Church collective, who believe Christ is the Son of God, divine in His origin and human only in His manhood. That He was the deliverer provided by God, He died on the cross, rose from the dead, ascended into glory, and as the living head of the Christian church occupies some point of space as our Lord, the man Christ Jesus.

All will see that a section believing in Christ in this way, is in a totally different position from that held by the unbelieving section of the race. For, in believing on Christ, Christendom is united with a humanly divine permanent objective existence, and holds that the scriptures or the church inspired of God, is the guide to regulate their lives in working out their own salvation in obedience to Christ, the vicarious sacrifice that God provided in His Son. With the unconverted—that is, "the intellectual believer," the motive at work in the intellectual combination inspiring, is, "do this and live," the Ideal conception implied being that faith must be accompanied by good works, so as to insure Salvation. These have not been born again, so they have not the personal experience of the inspiring power the Faith that worketh by Love possesses, in inducing the self-sacrificing service that love to an object begets; and they never think of applying the test that earthly love provides them with, in the willing service love to an object spontaneously generates.

Intellectual believers in the way indicated, are working out their own salvation, trusting to the personal merits obedience implies, and by doing so exposing themselves to the danger of being placed in the condition of having to pay the uttermost farthing. That might spring from the full consecration that obedience so rendered would indicate: which condition places those believing in the Christian records in a totally different and very much more responsible position from those who do not.

The idea conveyed in Matt. v. 21-26 on this point is making the individual responsible for the wrong act, when he is conscious of having acted unjustly, in being cast into prison and made to bear the consequences. This form of retribution intelligent beings are subject to who are conscious of having wronged a brother and have not agreed with their adversary. This is clearly the Saviour's meaning, and is a general proposition applicable to the unsaved human race as a whole. A general proposition rendered clearly intelligent in the graphic words of "with what judgment ye judge ye shall be judged, and with what measure ye mete, it shall be measured to you again." Though this general proposition applies to all unconverted, it places the intellectual Christian in a far more responsible position than the other, in being warned of the danger he is liable to incur, by our Lord, whom he justly believes to be of divine origin. When it is so, that Will is guided by motives, we have in this proposition the strongest of all motives to induce any one to do the right, viewed from the materialistic base, the human mind is now clearly proved to rest in. Strength is promised for any emergency to all who ask. The Lord's words are—"Ask, and it shall be given you, seek, and ye shall find, knock, and it shall be opened unto you. For every one that asketh, receiveth, and he that seeketh, findeth, and to him that knocketh, it shall be opened."—Matt. vii. 7-8. If the intellectual believer takes possession of these promises, he is armed for great emergencies, when enlightened by the rational conception on which the working of the general proposition is to depend, in the precept the words of our Lord convey in "Whatsoever ye would that men should do to you, do ye even so to them; for this is the law and the prophets."—Matt. vii. 12. This precept is addressed to men of considerable intelligence, rational beings capable of perceiving consequences, who are to be guided by a sense of justice, which makes them responsible for the effect produced, and are expected to regulate their actions accordingly: simply to regulate one's conduct toward others, in the harmony justice to self and to others indicate, guiding a class striving to work out its own salvation, trusting to the Lord's promised strength.

This precept does not, I think, affect the following rendering, though it may seem to do so. Suppose an unconverted man has done another a great wrong; because the injured one would not like to suffer himself again what he has suffered, would he be justified in letting the guilty
W

one escape unpunished, when acting so might generate selfishness and oppression in the other?

Remember, one of the good things God has to give for the asking, is wisdom and strength to act justly and rightly, and certainly an intelligent believer is supposed to ask this day by day, going onward in the promised strength indicated. It was to Intelligences acting and reasoning as human beings that our Lord addressed the words, "Do as you would be done to." Individuals acting thus, fulfil the law and the prophets. For it is when man does to his fellow-man what his fellow-man would have a right to do to him in similar circumstances, that makes the precept clearly intelligent, read in the light of the general proposition conveyed in these words "Judge not, that ye be not judged; for with what judgment ye judge, ye shall be judged; and with what measure ye mete, it shall be measured to you again."—Matt. vii. 1-2. Read in this light, a man desiring to do as he would be done to, in dealing with one who has wronged him, has to bear in mind that by letting the injury pass unheeded, he is not doing as he would like to be done to, as acting thus would leave the other liable to suffer the measure of the injustice he has measured out. 'Remember, it is not those converted I address thus. This being so, to compromise is the wise course to take. For to adopt the non-resistance creed where such consequences are involved, might be a most selfish and unjust course, in taking an unjust advantage of one who was responsible, to his own section of humanity, in the life to come for the measure of justice he had measured out. It ought to be apparent to all that the non-resistance creed can only be safely applied by the members of the church of the first-born, to whom no retribution can be made, because their sins have all been atoned for by Christ, and forgiven; therefore every member of this church is assured of eternal glory, a church in this world, though not of this world, yet left in this world, whose members are entitled to give away their natural life in carrying into practice the non-resistance creed. For this reason they have freely received that they may freely give away their earthly lives in glorifying Christ's name, His work, and His cause. As the only fruit of their conversion, they have at their own disposal to act thus, being in adoption one with Christ in God. In this way they may be said to give back to humanity what humanity gives in bestowing natural life freely on each without money and without price, when they adopt the non-resistance creed. It is thus seen how totally different are the responsibilities of the two classes that form Christendom. But for the section of Christendom that is working out its own salvation in the way it holds to be in obedience to Christ's command, who has revealed to them much of what does take place in the world to come governed by its laws, to adopt the non-resistance creed in the face of what has been revealed, might be acting a very selfish part. In my judgment the safest course for such to take would be that enjoined in Micah vi. 8—"To do justly, to love mercy, and to walk humbly with God."

As I have said, the case of the converted Christian is quite different. This class is animated by the new vitality which love to their Redeemer, as their recognised Deliverer, gives expression to; and, humanly speaking, may be so related to the race, as to call for some concession made by them to it, in return for the individual immortal existence that the law of generation and inheritance leads to. For example, they may forward race development in the moral and religious vitality that inspires such, as members of Christ's body, in glorifying Him, by infusing into the race the joy good works impart in strengthening these two elements. It is acting thus the converted become the salt of the earth, and when this action ceases, as said by Christ, so far as the world is concerned, they, the converted, are good for nothing but to be cast out and trodden under the foot of man—Mat. vi. 13.

Again, it is when the new form of vitality conversion confers is in active vigour, dispensing deeds of kindness, of charity, and love, inspired by the non-resistance creed, that the converted on our earth "so shine before men, that men may see their good works, and glorify their father which is in heaven."—Mat. v. 16. That the illuminating phase so indicated does in reality exist, as the source of a visible vibration to the disembodied spirit of our race, is just what might be expected as the manifestation of a natural law, when the vitality of this form of love is of a certain pitch, dispensing deeds of kindness on earth. Further, that the good works done by the intellectually believing section of Christendom does also glorify Christ on earth is certain. Though animated by a totally different motive, arising from a much less ardent form of love than that of the other section of Christendom, therefore there is a much lower phase of vibrating energy, issuing from such individuals, which, we may infer, cannot be clearly distinct to the disembodied spirits of our race. That the intellectually believing Church, created by Christ, will, as a whole, reflect Christ's glory made visible to the disembodied heathen in the good works its fruit disperses, may be safely inferred when viewed from the material base all rests in.

In this way does this section of Christendom stand related to the heathen world. Whereas, in the intensity of its love radiating from earth, does the converted—the church of the first-born—stand similarly related to the unconverted intellectual Christian church in its energy rendered visible to it. Each of the two sections of Christendon, called the body of Christ, in its own way we may infer, does reflect Christ's glory in the universe of space. For, in a general way, the intellectual believer holds Christ to be the Son of God and the Saviour of the world. So the church, as a whole, has in this intellectual combination the object Christ as a mental structure formed in the brain of each member of its community, which, if put in vital contact with Christ, in converting the individual by accepting the forgiveness He freely offers, would make that contact felt. The effect of this is to assure the individual of eternal life, so as to nullify the sentiment of fear, and generate gratitude and love to Christ for what He has done.

The condition capable of inducing this change is present in the brain of each member of the church as an intellectual combination embodying the ideal Christ. But, alas! the structure of this conception is in the form of a lifeless body, incapable of feeling, because deprived of the vital union that contact with Christ in conversion imparts. Therefore, viewed from the Christian standpoint, the soul of the individual is dead in not being in vital contact with the source of its life. The soul is animated by human nature, and as such has in its nature what may lead to the most depraved line of conduct. Though having the ideal structure of God the Son formed as an intellectual combination in the brain, ready to burst into vital activity at any moment, if "Sentient Personality" would but make the effort of grasping the free pardon our Lord makes offer of. An effort, if persisted in, will be speedily followed by the assurance that realised belief inspires in giving expression to the continuous flow of love divine, that emanates from Christ in uniting the ideal

Christ with the actual Christ in the felt communion of a soothing flow of love ; which induces the Ego to dispense with the pleasure the world can give during the short period of earthly life, in adopting the non-resistance creed, so as to infuse as much earthly joy as possible, into the contemporary human organism of humanity. An Ego born again during its earthly life, at death passes into the family of the adopted children of God, to be forever with the Lord. A distinction so great as this does conversion confer on its votaries, in transforming the intellectual believer into an actual Christian, in vital union with Christ, therefore adopted of God—and he enters heaven as such.

However, the intellectual believer must remember that in virtue of the eternal glory that holding the ideal Christ as a form of belief confers on him, it also confers corresponding duties, towards his fellow-Christians as well as towards the world at large. And such corresponding duties do make him his brother's keeper, in this that, by revealed truth, he is assured that the course of action he adopts on earth in the consequences arising therefrom during earthly life, does affect the individual's destiny in the eternal state. Further, that all Christians are bound to make that fact clearly intelligent to the unbelievers of their day, by applying the new light shed on this point by modern science so clearly giving proof of the material nature of the human Ego. There are endless ways for Christians to apply the new forms of thought that this fact develops so as to illustrate the truth that our Lord reveals to the race. It will give the old truth a new lustre it never possessed before, and will make mysteries involved in revelation clearly intelligent to all.

Christendom, in accepting the Christian records as a revelation from God in Christ, is in possession of a code of laws it is bound to give heed to in dealing with man. Possessed of knowledge thus revealed, the intellectual Christian is in danger of being beaten with many stripes, if he does not take heed to unfold to his fellows in clearly intelligent language the importance these records possess. However, before they can make the mysteries revealed clear and intelligent to others, it is very certain they must have a clear conception themselves of what is revealed, in adjusting the molecular properties of the brain to the new conditions ; so as to enable all classes to understand how modern scientific facts can be used to illustrate the old truths in giving them direct point and force. Take for example the truth revealed in these texts—Matt. xii. 36-37 ; Rom. xiv. 12 ; 2 Cor. v. 10—which treat of the responsibilities man is exposed to in the future life and let them be read in the light of the new ideas (formed of mental groupings) that scientific research has developed, and placed at the Christian's disposal for that end. They will enable Christians to form a clear conception of the material nature of the Ego, and the process that creates and develops it. Christians will thus find a new lustre added to the importance of revealed truth which far surpasses any conception that could previously have been formed of the nature and truth the passages referred to contain. For natural science clearly proves that the Ego is the production of sensation, and that moment by moment, from the first sensation at birth, we are building up the eternal sequence which conforms to soul, Ego, or inner man, that survives death and holds the forces together as the self-conscious Ego of the individual to which these passages quoted from the Christian records apply. Further, that each self-conscious Ego will be known as the beginning of life in me, in us, derived by the law of inheritance from our progenitors. Thus understood and applied, it proves the solemn responsibility.' attached to those whose lives effect the destiny of children, in the form and quality of vitality which the structure imparts in the functionary power of the brain. This will be self-evident when the conservation of vital energy is applied to explain the nature and form of the intellectual combinations building up the human brain. Where the vitalized forces, capable of developing intelligence, are stored up ready to start into activity in developing the Ego on the arrival of the first sensation from the external world.

Further, we may only have to apply the conservation of energy, so understood, to the brain of a child born of converted Christian parents, to solve the mystery of "Else were your children unclean; but now are they holy."—1 Cor. vii. 14—the text on which the salvation, by election, of a child born of a Christian parent is understood to rest. Anyhow, it is very probable that a child born even of intellectual Christian parents will at birth have an intellectual combination in the brain corresponding to, and developed of the truth Christianity enfolds, inducing tendencies not possessed by a child whose antecedents and parents are unbelieving heathens. In such combinations we have a centre ready to be evoked when the proper stimulus is applied. How far the election of the infant may be involved here, we cannot tell. Though in the forces Christian belief indicates we may infer the Ego of the infant carries with it properties that would lead towards Christian belief. Observe, brain organism viewed in the abstract must be a production of objective units as perceived subjectively by the Egos of our race.

In applying the conservation of vital energy to the forces of the organic brain at birth, we may safely infer, that if the structures that will develop Intellect, were analysed as sections of mind—if that were possible—just as the analyst analyses the contents of the stomach in the case of one suspected of being poisoned, these sections of mind would indicate their origin as the offspring of the lives that gave its form of intelligence an individual existence. For, assuredly, we may infer, if the forces that gave birth to Intellect were analysed as the energy of intellectual combinations, these mental images would proclaim the nature and origin of these combinations. Further, that the intellectual combination of energy, locked up in the brain at birth, will at death indicate its origin in the form of the vital force derived from its progenitors, we may safely assume. This much may be said of life and its laws, when applied to human intelligence, which creates immortal individual units of its own form of vital force, namely, the children born into the social organism on earth.

It is certain that a condition on which intelligence depends is the structure formed of intellectual combinations, transmitted by the law of inheritance in the built up human brain. That the brain organism develops human intelligence, when the proper stimulants are applied, is so. These facts, clearly within our reach, prove intellectual combinations to be transmitted forms of the objective world to the brain of the subject, where the social organism play the most important part. That these transmitted ideas carry with them into the recesses of the psycho-intellectual activities of the brain the emotions that accompanied their origin, is true; and they are the vitalised elements that appear in the brain as ideal combinations, and as such, have an immortal existence conferred on them in being seized by Sentient Personality. Such is the combined action that the human nervous system creates in creating its Ego. As the brain is proved to be built up of such vitalized objective forms, it seems possible, in the spiritual sense of the word, to analyse them, by applying the test conveyed in the laws of logic, to explain the ideas and their emotions that form the brain.

Further, when these ideal intellectual combinations possess the power of reproducing their own forms of vital energy, which, in functioning, emit the emotion that accompanied them, we have in these conscious states an Ego ever capable of feeling, therefore a self-endowed form of Immortality. For to live is to feel, and to feel is to live. This immortality is inherent in the Ego itself, and confers a like boon on every sensation that the human form has given birth to, in finding a habitation in one or other of the Egos of the race. If we add to this proposition, what is probably true, that the Ego builds itself of sensations in the human form of the universal ether, and that every sensation adds its influx of such ether in developing the Ego, we have conditions to which we can justly apply the term conservation of vital ether—say energy. In analysing the capacity of the Ego as a whole, or the capacity of each sensation or group of sensations—we use the term capacity to indicate the force or power of each or of all combined—as the potential vital energy each human Ego had generated and can emit in functioning. Each Ego, in functioning, is understood to emit the emotion that accompanied the intellectual combination when formed.

It might be well to state here that I hold the term ether or energy, whether viewed as a vitalised force or not, to be the subtle fluid emanating from the sun, as well as from all luminous bodies in space, thus filling space with their own uncondensed substance, the radiant matter of the luminiferous ether everywhere present. A portion of this ether is vitalised, and in its way locked up in forming the immortal human Egos. So they may justly be called the vitalized portion of the luminiferous ether which, in functioning conscious states has taken the abiding human form, and as such is the habitation of the disembodied human soul, ever capable of feeling, therefore immortal in functioning conscious states, as well as in its substance the ether. We justly apply the term ether, so qualified and understood, to indicate the human instrument of progress that builds up the unsaved section of the human race; though we cannot apply these conditions in organic form or substance to hold good in the converted Christian section of the race, for the reason that this section is Divine in its Adoption and its members may not continue human in their form, or even continue to be formed of the universal ether, for they are divinely adopted and are one with Christ in God.

The subject matter of this chapter being the Intellectual believer, who takes as his motto—*do good works and live*, therefore what mostly concerns this class, is how best to occupy their time, so as to insure their eternal well-being, in being eminently fruitful in the good works to which they trust, as every one of these are immortal as such. To strengthen this point was the object I had in view in referring to brain organism as I have done in this chapter. The class referred to have, in the Christian records, the code of laws they are to be judged by as a race led onwards through eternity by the Son of God they honoured by confessing Him before men on earth, animated with the instinct of doing well for one's self and acting justly to each other.

Let a race so destined ponder on the words spoken

by our Lord " Woe unto you that are rich, for ye have received your consolation."—Luke vi. 24. These words place the rich and poor in contrast, by pointing out the advantage the rich have over the poor in this world, in having their comforts provided for, which leaves the time of the rich at their own disposal, to occupy very much as they please. Whereas the poor have to make their bread by their own exertions it may be, in providing the rich with the comforts and luxuries that surround them. Contrasted thus, the rich Intellectual believers have much consolation provided for them by the poor, and in many cases live an idle useless life, while the poor are earning their daily bread serving them. Thus far the rich have all the advantages.

But how strangely different the contrast becomes, when we pause to consider the advantages derived in the conservation of vital energy that the poor have conferred on them, in the liberated energy by which the Ego builds itself up during the earthly life of the individual in, we shall say, the luminiferous ether vitalized thereby. Conditioned thus, it confers on the disembodied Ego of the poor the potential capacity of generating the equivalent of the energy liberated during earthly life in doing conscientious work. In contrasting the rich and the poor in this way from the standpoint of Christian morality, I do not for a moment infer that energy spent in doing work not conscientiously done, would confer the advantage these conditions employ. It is when we view the potential energy treasured up in the formation of the Ego of the poor intellectual Christians as the equivalent of the honest labour they bestow in providing the comforts of the rich, that we comprehend the full force of our Lord's warning words, " Woe to you that are rich, for ye have your consolation."—Luke vi. 24.

By employing the material views the intelligence our age provides us with to explain and illuminate what is revealed, we can make the words of life intelligent to the non-Christian world, in a way impossible till now. Just note the strong appeal the rendering of the passage referred to makes to the Intellect of our age, in the explanation it gives of the danger arising from the idle life wealth often leads to, as such stand related to man in the light of eternity. The general proposition may be applied in a much broader sense indicating the favour conferred on Protestant Britain in the luxuries provided by the labour of heathen nations, put in contrast with the return Britain makes in sending missionaries to the heathen nations to convey to them the glad tidings that the Christian records impart. In accepting what we use up of heathen labour in this way, we increase our responsibilities many fold—responsibilities Britain is bound to acknowledge and return apart from the obligation resting on it as a Christian nation, to diffuse the knowledge of the gospel of peace. And, true it is, that the general proposition, applied to our race, included all in the energy that the immortal Egos forming that race unfold. It includes every iota of the vitalised energy that the human organism, in emitting sensations, gives birth to.

Much more might be said of the responsibility resting on individuals and nations—and specially so on Intellectual Christians—viewed in the light that revealed truth gives, when illuminated by the intelligence that the students of natural science have added to our knowledge. This class of men have often been greatly maligned by Christians. The Christian church constantly forgets the practical lesson taught by St. Paul, " We can do nothing against the truth.

but for the truth."—2 Cor. xiii. 8. This general proposition is deduced by St. Paul to indicate the fact that truth in the abstract, as seen from the human standpoint, is ordered of God.

Further, if our Lord's object in revealing what He does in the Christian records of man and his destiny, was to enable Christians to apply the laws the sciences rest in, to explain how what is revealed of man's future was to be accomplished by the laws of nature so directed as to secure that end. Viewed thus, the student of Christendom was intended to stand between unbelievers and his class to apply for that purpose the truth the student of nature provides— " Thus unfold the banner of the cross, and honour all His laws "—in a way not dreamt of less than a century ago. Let us Christians firmly rest in this general proposition, written in letters of light, ever visible, and applicable to what can be said of revealed truth in the light the scientific investigations of the age provide.

Much of this illuminating work of the future must rest on the intellectual Christian church, every member of which is united to Christ in the forces forming the Ideal Christ, who is the God of Humanity in the brain, so in that respect, they are in a totally different position to that occupied by the unbelieving portion of the race. The intellectual believer is thus well qualified for the work of compiling sets of truth I assign him. For each, in his way, is united to the object, Christ, " the God of the whole earth " —Isaiah v. 4-5—therefore insured of an eternal existence. This is the position Christ the Son of God now occupies to the human race. To make all that is Revealed even in the Christian records, plain and intelligent, is a very important work conferred on the Church of the future, requiring considerable intellectual power as well as force of character. Those engaged thus will do well to note the words of the Redeemer addressed to the race—" He that overcometh shall inherit all things."—Rev. xxi. 7. For the strength imparted is of eminent importance to the Intellectual Christian Church that leads, as well as to the section of the race that follows.

CHAPTER XV.

MYSTERIES OF CHRISTIANITY EXPLAINED IN SCIENTIFIC LANGUAGE.

IT is to the conception on which the science of Biology rests that we must turn for an explanation to make the mysteries revealed in the Christian records intelligent to all. For example, Biology proves that the natural course life takes is that of following the lead of pleasure.

This Law of following the lead of pleasure conforms to Christianity in this that the emotional nature being stirred to its depths by love to Christ in conversion, the convert is compelled to give expression to that emotion in striving to serve the object loved; while the emotion of love predominates, it generates the state of mind in the Christian convert to which the law of necessity is applicable. It is the Law governing Faith working by Love. Christianity can only be approached as a science when its precepts and laws can be explained in the language of the science of Biology, and that Christianity will admit of this, I confidently affirm. Therefore, if this is possible, all will admit that it is of the greatest importance to humanity that the science of Christianity be understood and promulgated. For the result arising therefrom would be equally beneficial in furthering man's spiritual wellbeing, as well as insuring his temporal advantage and peace of mind. It is evident to me that St.

Paul anticipated such a science when he divided our race into three species, represented by the third heaven referred to in 2 Cor. xii. 2, where the sentiment animating each would be to induce each section to act from a different motive.

Christianity being a new dispensation created by Christ's life, death, resurrection, and ascension, it is the revelation contained in the Christian records that specially concerns Christians, and must form the base of a Christian science, with its motto of "resist not evil." A science of Christianity was only possible when the race had so far advanced as to be able to classify the phenomena of nature in building up the sciences, of the observed and demonstrated facts nature provided, so as to apply the forces of nature to show how the mysteries involved in their agency may have been employed to produce the Christian miracles; as well as explaining the effect conversion produces on mind in bringing it into the harmony of vital union with Christ which the "being born again" bears witness of, in inducing a sentiment which finds pleasure in serving Christ as the object of love.

Christianity takes to do with the immortal soul created of conscious states, and we have seen that "primarily" conscious states are derived from the objective world, and carry with them the emotions that accompany them at their origin. I hold it permissible to believe an Ego or soul, so defined, to be built up of luminiferous ether, which, when disembodied as such in functioning, gives expression to the conscious states, developed during natural life, and the correlative of consciousness, the phenomena of which conscious states are forms. Through this process the ether becomes vitalized in assuming the Human Form, and provides the immortal

x

part of man, which enables him, as a disembodied spirit, to penetrate everywhere, yet retaining his human personality; which was given birth to in the first emotion the organism in relation with its environment created, in vitalizing and transforming the section of the ether then present as a conscious state into the immortal Ego.

When we have a material human soul or Ego formed and endowed thus, which our Lord tells us is born of the flesh—flesh; which cannot cease its activity on the death of the organism, but continues to function conscious states— in such an Ego we assuredly have a base for the science of Christianity to rest on. This science must find its work in pointing out how the laws of nature can be applied to accomplish the future conditions which, revelation indicates, have yet to be fulfilled in the history of our race, as well as to anticipate how the laws of nature could have been so directed as to produce the Christian miracles. For example, what law of nature did our Lord use—for nature is one—to produce the loaves and the fishes. Are not these organic elements present in or on our planet, which, in obedience to our Lord's command, united to produce organic matter formed into loaves and fishes, required to feed the hungry multitude? Our Lord thus commanded nature to do what our men of science do in the laboratory, guided by intellect in producing the substances they want to form, either organic or other. In viewing the Christian miracles from this point Christians are justified in maintaining, there was no break in the continuity of nature. In the future to act thus, may become a common practice, judging from the words of our Lord in John xiv. 12-13. Let that be as it may, in viewing "nature as one," and reasoning thus, the science of Christianity will make great progress.

By applying biology, including human physiology, to explain truth revealed in the third chapter of John, we get a clear conception of what our Lord means, when he defined the human mind as one in substance with the body, and called it flesh, put in contrast with the new spiritual sense conversion develops, as the equivalent of the heavenly sentiment that union with God in Christ begets.

The Science of Christianity, originated by our Lord, rests on the materialistic conception of mind that biology advances, called by our Lord flesh, when He indicated the necessity that rested on the natural man to be born again before he could be saved. That is, in the efficacy conversion imparts, enabling the individual to realise as a personal experience that the kingdom of heaven is within him—the fruit of the new sentiment our Saviour calls spirit.

Thus, then, the work of the student of Christian physiology is to define the mental state that marks the distinction of a converted individual put in contrast with one not converted, therefore unsaved. The first class are by our Lord said to be born again—created anew—in being inspired by a heaven-born sentiment, the latter remaining in their natural state. Surely a distinction so great as this may be defined in language clearly intelligent to the weakest capacity.

This is a personal experience, indispensable to every student or teacher of Christian physiology, otherwise he is a wholly incapable guide, in not having acquired the most rudimentary knowledge of the subject he professes to be qualified to teach and instruct others in. That this is so must be apparent, when it is clearly proved that the fundamental separation of the Intellect is into three such simple divisions as Discrimination, Similarity, and Retentiveness, put thus by Dr. Bain :—"(1) Discrimination, the sense of Feeling or Consciousness of Difference ; (2) Similarity, the sense of Feeling or Consciousness of Agreement ; and (3) Retentiveness, or the power of Memory or Acquisition." With Intellect thus simplified, surely the Intellectual distinction that marks a change so great as that of "being born again" must be of such a nature as to enable the student of Christian physiology to define in clear enough language the distinction that separates the converted individuals forming the Christian church from the unconverted race.

In adopting this process the student of Christian physiology is dealing with the human Intellect built up of Discrimination, Similarity, and Memory, just as a man of science would deal with properties of a not very complex compound he was analysing. For when in the case of the Intellect we substitute the feeling and the felt, for the properties of the physical compound being analysed, in defining the mode in which a sinner saved by grace (that is by favour) feels himself affected towards Christ as his substitute, whom he loves, therefore finds pleasure in serving, put in contrast with how he felt toward Christ before his conversion as the originator of Christianity, toward whom he was in a certain degree indifferent. This being so, I ask one capable of judging, have we not a mental state as clearly marked in its own way, as the conditions marking the physical analysis, in how such mental states differ and agree, put in contrast with the analysing process of a not very complex compound. For we have in both cases a material base capable of being analysed it its own way. As has been said of the Intellect by Dr. Bain, in his "Mind and Body," in "Discrimination, Similarity, and Retentiveness, we have an ultimate analysis of the mental powers, their numbers cannot be increased or diminished ; fewer would not explain the fact, more are unnecessary. They are the Intellect, the whole Intellect, and nothing but the Intellect. Remember, it has been already explained that Ideas carry their emotions with them, which, in thought, reappear as such. Therefore, we know that all intellectual combinations that move Sentient Personality have their emotional side, and in these emotions we have the definite properties of intellectual complexity which mark the distinction in the Intellect of a converted Christian from the Intellect of a man in his natural state. In treating the subject in this way, we have a clearly distinct conception of the mental process in the new condition conversion creates, as the special experience marking the distinction between a man in his natural state and a man born of the spirit. The chief feature that marks the distinction, in one having accepted Christ's free offer of forgiveness, is the emotional nature being animated by the love to the Redeemer gratitude inspires. In this form of love the converted Christian is so united to Christ as to form part of His body in his sensations being transmitted to the Saviour, his head, just as our bodies transmit the impressions of their surroundings to the brain, through the nervous system. In this case the nervous system is the vibrating link that unites the brain and the world in carrying impressions to the soul, Sentient Personality; whereas with the Christian it is the sentiment of love vibrating in unison with its source, the Saviour, that unites the redeemed one with Christ his Lord. The Intellectual conceptions conveyed from the Christian records to the brain through the medium of the senses develop the ideal conceptions from which all spring, for, in this way, is the activity of the heavenly sentiment established between Christ and His redeemed ones. The sentiment in its fulness is the spirit of adoption, which frees from the bondage of fear. This mental state is graphically put by St. John in the "there is no fear in love; but perfect love casteth out fear; because fear has torment. He that feareth is not made perfect in love." Followed by the reason that induced such love, given in the graphic words, "we love Him because He first loved us."—1 John iv. 18-19. For, love begets love, and such is the union established between Christ in heaven and His people—His spiritual body—on earth.

The union is effected through the medium of the universal ether—as the conducting agent—between the saints on earth and the Saviour in heaven. In this way, the Intellectual combination, which forms an Ideal conception as a conscious impression in the human Brain, impresses itself on the ether as such, and is thereby wafted onward through space to the point which the Redeemer—in the human form as the man Christ Jesus our Lord—occupies, and which is thereby participated in by him, surrounded as is indicated in the Revelations with the seven churches, typified in the seven stars, conditions which give expression to the material nature of all. For nature is one. Probably all is formed of the universal ether fastened so as to represent both conditions typified in the seven stars in His right hand called the seven churches, which indicates the material nature of the ether, which is the base that forms the connecting rod between Christ and His people. Every member of His spiritual body on earth is united thus, in the current of vibrating energy, passing from the human brain on to the person of the Redeemer, carrying the Ideal conception and its equivalent sentiment in its grasp, thus making the action and counter action that takes place between Christ and His Redeemed ones apparent to the saints on earth "in felt communion." This union rests in the similarity of sentiment and pitch, that unites both, thus forming one instrument, which vibrates in unison, united by the universal ether, which wafts the ideal present in the brain onward through space, to the abode of the Risen Lord, the Saviour in heaven. The material medium that effects this union, is the universal ether that unites both. A form of which is the medium that supplies the material referred to by John in Rev. i. 19-20, representing the things which are, and the things which shall be hereafter, and typified in the seven golden candlesticks, representing the seven churches, and the seven stars, the angels of the churches, with Christ having the seven stars in His right hand.

In reasoning in this way, we get an intelligent conception of what was taking place between Christ and the seven Churches of the Revelations—as perceived by John —Churches which Jesus warned and instructed by the hand of His beloved disciple. For the revealer of truth, called the Spirit of God, is the intellectual combination forming the moving current, accompanied with their emotions, carrying the conceptions or ideas to and from heaven and earth. In much the same way the conceptions embodied in human intelligence are represented in the social organism, and transmitted to the individual brain in the moving current of vital activity animating the individual to be interpreted in the brain by Sentient Personality as warnings and instructions conveyed to Sentient Personality, from the social organism of which Sentient Personality forms part.

It thus comes to pass that the mysteries surrounding revealed truths may become so plain, that he who runs may read, when such truth is explained in the language of the intelligence which humanity provides. For example, the

Saviour communicated to John the message He wished to convey to the race. Those animated by the Spirit of God are those converted who are taking their instructions from Christ in striving to regulate their lives by the standard laid down in the Christian records as Christ's message to them. Whereas the unconverted are animated by the human intelligence developed by the social organism. The social organism is the source from which the instructions that move them spring, guided in a general way by the voice of public opinion; whereas the converted, forming Christ's spiritual body, in so far as they are living up to their privileges, are striving to regulate their lives according to Christ's teaching. They have His voice sounding in their ears, in "Love not the world neither the things of the world. If any one love the world, the love of the Father is not in you."—1 John ii. 15.

But the unconverted, the natural man or class, are striving to regulate their lives in conformity to the usages of the world, the individual desire being to enjoy as much of the pleasures of the world as is possible and profitable. This is natural, for to strive to secure a pleasure is the vitality our planet has given birth to.

My aim for contrasting the two classes thus is to give a scientific explanation of the struggle Paul endured, and relates in Romans vii. 14-25. When animated, as related, Paul was striving to overcome the vital force that his natural life was built up of and induced, by nullifying that phase of energy by the power his spiritual nature generated through union with Christ. He employed this vitalised force to overcome the desires of the natural life which had built up his organism. Such are life and its laws both natural and spiritual. Remember, it is contrast that gives us our

Intelligence, for we do not know anything of itself but only the difference between it and another or other things. In such distinctions science rests, and the Science of Christianity is no exception, as we have just seen.

Thus, then, any one may comprehend the strong necessity to maintain the struggle of the will against a strong present appetite, which Paul had to encounter, related in the seventh chapter of Romans. In this incident we have Paul represented as Sentient Personality, the true life of the organism, drawing from the blood its energy to secure the purpose desired strengthened by our Lord. The energy drawn from the blood is the energy of human nature, but in Paul's motive and nature being changed, the energy is spiritualised, and as such is the new form of vital energy that builds up the new man, and enables Paul to overcome.

You see how Paul's new motive changed his nature, and placed him in conflict with the natural life of his organism. Placed in contrast, thus stands the natural man of the race and the spiritual man Christianity produced, in such a way as to simplify all that Christianity has to say. "Contrasts" involving the greatest consequences the race has, or can have, conferred on it. For to the one section, the world is everything; to the other, the Kingdom Christ has gone to prepare, which they enter at death, is everything. To the first class the world is all and all, whereas the second are striving with their might, not to love the world or the things of the world. For such is the scientific explanation of the struggle that must spring from the contrasted forces of such a nature. These contrasted forces are defined in the clearest possible terms as flesh and spirit. For, assuredly, it is the very flesh that builds itself up, as the equivalent of conscious states forming the organ of the carnal nature—

mind—that has to be conquered and overcome by the sentiment Christianity induces in developing an organic form of mind, which is of heavenly origin, in harmony with its own heavenly born spiritual nature, animated by the sentiment of Love to the Redeemer ensured of the "I can do all things by Christ strengthening me." "For there is therefore now no condemnation to them which are in Christ Jesus." "For the law of the spirit of life in Christ Jesus has made me free from the law of sin and death." (Revised Version) Romans viii. 1-2. These pathetic words provide the strength for the contest. They are sure to bring it to a successful issue; or, rather, I should say, end the contest, by enabling the individual to feel he is free, and inspired by the desire to serve. It was the realization of belief thus indicated, that Justification by Faith induces and inspires, that enabled Paul to feel free.

And, glory be to Jesus' name, we can offer this free pardon to all, even to a sinner so vile, that nothing short of the life-blood of his innocent victim, satisfied his love for self-gratification, leaving his victim to drag on a heartless lifeless existence, an outcast from society, whose only choice rested in being starved to death by inches, or to live a life even worse. Yet, to a wretch so vile as to cause such misery, at the very gate of death, we can offer a free pardon, assured that in the Kingdom of our Lord this free pardon, if accepted, will animate with love to God, generated by gratitutide that changes the cardinal nature and fits for heaven. But not by blotting out the past history of a sinful course, so as to leave an earthly life in that far a blank, but by inspiring with the gratitude and love forgiveness generates. For every thought that passed through the individual's mind on earth is crystallized in Sentient

Personality as a unit of a human soul or Ego, such being the law that develops the immortal self-conscious units of our race.

How terrible these realities are for a soul unsaved to realize, just entering as a living unit into eternity. What comfort could the most tender-hearted give if we had not a free pardon to offer? What consolation apart from that have we to offer? But in the sentiment the free parden develops, we have the spirit that quickeneth. Of it our Lord said—placing it in contrast with the fleshly organ of mind—" The flesh profiteth nothing; the words I speak unto you they are spirit and they are life."—John vi. 63. Such is the quickening power the converted one, even at the eleventh hour, carries with him, however sinful his organ of mind may be in having this sentiment of love divine infused into it. Mind has what quickeneth, animates and inspires in heaven, the new life our Lord imparts " In faith working by love."

It is so that the power of mind, perceiving the properties of matter includes all that conforms to human intelligence. Mind, the material product of the mental structure of natural man, viewed in the abstract, is the human unit called by our Lord flesh, of the earth, earthly, having only hope as its immortal sentiment or portion; therefore, when separated from the body it lives, and it hopes to live—it can rise no higher, it can go no farther—it may be immortal, or it may not; and of this for certain the natural structure of human mind can never know, except insurance comes through the evidence Revelation imparts.

Now we have to put in contrast with this material structure of mind, the new influence that comes in conversion, which is of a spiritual nature, called by our Lord Spirit, definite as that which is born of the spirit, spirit, the living thing working from within. The ideal conception unfolded in spirit is the divine life flowing directly from God through Christ which animates at conversion, thus quickening, so as to beget the new sentiment that divides the race. The discriminating power of the Intellect, thus illuminating Christians, as to the source and nature of the new influence, explains the mystery in the language of science. Viewed from this point, there is no mystery thus far, just a new mental state, of great magnitude has been perceived by the Intellect classified and recorded as a divine aspiration. It may be justly explained as the emotion of love, creating the endless flow of pleasure in the vital activity that sustains the immortality of eternal life in Jesus. In adopting this line of argument, Christians can classify very clearly the intellectual distinctions that mark the term flesh and spirit, and show that the human mind developed by the body is one in the substance of energy with it. Our Lord calls it flesh; Paul the carnal mind. Immediately the spirit of life, which union with Christ imparts, flows into a carnal man, it raises him above earth and the things of earth. It makes the individual indifferent to the pleasures of the world, in being animated by the purer higher joy of the adopted child of God. A mental state, justly called spiritual, in coming from God through Christ. Without Christ as the objective existence that bridges the gulf between, this sentiment, if possible, would be quite unintelligible, of which no scientific or rational explanation was possible.

The struggle that follows conversion is the spiritual life striving to take the place occupied by the self-regarding instinct of human nature, for when love to Christ waxes cold, human nature craves for earthly pleasure, that the higher life in a healthy state is indifferent to; whereas desire or craving generates mental conflict, which lowers the general vitality. It is when the craving or desire dies away that the mental struggle ceases. Thus understood, the realization of belief indicated in the eighth chapter of Romans, in its way, nullifies the desire, and with it the struggle ceases, by the believer realizing that all he desires is his in Christ. For such is the response Sentient Personality gives, in responding to the realization of belief, filled with joy at the announcement that all the good things Christianity offers are true—are the heritage of the Ego's own. This sentiment nullifies the desire for earthly pleasure.

Much that is said in the eighth of Romans is so plain to the converted—therefore adopted child of God—that he who runs may read. Assuredly, to him the mysteries of Christianity are explained in the simplest form of language.

Viewed from the point of Psychology, my plea is that the sentiment conversion confers, is the only efficient agency that fits a man for preaching the gospel. In proof of this, I quote the following hymn, because it was written by an unlearned man, a member of the Society of Friends, and breathes the very spirit of devotion.

ON PRAYER.

While Praying's thought an *Art* so happy,
   By a few who others rule—
JESUS teach me its importance
   In Thy self-denying schooL

Prayer's the sweetest, noblest duty—
   Highest privilege of man ;
God's exalted—man's abased :
   Prayer unites their natures one.

God *alone* can teach His children
    By His spirit how to *pray*;
Knows our wants and gives the knowledge
    When to ask, and what to say.

Why should man, then, manufacture
    Books of Prayer to get them sold?
Sad delusion—strive to barter
    Christ's prerogative for gold.

Where's the book, or school, or college
    That can teach a man to pray?
Words they teach devoid of power:
    Learn of Christ, for He's the way.

Why ask money from the people
    For those barren *Books of Prayer?*
Paper, ink, and words are in them;
    But, alas! God is not there.

Those who search will surely find Him,
    Not in *Books*—He reigns within;
Formal Prayers can never reach Him,
    Neither does He dwell with sin.

Words are free as they are common,
    Some in them have wondrous skill;
Saying *Lord* will never save them—
    Those He loves who do His will.

Words may please the lofty fancy;
    Music charm the itching ear;
Pompous sounds may please the giddy—
    But is Christ the Saviour there?

Christ's the way, the path to heaven—
    Life is ours, if Him we know;
Those who can pray, He has taught them—
    Those who can't should words forego.

When a child wants food and raiment,
    Why not ask his parents dear?
Ask in faith, then—God's our Father,
    He's at hand requests to hear.

Prayer's an easy, simple duty—
    'Tis the language of the soul;
Grace demands it—grace receives it—
    Grace must superintend the whole.

God requires not bod'ly postures,
    Neither *words* arranged in form;
Such a notion pre-supposes
    That by words we God can charm.

God alone must be exalted;
    Every earthly thought must fall;
Such the prayer and praise triumphant;
    Then does God reign over all.

Every heart should be a temple—
    God should dwell our souls within:
Every day should be a sabbath:
    Every day redeemed from sin.

Every place a place of worship;
    Every time a time of prayer;
Every sigh should rise to heaven—
    Every wish should anchor there.

Heart-felt sighs and heaven-born wishes,
    Or the tear-uplifted eye—
All are prayers that God will answer;
    They ascend His throne on high.

Spirit of prayer! be thou the portion
    Of all those who wait in time;
Help us, shield us, lead us, guide us;
    Thine the praise, the glory thine.

Preaching the gospel with effect necessarily includes this spirit of devotion which is a sentiment peculiar to the race under similar circumstances, and is a Christian mystery no longer; but can be recognised and explained by Christians as the felt communion union with Christ proclaims itself in, to each member of His body. In the language of Christianity thus clearly does the science of Christianity enable its votaries to illuminate the Bible.

True it is, that desire—mental conflict—ceases when something greatly supernal to the condition desired is bestowed. In St. Paul's case it was the full assurance of an eternal heritage forthcoming — entered at death—of a most attractive and desirable nature, the thought of which creates intense longing to inherit.

It is being in possession of this sentiment that qualifies a man for becoming a minister of the gospel. By insisting on a college course, may have the effect of wholly damping the ardour of a young convert—an ardour seldom if ever regained.*

---

*Except some very stirring event occur, such as took place at the Disruption of the Church of Scotland, when over 400 of the most devoted and evangelical section of the clergymen of the church seceded, and by this personal sacrifice secured for Scotland the blessing of the evangelical preaching which the teaching and example of such a noble band led to. The noble band who, by the erestian spirit displayed by the Government of the day, were either compelled to disregard the dictates of conscience or sever their tie with the State Church, which tie—to the strength of their Christian principles may it ever be spoken—they unhesitatingly did sever, and formed the Church of the Disruption. The struggle that followed is graphically unfolded in the annals of the Disruption.

The sympathy that united pastor and people in the struggle that ensued was graphically described to me by a disruption elder's wife, in

MYSTERIES OF CHRISTIANITY EXPLAINED. 385

Indeed, the eighth chapter of Romans is just what any similarly constituted minds would write in giving expression to the generalizations and inferences the subject suggested. The references to prayer made in the twenty-sixth and twenty-eighth verses are much simplified when we perceive that what is really meant "by the spirit itself making intercession for us with groanings which cannot be uttered," is the sentiment of adoption inducing the converted believer to strive thus earnestly to be conformed to the will of God, whatever happens, resting in the full assurance "that all things work together for good to them that love God, to them that are called according to his purpose." The mental state the prayer gives utterance to indicates a great mental struggle arising from a strong desire or craving for something not likely to be attained; dying away in the desire for submission, and that submission attained in the groans that cannot be uttered, succeeded by the soothing flow of peace inseparable from unreserved submission as the manifestation of one led by the spirit of God. This experience must end in the meek and lowly finding rest to their souls; for the spirit of the intercession of adoption in the unutterable groan ending thus calmly and peacefully, is the sentiment of adoption nullifying the opposing force. For assuredly, the struggle began by the two sets of antagonistic forces making their presence felt in

comparing how neglected she had been—a helpless invalid for, I think, 20 years—and during that time never once visited by her minister, with the kind sympathy shown her and her husband about the time of the disruption by Dr. Candlish, who was in the same excursion boat, who came, and sat down beside them, conversed with them, ending in a glow of enthusiasm with " but these were the glorious days of the disruption,"—her face brightening up with the enthusiasm the recollection recalled. This incident proves how strong the ties of sympathy were.

Y

the brain,—the one the activity of self-conservation, striving to secure a personal end, the other the activity conversion develops that induces a desire to submit to the will of God. It is by placing the ideal conceptions that indicate antagonistic forces in contrast, that we get to perceive the intellectual conception which explains the condition of both sets of forces, so as to simplify the mysteries Revelation unfolds conveyed in the terms Flesh and Spirit.

The contrasts thus indicated provide Christianity with its Scientific Base. In this base the human mind is recognised as representing the surroundings of that body ; and as such the individual mind is viewed as a unit of force regulated by the energy of self-conservation, for such is Sentient Personality so inspired. This conception indicates the material base of mind in the abstract, which in conversion has a new influence —called spirit—infused into it from God through Christ, which animates with love to God and inspires Sentient Personality, to seek first of all the glory of God. With two such forms of vital force totally distinct in their nature and action, we may well claim for Christianity a scientific base : as in this conception we have the consciousness of points of contrast and points of agreement, conditions which must be conformed to before a science is possible. But with these conditions satisfied, we have a base provided for the most sacred of all sciences, namely, that of Christianity, the development of which cost the life-blood of the Son of God, for in nothing short of this does the science of Christianity, "that is rescue by substitution," rest.

So let us go to the root of the matter, in proclaiming the fact that in the first sensation the infant organism gives birth to, it creates its Ego, Sentient Personality, of the subtile fluid liberated by the organism and vitalized by the conscious shock. In this conception, we find the vital force created which henceforth will regulate the play of that organism, as the vitalized fluid of conscious states the body liberates in adding moment by moment its vitalized atoms of radiant matter, which develops the Ego of the sequence of conscious states that follow. For the fluid—the energy of radiant matter—liberated by the organism as conscious states, is the Ego, the inner man that survives death, and holds together all through eternity, so graphically put by St. Paul in 2 Cor. v. (Revised Version), in the " we know that if the earthly house of our bodily frame be dissolved, we have a building from God, a house not made with hands, eternal in the heavens. For verily in this we groan, longing to be clothed upon with our habitation, which is from heaven," &c. This building from God, not made with hands, is the conditioned organism of the bodily frame conversion formed and fashioned, decreed

"To sound in God the Father's ears,
No other name but Christ's."

This is the nature and sentiment conversion creates in creating the spiritual organ, the house not made with hands, the eternal habitation from heaven, that is the inner man union with Christ creates, who survives death, formed of a section of the ether—everywhere present in nature—a section which in this case had a new life-action infused into it called spirit, which forms the new man. Remember, I hold ether to be radiant matter, the uncondensed substance emanating from all luminous bodies. It makes its presence felt in electricity, magnetism, light, heat, &c. A section of this fluid, ether or energy, vitalized by the human organism creating Sentient Personality, comprises the immortal units of our race; and it is with these Christianity has to do.

The energy of conscious states in life vitalized and liberated by the organism in nerve current which develops Intelligence in developing Sentient Personality is the Ego, an activity which gives expression to one of the forces of nature that is ever increased by pleasure, therefore the desire to secure a pleasure is the will or strongest power in it, that starts into activity whenever a pleasure is to be secured or a pain repelled, because pain lowers its vitality. Inspired thus is man in his natural state. One of the things the science of Christianity has got to do, is to show how self-conservation, this pleasure seeking property, which leads to oppress the weak where a pleasure can be gained, is to be neutralized by inducing Sentient Personality to act differently. So as to do this, the science of Christianity has to define the nature of the vital force God in Christ provides, which so animates Sentient Personality as to make the Ego more or less indifferent to earthly joy. This is done by the Christians being in possession of the evidence the new sense manifests, namely, that of finding pleasure in serving Christ, because they love Him. To act thus is Christian Life and Work, the heaven-born fruit of the spirit, which conquers in generating "love, joy, peace, long-suffering, gentleness, goodness, faith, meekness, temperance. Against these there is no law. They that are in Christ have crucified the flesh with the affections and lusts."—Gal. v. 22-24. In this way the science of Christianity can place in clear and forcible terms the mental state developed by the new sense conversion imparts put in contrast with the "flesh lusting against the spirit, and the spirit against the flesh, which are contrary the one to the other."—Gal. v. 17. For nothing is a more certain experience to a converted Christian than that the mental state giving expression to the two opposing sets of forces is totally different and opposite.

Thus, then, the ministers, the exponents of this sacred science have a work of great responsibility resting on them in making such distinctions clear and intelligible, so as to leave no reasonable doubt what the fruit of the spirit, the evidence of conversion is. First having partaken of this fruit themselves, let them never cease to notify that all springs from love to Christ, generated in conversion, a source of pleasure far greater than any the world can provide. Let them proclaim in language clear and distinct the fact that the other, the unconverted class, is wholly dependent on the world for their source of pleasure.

Christendom was created when our Lord was humanized —that is, developed a human being, through a Divine agency called " the word made flesh and dwelling amongst us." He was born of our race, therefore He took our form, our nature, and our phase of intelligence, He developed, through the agency of the miraculous conception, a human being as any other of our race is developed. In this way, His divine nature comes to act and react through a human medium. Viewing our Lord's earthly destiny from this point, it is clear the term Word applied to Him by John, was by John used to indicate a divine intelligence, and as such was a term very clearly conveyed in the intellectual conception John used, when he said all things were made by him, and without Him was not anything made that was made. For, humanly speaking,—it is intelligence that makes everything—without intelligence nothing can be either understood or made. John in this way makes it clear to human intelligence that Christ the Son of God was the source from which revelation springs, and in His manhood embodied all that had hitherto been revealed. Thus, then, in the Christ of Christianity made flesh, and dwelling among us, issued in the Christian era. The era whose end is not yet, and never can end, since our Lord has taken the human form, as a divine intelligence, gives expression to the Will of God, through it, as the second person of the Trinity, who renders the whole case clearly intelligible in the language that humanity provides, indicating the condition John terms "Word." It may be put thus. Christ, the only begotten of the Father, was the divine being formed of the intellectual combination embodied in Revelation who appeared in the human form, and who in functioning gave expression to the will of God. For, in every action of His earthly life, His aim was—and His character declared it— to do the will of God. This was to Him an instinct. Yes, the instinct that redemption came through, typified in the vicarious sacrifice working all through nature, which finds its climax in the redemption purchased by our Lord. To put the case thus: we are to understand by the terms "Word," Intelligence, God, the first cause from whence emanated nature, possessing all potentially that our race embodies: human intelligence as well as all phases of intelligent beings and systems which may be, or will be, in the universe. For all was designed by God, and by Him decreed to be developed by nature. In this way intelligence was prior to matter, in nature emanating from the triune God, as the agent decreed to develop all.

As Christians, we may state the case thus. Nature is an imminence from God, whose only-begotten Son, our Lord, adopted the human form and phase of Intelligence. He was "in the world, and the world was made by Him, and the world knew Him not."—John i. 10.

Human mind, viewed in its collective form, embodies the intelligence of the race. And human intelligence includes all that our race knows of matter, and in its Egos it carries that knowledge into eternity as the heritage of the race. You will note these Egos of the race are the subjective product which represents objective nature as human beings see it; and in Sentient Personality the human beings of our race are capable of reproducing in their own way natural phenomena. The human Egos built of the luminferous ether is man as nature appears to man.

Every iota of nature, including the incidents of the social system, perceived by a human Ego, has in that vitalized unit of mind-force a duplicate of nature's doings. Created by the human organism and its environment, Ego transforms a portion of the luminferous ether into a subjective human unit of intelligenec, which contains all that Ego knows of the objective world as an abiding form of human intelligence representing incidents that took place on our planet during his time on earth. These abiding forms, constituting Sentient Personality, are the life of man, called the light of man.— John i. 5. A term when viewed from the standpoint of present knowledge, which must be understood to indicate the form of individual life into which Immortality enters.

It is so that the organ of mind, formed of a section of the universal ether, is vitalized in the shock that accompanies consciousness, including the ideal conception then present in conscious mind. Consciousness mind in this way takes the human form as the vitalized luminiferous ether forming the Ego. For such is the disembodied form of mind-force that the human race embodies in its Egos. This is the very process referred to by St. Paul in 1 Cor. xv. 44-47, whereby Adam was made a living soul. The natural man is of the earth earthly. The soul or Ego is indicated by St. Paul as the equivalent of the natural life, and may justly be called spiritual body to distinguish it from the body we lay in the grave or cremate. Thus formed, the human race live as immortal units in one or other point of space. Man in his natural state forming his section of the social organism, and all that that includes, is regulated by "with what judgment ye judge, ye shall be judged : and with what measure ye mete, it shall be measured to you again"—Matthew vii. 2—into which the new gospel of "he that overcometh shall inherit all things" enters. It develops in strengthening the sentiment of hope. Hope is the immortal heritage of our race, the stimulating power in the consoling words I have quoted which receives a new impulse. Thus viewed, the wail of poor suffering humanity has a totally different significance. For finally the wail of even the greatest oppressor suffering the consequences his life leads to, is to cease through the power the new gospel infuses, in the "He that overcometh shall inherit all things." Thus, then, the wail of him who was the greatest oppressor, will in eternity be made to be the shout of a conqueror as he gathers strength to overcome—though this must be accomplished as the fruit of great suffering.

For it is so that the wail of the oppressor suffering the penalty his sins entail, will eventually become a spur (notwithstanding the suffering accompanying the effort), to spur him on to higher and higher attainments as the end God's design takes to purify man in leading him upward and onward, Morally, Religiously, and Intellectually. For our Lord must reign till He has put all enemies under His feet. The last enemy to be destroyed is death—1 Cor. xv. 21-28—where death must be understood to signify pain, and life to signify hope, in mind-force striving to attain its Ideal in developing the human Intellect. The unsaved section of the race, animated by hope, is organic mind formed of luminiferous ether in giving expression to conscious states on earth; units of energy vitalized in having become the habitation of a human soul, which does not die, but lives evermore, a race which has yet to be delivered up by the Son to the Father. The Son is the Second Adam, the quickening spirit, by whose purifying power all is accomplished. Thus, then, the unsaved section of the suffering mortals of earth, called in the Scriptures the last or condemned, even their groan and travail of pain merely represent an incident in their life; however painful that may be, they nevertheless are on their way to a higher and higher Religious, Moral, and Intellectual development, which eventually will add to human happiness.

Concrete humanity, with its countless millions who have got their immortality from our planet, and lived their little life on earth, in poverty, in ignorance, and in woe, shall yet share in the glorious result of the splendid destiny of their race, secured through our Lord's vicarious sacrifice, who in a sense is the propitiation for the sins of the whole world—1 John ii. 2—who has secured race development by securing conditions which neutralize its possible degeneration.

Evolution Illuminating the Bible.

By HERRIOT MACKENZIE.

Opinions of the Press.

"It is not easy to give an idea in a few words of a work like Mr. Herriot Mackenzie's 'Evolution Illuminating the Bible,' full as it is of close scientific or quasi-scientific discussion and reasoning. . . . But perhaps we should not be far wrong if we say that its aim is to reconcile the extremest materialism with religion, and to show that there is nothing in the doctrine of evolution which even the staunchest Bible Christian need fear. 'It is evident,' says the author in his preface, 'that the materialistic views advanced by our leading men of science are causing a class of Christians much anxiety. One object I had in writing this volume was to draw the attention of this class to the fact that our Lord clearly advanced such views when He defined man in his natural state as a unit of Body and Mind—classed by Him as born of the Flesh is Flesh—put in contrast with the new sentiment conversion imparts, defined as one 'born of the Spirit, Spirit.' John iii. 16. Cabannis taught that thought is a secretion of the brain, and Mr. Mackenzie, who writes that 'there is no longer any doubt of the mental structure being of a material form.' seems to stop no way short of this celebrated dictum. The loss of brain substance can so far be measured as a secretion from the brain during mental work; further, the heat developed is perceptible and measurable by thermo-electric apparatus.' Nevertheless, he recognises a spiritual principle under the name of the Ego, a conscious personality, not, however, antecedent to the body, but created by the vitality operating in the blood, yet not perishing with the body but surviving it. To follow the author minutely in his curious speculations *is of course* impossible here. It must be admitted, however, that he seems to have a good acquaintance with recent scientific literature dealing with the relation of mind and body, and must have thought deeply on the subject of which he writes. . . . It is dedicated—without permission—to Professor Huxley, 'as a token of admiration and a tribute to his genius.'"—*Scotsman.*

"The writer of these pages hastens to reassure her readers or rather her fellow 'converted Christians' that Materialism has the sanction of Scripture. She finds the germ of it in the words of our Lord to Nicodemus, and its fuller exposition in the eighth chapter of the Epistle to the Romans. Evolution and the Bible mutually illuminate each other."—*Bookseller.*

From Messrs. Simpson, Marshall, Hamilton, Kent & Co. "Evolution Illuminating the Bible," by Herriot Mackenzie.—"'It is evident,' says Miss Mackenzie, 'that the material views advanced by our leading men of science are causing a class of Christians much anxiety; but the author is not among these. She dedicates her book boldly to Professor Huxley, 'as an admiration and a tribute to his genius,' and though an earnest Christian herself, has written a book to show the class referred to that their fears are groundless; that we have the highest of all authority for accepting the material views advanced by such authors as Spencer, Bain, Huxley, &c.

"Those who are familiar with works on these lines will anticipate the nature of Miss Mackenzie's reasoning."—*Publisher's Circular*.

"Evolution Illuminating the Bible," by Herriot Mackenzie, is an attempt to show that the material views advanced by our leading men of science were clearly advanced by our Lord in His words to Nicodemus about the new birth. The book is not easy reading, and is based on the hypothesis that spontaneous generation is possible. . . . Our authoress regards 'Light as a disturber of elements' the most probable force to originate the vaguest possible form of sensation—which is life."—*Literary World*.

"One of the most singular among the recent books which have been published is Mr. Herriot Mackenzie's 'Evolution Illuminating the Bible.' Mr. Mackenzie is so great an admirer of Huxley, the high priest of Agnosticism that he dedicates this volume to him; and yet his faith in Evangelical Christianity is as devout and unquestioning as that of a Highland Free Church Elder. He is an out and out materialist, and professes to find materialism as one of the corner stones of Christ's teaching. How he reconciles this doctrine with a future state, readers must find out for themselves. It is impossible to indicate in the short space at our disposal the drift of Mr. Mackenzie's general argument. It is able. . . . Messrs. John Menzies & Co. are the Edinburgh publishers."—*Northern Ensign*.

"Miss Mackenzie dedicates her book to Professor Huxley, as 'a token of admiration and a tribute to his genius.' That eminent scientist says somewhere, 'that the crassest materialism is consistent with the airest idealism;' and he confesses to have a lingering affection for the old materialistic view that the brain secrets thought somehow in the same way as the liver secrets bile. It has often been deplored that no writer ever appeared to set about the difficult task of reconciling the theories of the physical philosophers and of the airy idealists, and of harmonising the discordant opinions of Professor Huxley and Mr. Herbert Spencer on the one hand, and of Messrs. Moody and Sankey on the other. By most people it is generally believed that these couples are metaphorically at daggers drawn on such subjects as God, the Universe, and the origin and destiny of man, but in Miss Herriot Mackenzie's opinion such is not the case. . . . . Miss Mackenzie comes boldly forward and publishes what will be either an epoch making book or the reverse. She concedes at the outset everything to her opponents, postulating only a soulless, godless universe filled with all pervading ether; and at the close she forces the Agnostic into a corner, compelling him to accept without reservation, qualification, or modification, all the doctrines of popular Evangelical Theology. Some critics who look more to processes than to results may be apt to raise objections here and there to Miss Mackenzie's logical methods ; but these are small and insignificant matters compared with the great object aimed at, viz., showing that the principle of Materialism leads ultimately to Methodism, and those of Evolutionary Agnosticism to Scotch Presbyterianism.

"Miss Mackenzie, in the beginning of a book of about 400 pages, shows how the transition from lifeless matter to organism is accomplished by means of the heat and light of the sun. The origin of consciousness is next traced to the simple fact that plants notice the presence and absence of the sun. After this the development of intelligence is easy. All notions of right and wrong follow as natural consequences of sensitiveness to pleasure and pain; while, last of all, the growth of the immortal soul is demonstrated to be connected in some way with the universal ether filling all space. . . . . When so much is accomplished, the origin of life, of consciousness, and of the soul made perfectly plain to the most rudimentary understanding, there is no need to explain in detail the steps by which Miss Mackenzie at last reaches the conclusion that each and all of the doctrines of Evangelical Theology harmonise with, and indeed are but logical sequences of the principles professed by Professor Huxley and Mr. Herbert Spencer. As our authoress says, after one has followed her argument, 'the process of Christ's resurrection is simplicity itself.' . . . Miss Mackenzie has evidently read extensively in the subjects of biology and of organic evolution generally. Her scientific knowledge is up to date. . . . . Altogether, this is one of the strangest books we have read for a long time. Audacious in its conception and its scientific conclusions. . . . Miss Mackenzie's ironical treatise on the Bible and Evolution is certainly the most unique book of its kind."—*Banffshire Journal, Aberdeenshire Mail, Moray, Nairn, and Inverness Review.*

"In admiration of the Disruption it cannot be excelled. It also accepts the rankest materialism, and reconciles it to a very simple evangelicalism by denying to all men any spiritual nature whatever prior to regeneration."—*Dundee Advertiser.*

"'Evolution Illuminating the Bible.' . . . The author appears to admit the extremest theories of materialism, as far as Body and Mind are concerned, in order to introduce a third element, as he puts it, 'Born of the Spirit, Spirit.' Several chapters are devoted to a review of Modern Physiology and Physiological Psychology. . . . (Example of) the author's style: 'Christianity takes to do with the immortal soul created of conscious states, and we have seen that primary conscious states are divided from the objective world, and carry with them the emotions that accompany them at their origin. I hold it permissible to believe, an Ego or soul, so defined, to be built up of luminiferous ether, which, when disembodied as such in functioning, gives expression to the conscious states developed during natural life, and the correlative of consciousness the phenomena of which conscious states are forms.'"—*Westminister Review.*

"'Evolution Illuminating the Bible' is a study written with a set purpose. The author attempts to prove that there is really nothing in the theory of Evolution which is at variance with the teaching of the Scriptures. 'It is evident,' says Mr. Mackenzie, 'that the material views advanced by our leading men of science are causing a class of Christians much anxiety.' Why this class does not approve of the scientific opinion, he does not understand, for 'our Lord clearly advanced such views when He defined man in his natural state as a Unit of Body and Mind.' . . . 'That which is born of the Flesh is Flesh,' put in contrast with the sentiment 'one born of the Spirit is Spirit.' It is the immense difference between Body and Mind that the author dilates upon, and his reasoning, while ingenious, is very unusual. This remarkable book is dedicated to Professor Huxley 'as a token of admiration and a tribute to his genius.'"—*John O' Groat Journal.*

"The author's object, according to his own statement, is 'to draw attention to the fact that our Lord clearly advanced such views (that is, the material views of leading men of science), when he defined man in his natural state as a unit of Body and Mind.' . . . Classed by Him as 'that which is born of the Flesh, Flesh,' put in contrast with the new sentiment conversion imparts, defined as one 'born of the Spirit, Spirit.' Mr. Mackenzie believes in spontaneous generation—'light originated life, sensation is created by the shock produced in parting atoms of a very stable compound molecule.' 'The vital force inherent in the human form at birth awakens into consciousness, and creates the soul of the first sensation.' The Christianity of the future will be moulded by the operation of the materialistic views, which will explain all mental terms in form of matter."—*North British Daily Mail.*

"We shall not profess to review this work, which is best left to make its own way. The views of the writer are so peculiar that it would require far more time than we are able to afford to enter into their merits or demerits. . . . We would not care to stand in the way of a new light, if new light it is, and therefore would earnestly recommend the reading public to procure the book and judge for themselves."—*Brechin Advertiser.*

"The author wishes to show that the immortal part in man is gradually evolved from material conditions, but being evolved in this life it is then indestructible."—*Independent.*

"This volume gives, undoubtedly, evidence of considerable thinking power and knowledge of biology."—*Glasgow Hearld.*

"'Evolution Illuminating the Bible,' by Herriot Mackenzie, is a praiseworthy and thoughtful attempt to treat the subject, so far as relates to religious matters, in a legitimate way."—*Church Times.*

EDINBURGH AND GLASGOW: JOHN MENZIES & CO.

LONDON: SIMPKIN, MARSHALL & CO.

"This is a singular and remarkable book. On professedly scientific grounds the author has adopted the materialistic views of Professor Huxley (to whom the book is dedicated), Herbert Spencer, Professor Bain, and other scientists—views generally regarded as opposed to the teachings of the Bible, and yet in this book he powerfully applies these same conceptions to the elucidation and enforcement of Evangelical Christianity. The theory of Evolution, which not a few consider to be anti-Biblical, he holds to be illuminated by the Bible, and the Bible illuminated by it. The most startling part of the argument is that in which he applies the Evolution theory to the exposition of our Lord's teaching on the all-important subject of the new birth and its necessity. He finds proof of his thesis in his words to Nicodemus: "*That which is born of the flesh is flesh; and that which is born of the Spirit is spirit,*" and also in the general teaching of St. Paul. On this subject of regeneration by the Holy Spirit he utters no uncertain sound. He describes it as "a change so momentous and of such vast importance, as far to surpass anything that could happen to a human being hereafter, even during that immortal individual's onward existence through eternity;" and he affirms that "much that is said in the eighth chapter of Romans is so plain to the converted—therefore adopted child of God—that he who runs may read. Assuredly," he adds, "to him the mysteries of Christianity are explained in the simplest form of language." Unfortunately, in dealing with these mysteries, the author's style is not simple; and this, combined with the exceedingly abstruse character of the argument will, we fear, limit his readers to "the few and the fit." Those, however, who will take the pains to carefully study and weigh his arguments and lines of thought will find a rich reward in many a fresh view of old truth and in the confirmation of faith in revelation and in the religion of the Bible. On the great cardinal doctrines of the divinity and atoning work of Christ he is equally outspoken and orthodox. " All that revealed truth ever imparted to our race," he declares " was embodied in the person of our Lord Jesus Christ, who eame to atone for sin by means of vicarious sacrifice ;" and on page 268 he ably shows that vicarious sacrifice " is an eminent law of the constitution and development of the social organism." We regret we have not space to show how, starting from materialistic conceptions of humanity, he arrives at the Christian doctrine of immortality and eternal life, or his treatment of prayer and law, or the application of his principles to the ethics of the Gospel. In all these subjects he shows himself to be not only an earnest believer in Divine revelation, but a *Christian of no ordinary spiritual knowledge. And the freedom with which he handles biological and other sciences in the prosecution of his great and noble object is instructive.* The concluding chapter, entitled " *The Mysteries of Christianity explained in Scientific Language,*" is a fitting elose to this singular book. From what we have said our readers must not suppose that we agree with the materialistic views of the author. We do not ; but his object is so good, and his maintenance of the great facts and doctrines of the Gospel is so earnest, that we have been able to speak much more favourably of the work than otherwise we might have done, if noticing it purely as a " scientific production."—*Christian Age.*

www.ingramcontent.com/pod-product-compliance
Lightning Source LLC
Chambersburg PA
CBHW022110290426
44112CB00008B/624